SURVIVAL SCOUT

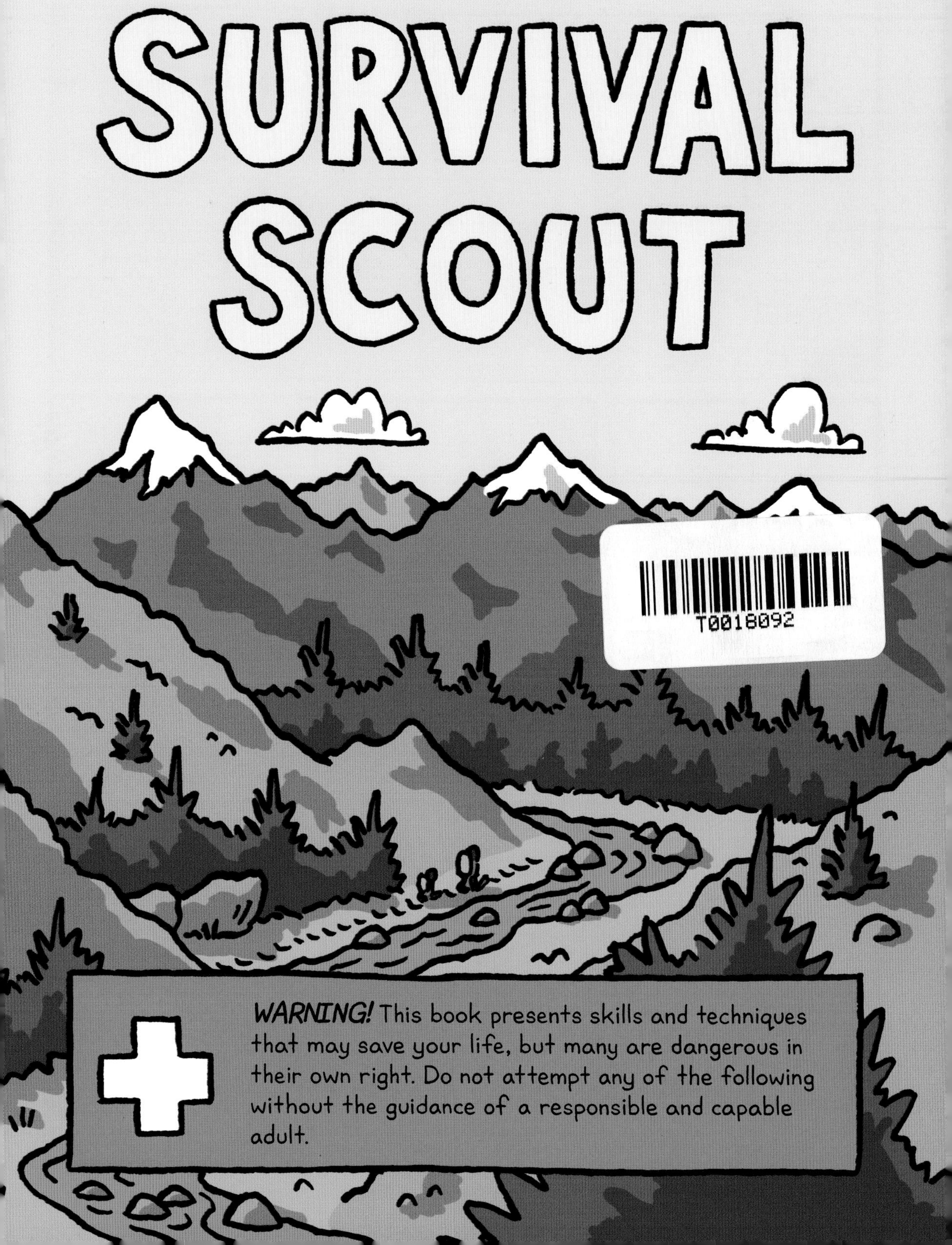

WARNING! This book presents skills and techniques that may save your life, but many are dangerous in their own right. Do not attempt any of the following without the guidance of a responsible and capable adult.

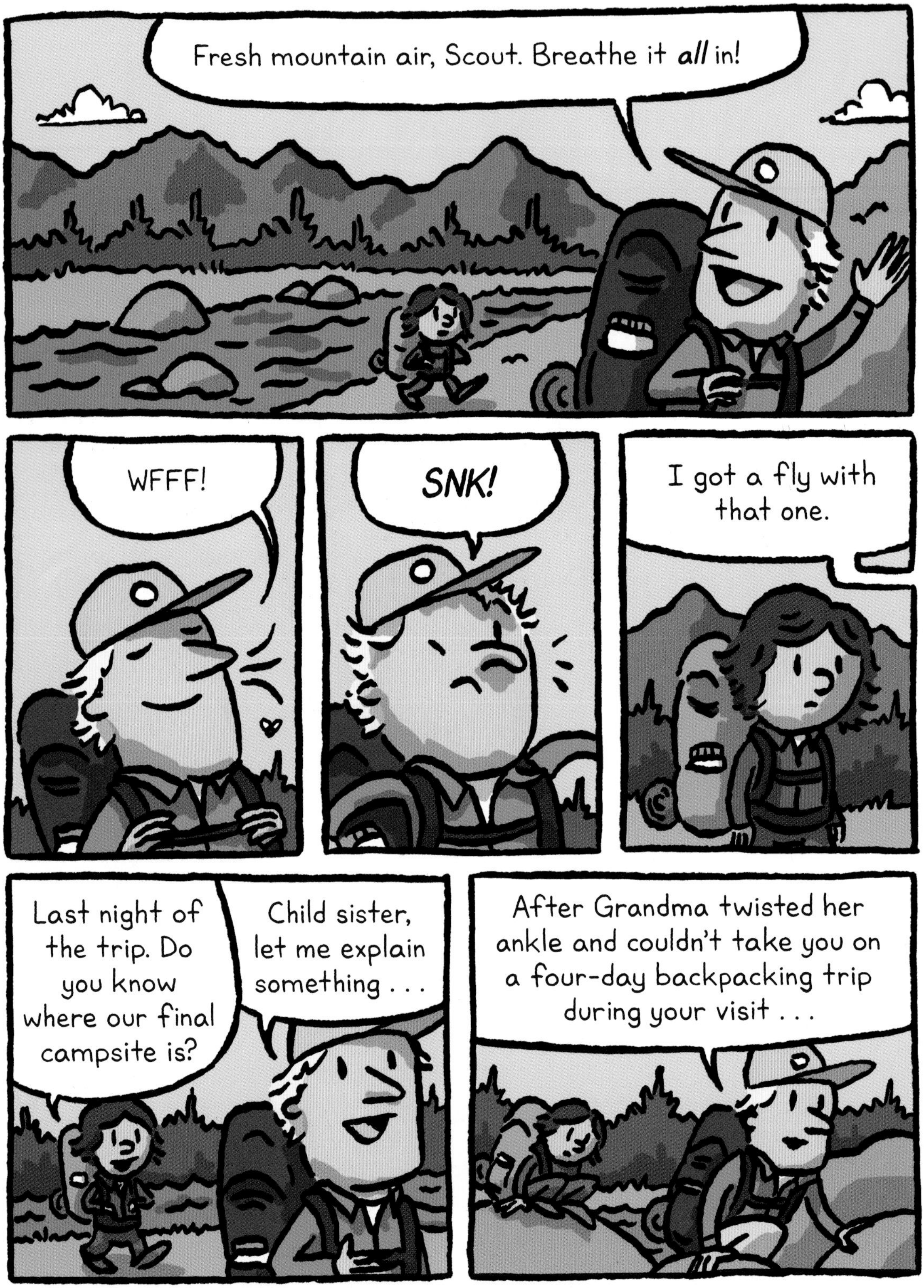
Fresh mountain air, Scout. Breathe it *all* in!
WFFF!
SNK!
I got a fly with that one.
Last night of the trip. Do you know where our final campsite is?
Child sister, let me explain something . . .
After Grandma twisted her ankle and couldn't take you on a four-day backpacking trip during your visit . . .

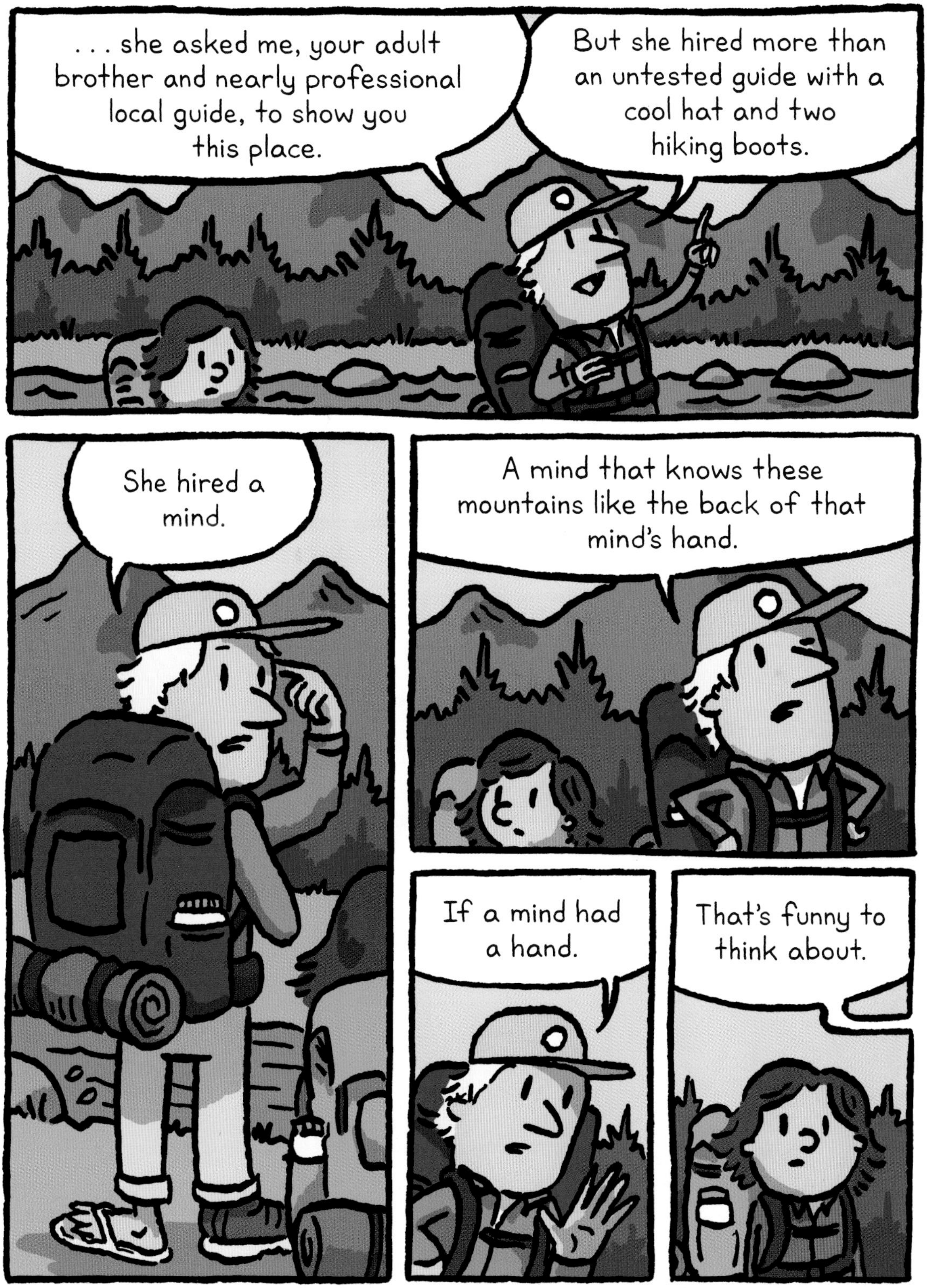

. . . she asked me, your adult brother and nearly professional local guide, to show you this place.
But she hired more than an untested guide with a cool hat and two hiking boots.
She hired a mind.
A mind that knows these mountains like the back of that mind's hand.
If a mind had a hand.
That's funny to think about.

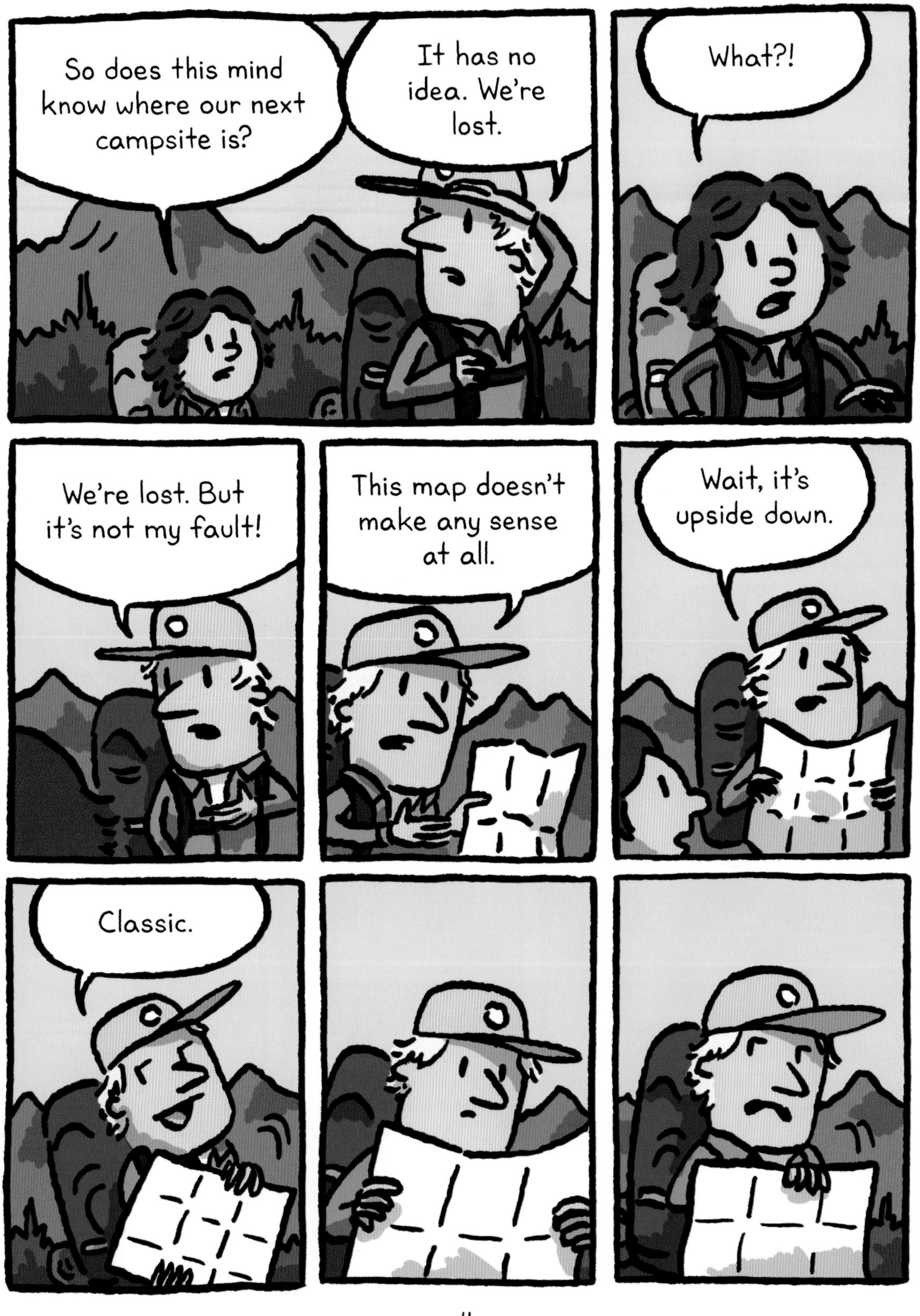
So does this mind know where our next campsite is?
It has no idea. We're lost.
What?!
We're lost. But it's not my fault!
This map doesn't make any sense at all.
Wait, it's upside down.
Classic.

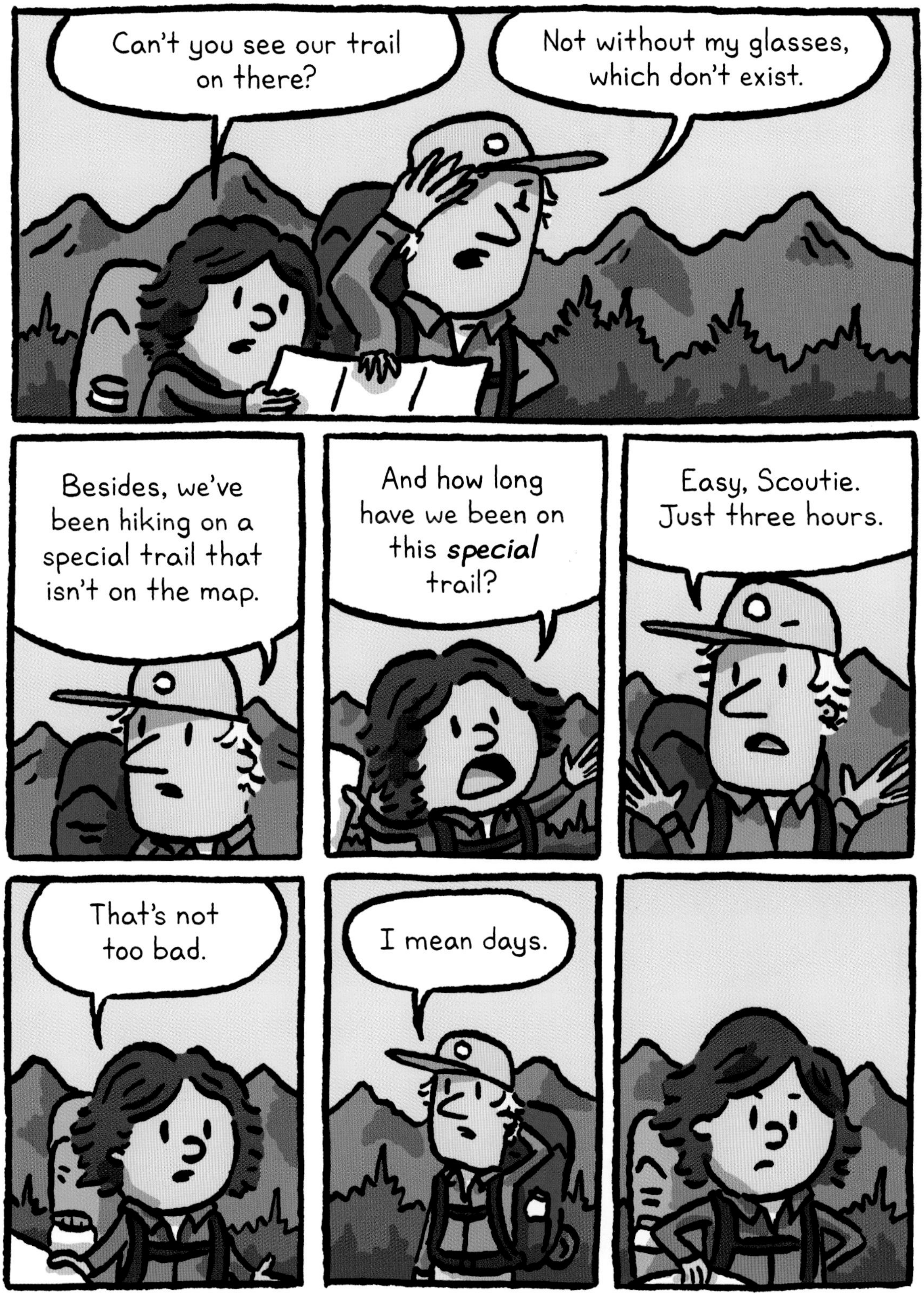
Can't you see our trail on there?
Not without my glasses, which don't exist.
Besides, we've been hiking on a special trail that isn't on the map.
And how long have we been on this *special* trail?
Easy, Scoutie. Just three hours.
That's not too bad.
I mean days.

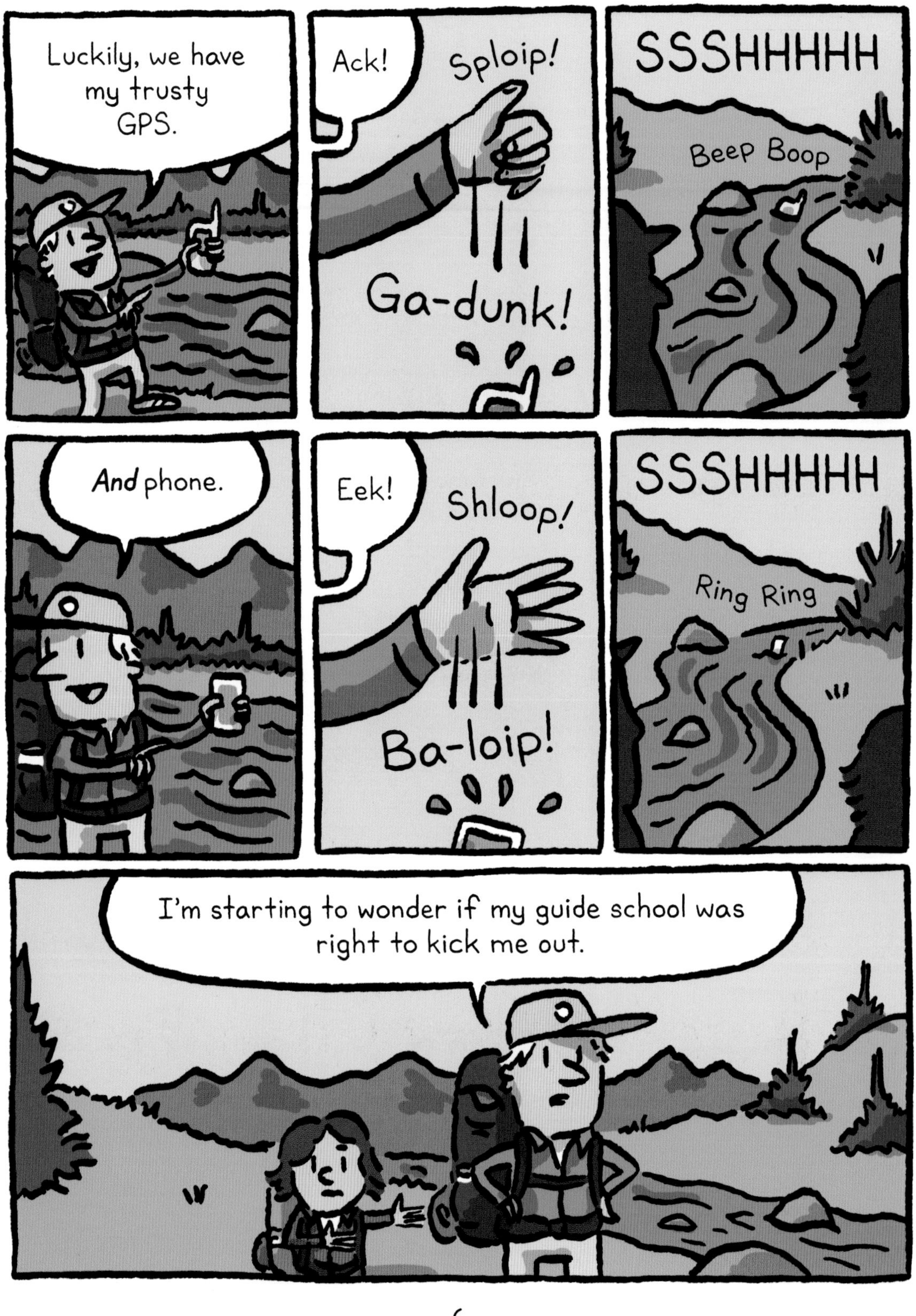
Luckily, we have my trusty GPS.
Ack!
Sploip!
Ga-dunk!
SSSHHHHH
Beep Boop
And phone.
Eek!
Shloop!
Ba-loip!
SSSHHHHH
Ring Ring
I'm starting to wonder if my guide school was right to kick me out.

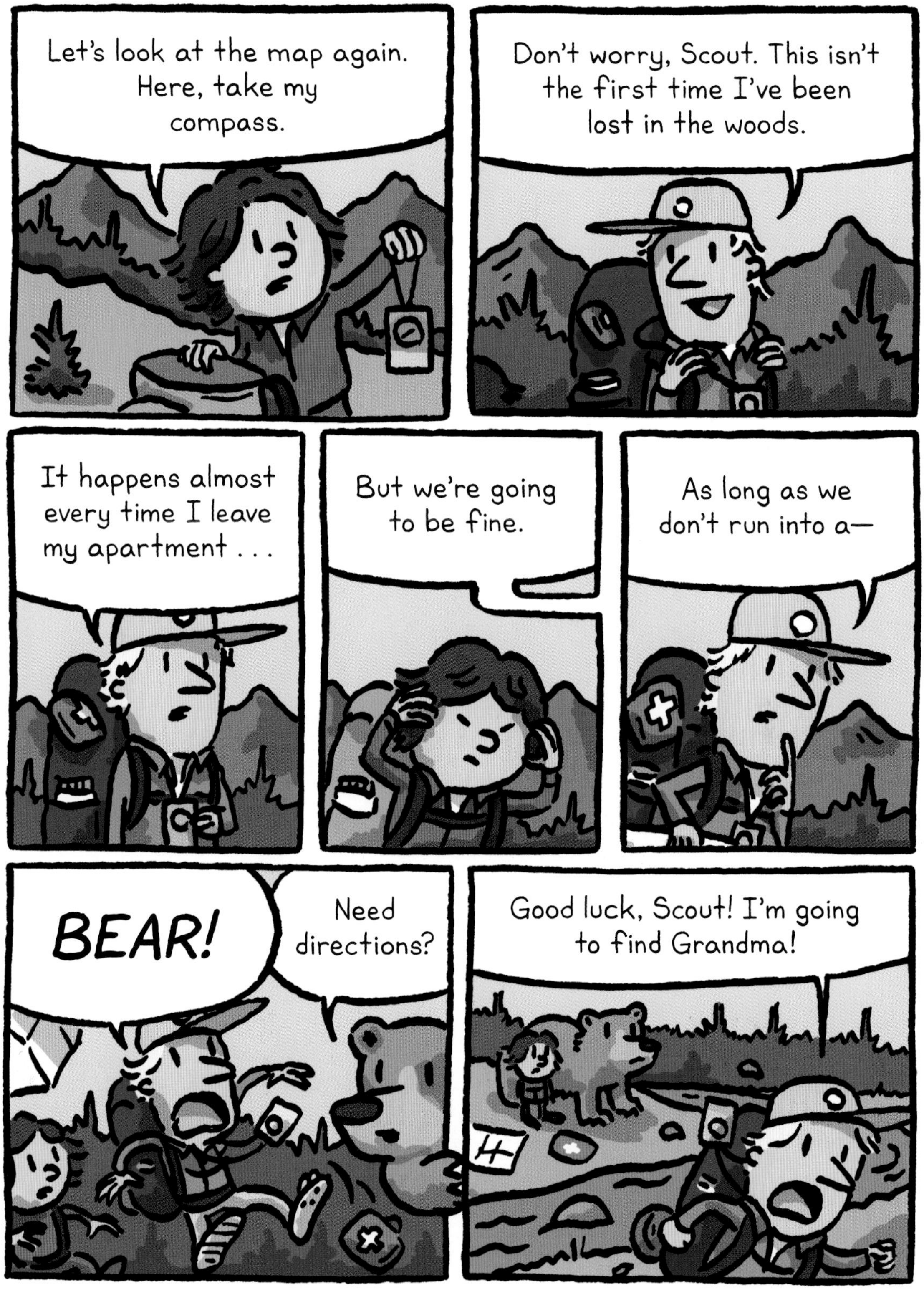
Let's look at the map again. Here, take my compass.
Don't worry, Scout. This isn't the first time I've been lost in the woods.
It happens almost every time I leave my apartment . . .
But we're going to be fine.
As long as we don't run into a—
BEAR!
Need directions?
Good luck, Scout! I'm going to find Grandma!

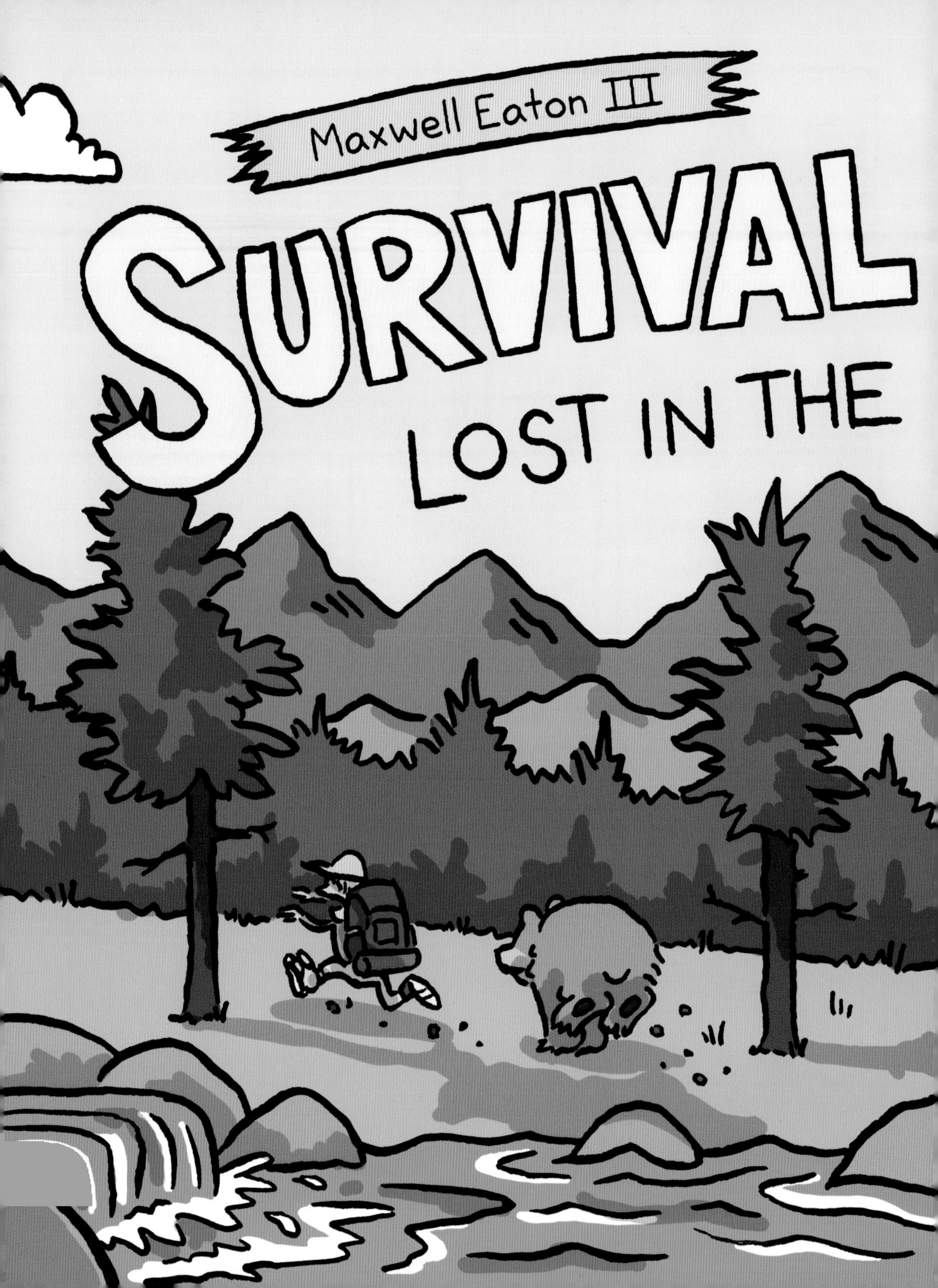
Maxwell Eaton III
SURVIVAL
LOST IN THE

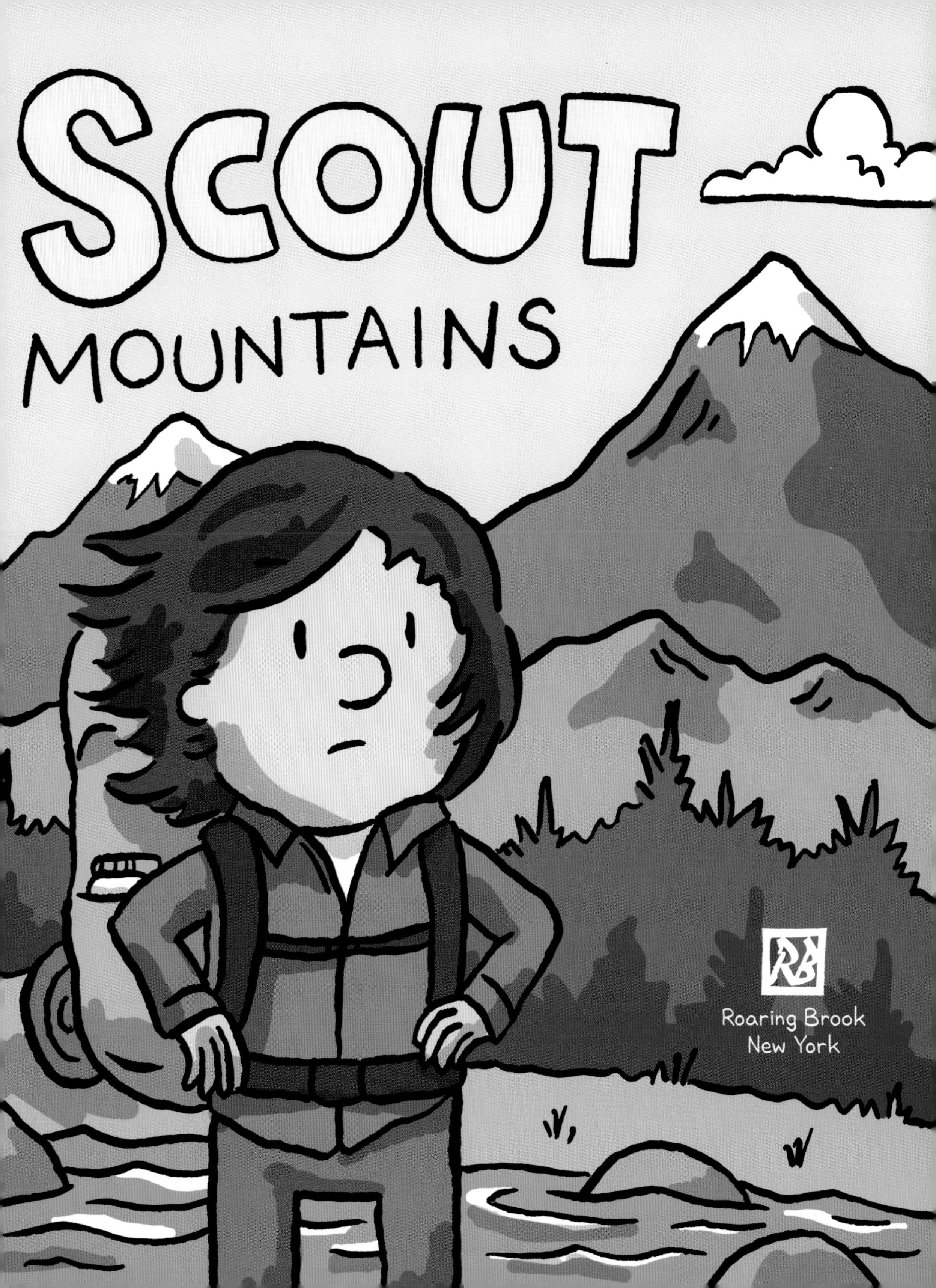
SCOUT
MOUNTAINS
Roaring Brook
New York

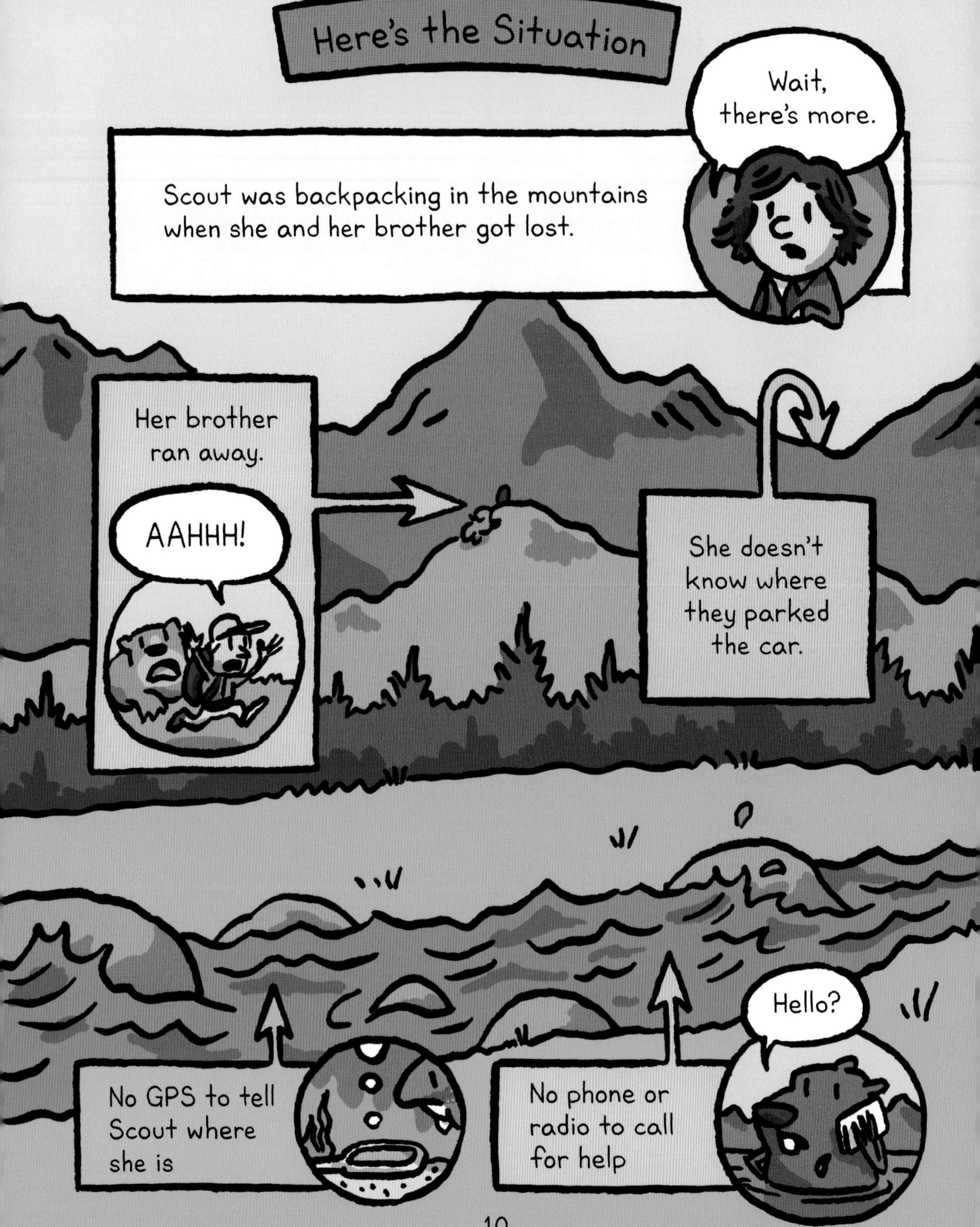

Here's the Situation
Scout was backpacking in the mountains when she and her brother got lost.
Wait, there's more.
Her brother ran away.
AAHHH!
She doesn't know where they parked the car.
No GPS to tell Scout where she is
No phone or radio to call for help
Hello?

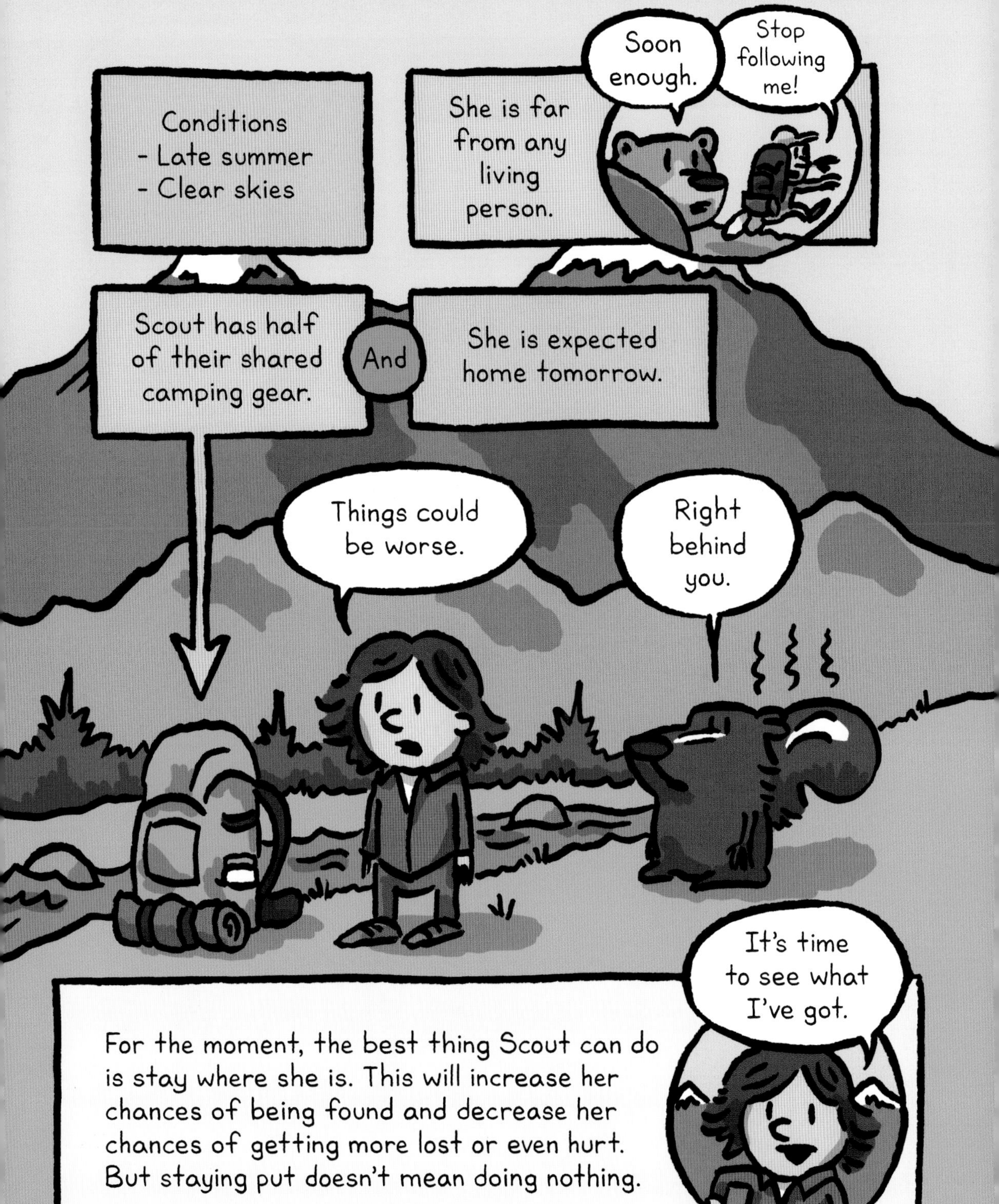

Conditions
- Late summer
- Clear skies
She is far from any living person.
Soon enough.
Stop following me!
Scout has half of their shared camping gear.
And
She is expected home tomorrow.
Things could be worse.
Right behind you.
For the moment, the best thing Scout can do is stay where she is. This will increase her chances of being found and decrease her chances of getting more lost or even hurt. But staying put doesn't mean doing nothing.
It's time to see what I've got.

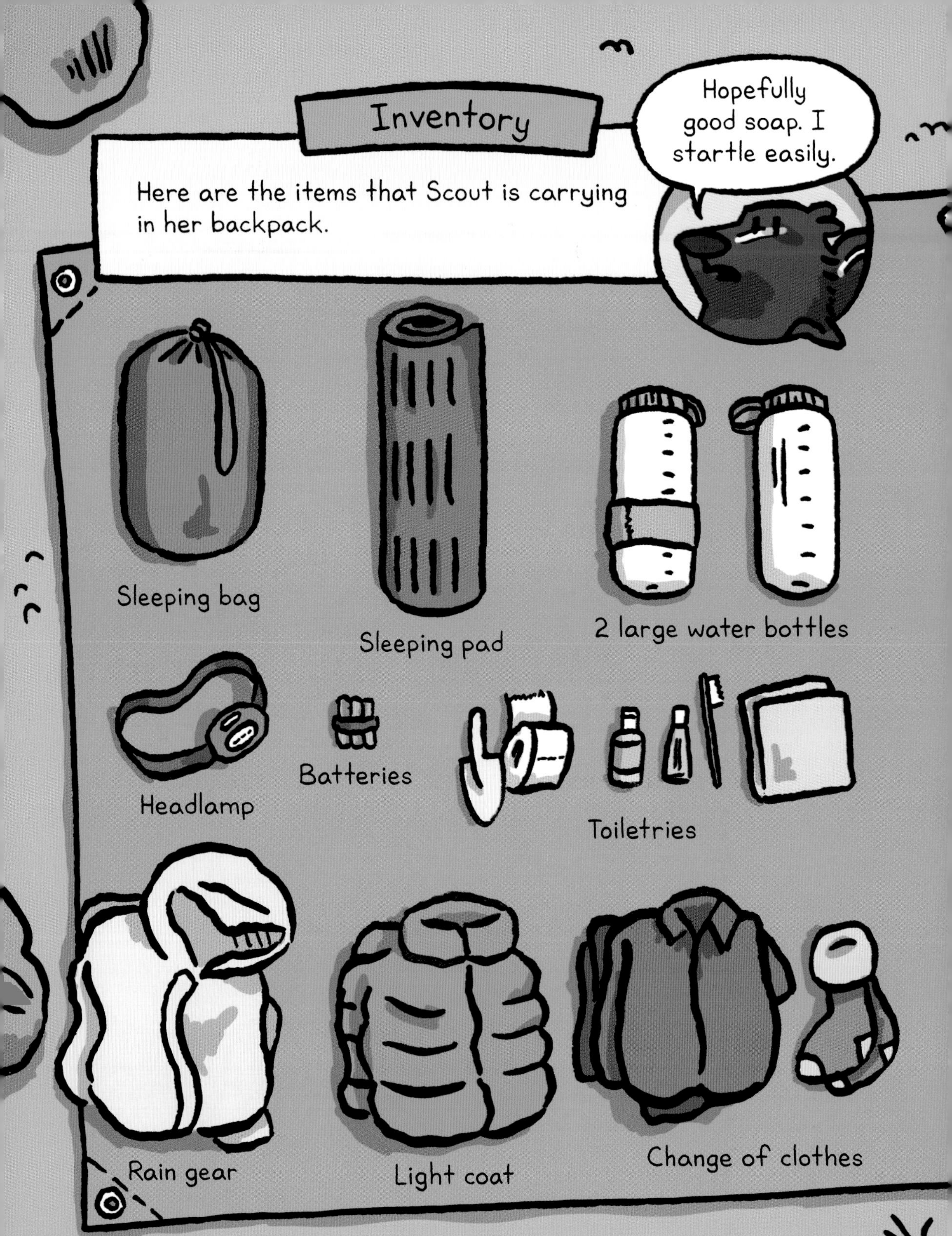
Inventory
Here are the items that Scout is carrying in her backpack.
Hopefully good soap. I startle easily.
Sleeping bag
Sleeping pad
2 large water bottles
Headlamp
Batteries
Toiletries
Rain gear
Light coat
Change of clothes

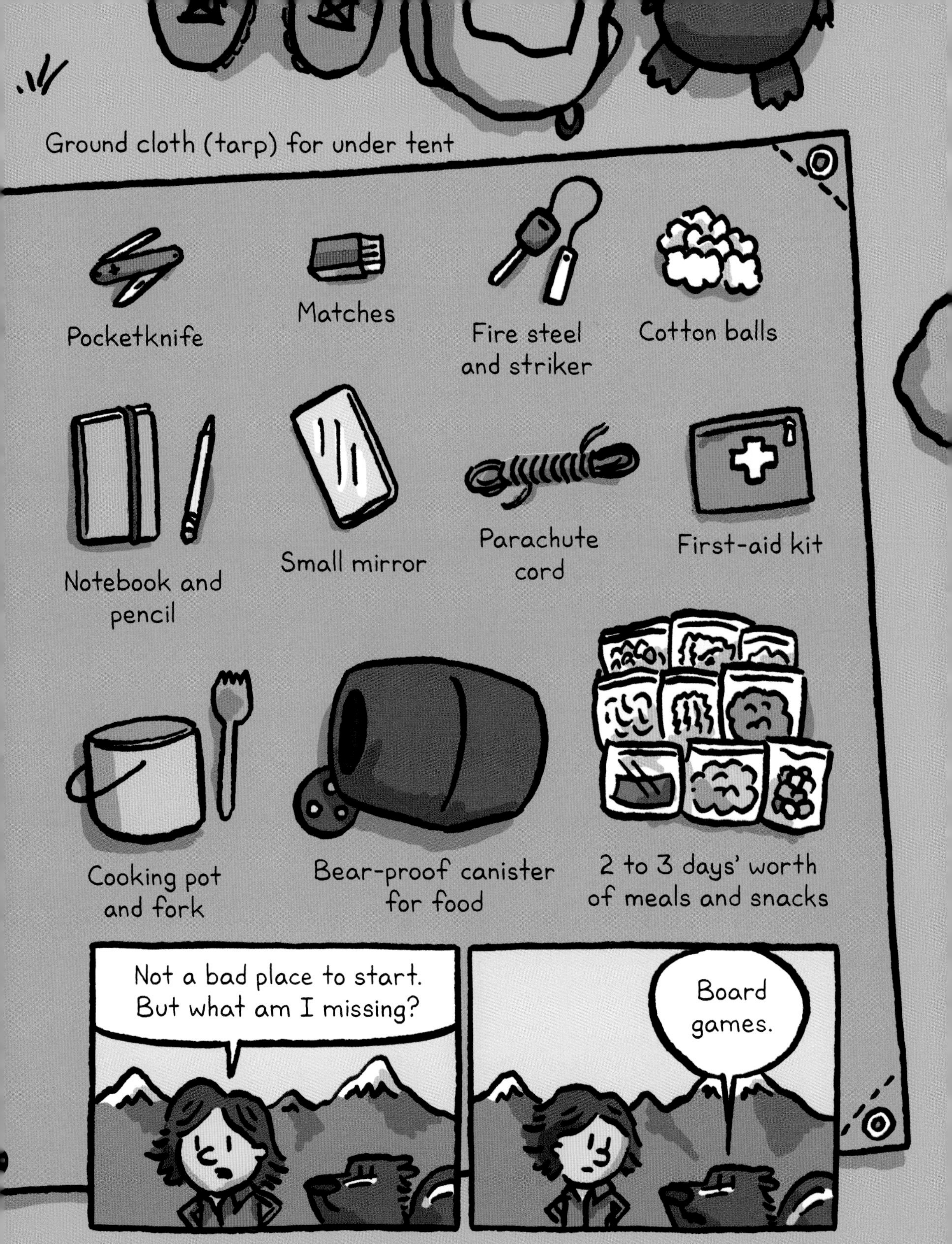

Ground cloth (tarp) for under tent
Pocketknife
Matches
Fire steel and striker
Cotton balls
Notebook and pencil
Small mirror
Parachute cord
First-aid kit
Cooking pot and fork
Bear-proof canister for food
2 to 3 days' worth of meals and snacks
Not a bad place to start. But what am I missing?
Board games.

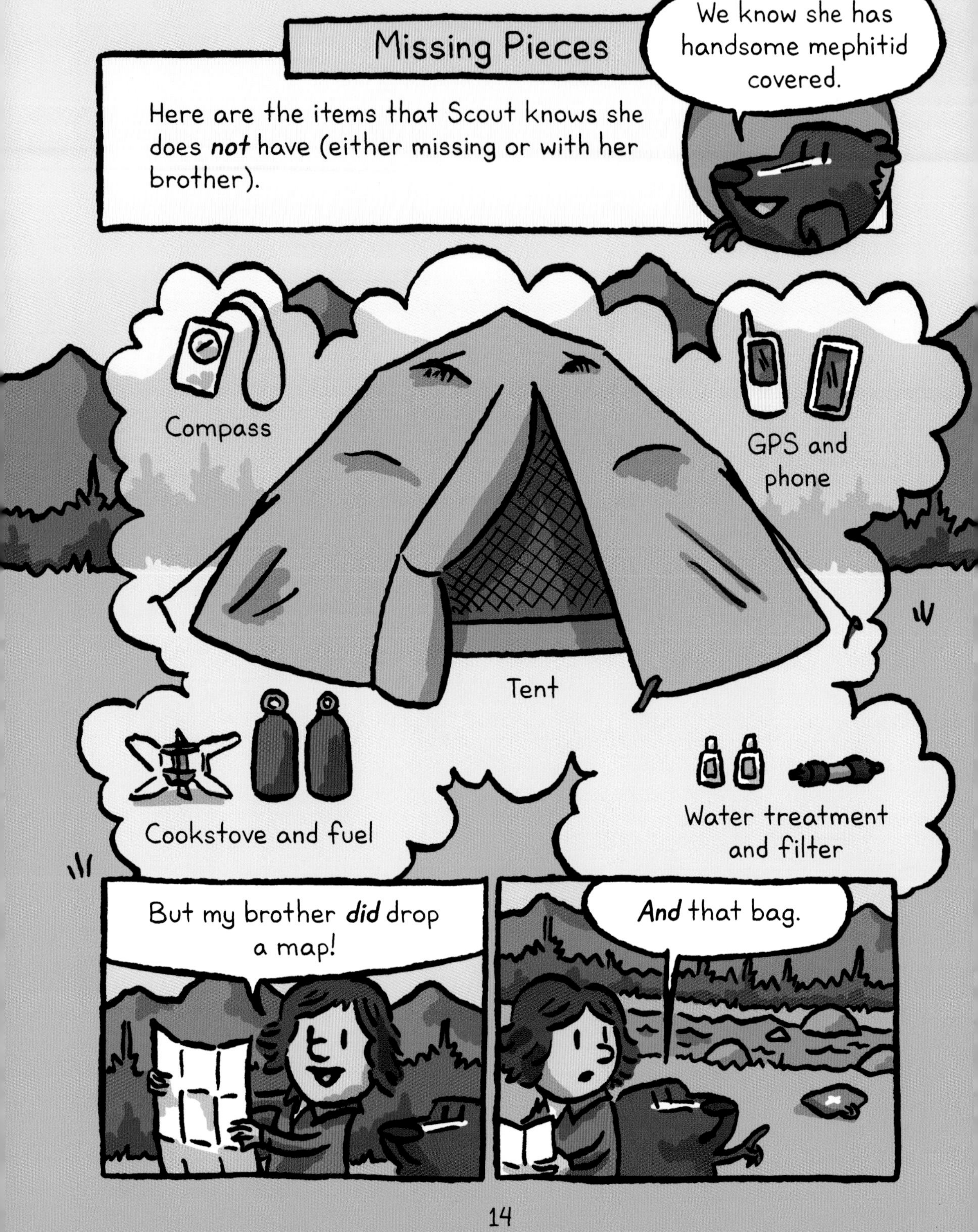
Missing Pieces
Here are the items that Scout knows she does *not* have (either missing or with her brother).
We know she has handsome mephitid covered.
Compass
GPS and phone
Tent
Cookstove and fuel
Water treatment and filter
But my brother *did* drop a map!
And that bag.

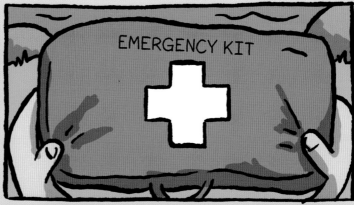
EMERGENCY KIT

This could be useful.

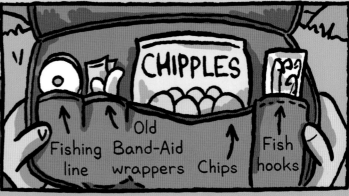
CHIPPLES

Old
Fishing Band-Aid
line wrappers Chips Fish hooks

His tackle box.

Ooo, Chipples.

I wish I had those Chipples.

Inventory aside, the most important possessions are knowledge, preparation, and a positive state of mind. And Scout has all three.

A working phone would still be nice.

So what's next? This is exciting.

Priority 1: Shelter

Scout's biggest concern now should be protecting herself from sun, wind, and rain. A passing shower or approaching dark could cause hypothermia, where the body's temperature falls below normal and can't recover. It is a deadly condition.

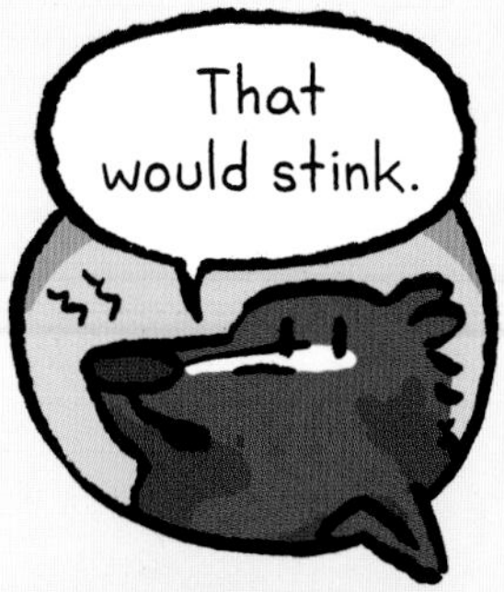
That would stink.

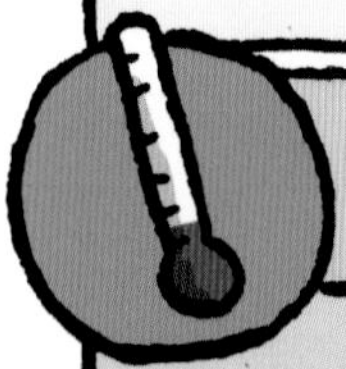

Hypothermia can be caused or made worse by . . .

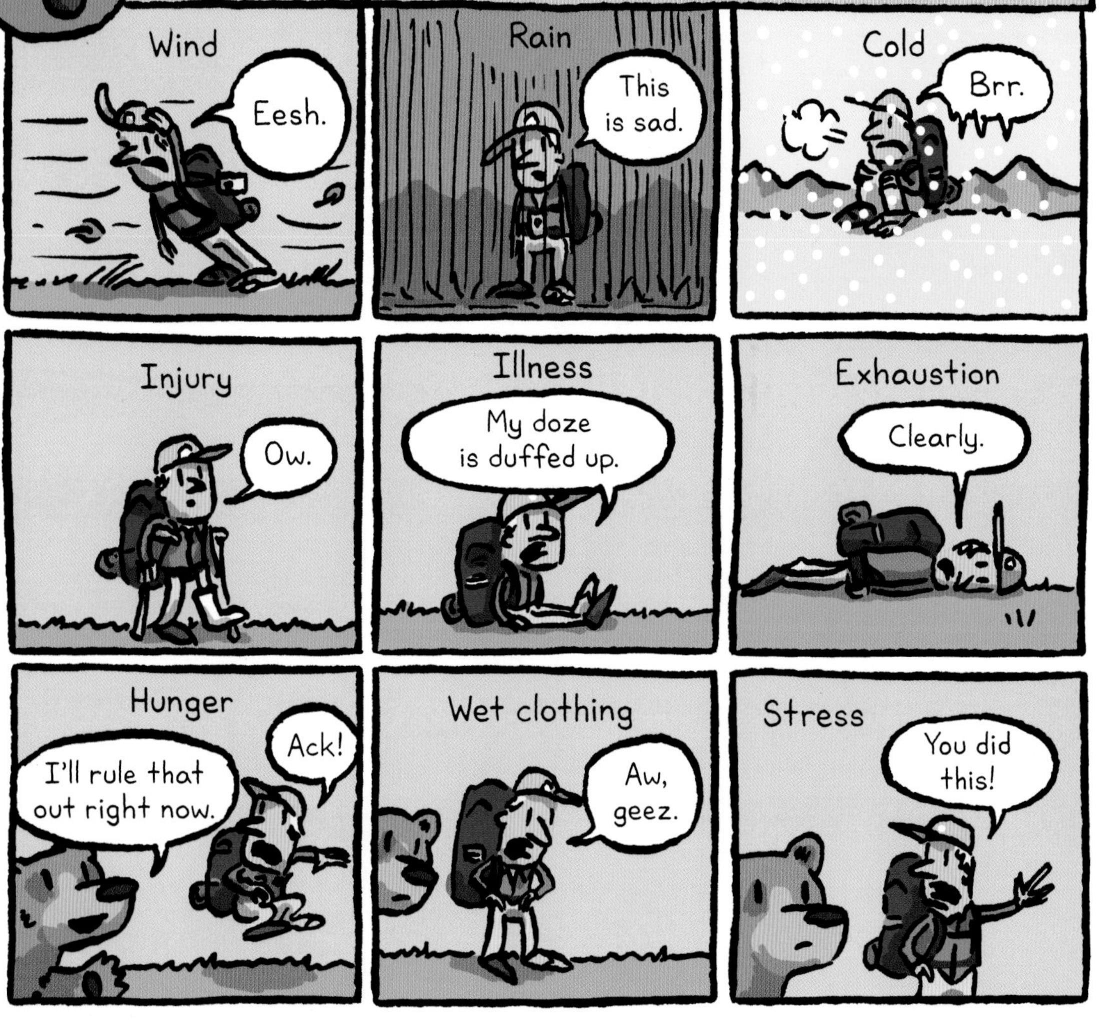
Wind
Eesh.
Rain
This is sad.
Cold
Brr.
Injury
Ow.
Illness
My doze is duffed up.
Exhaustion
Clearly.
Hunger
I'll rule that out right now.
Ack!
Wet clothing
Aw, geez.
Stress
You did this!

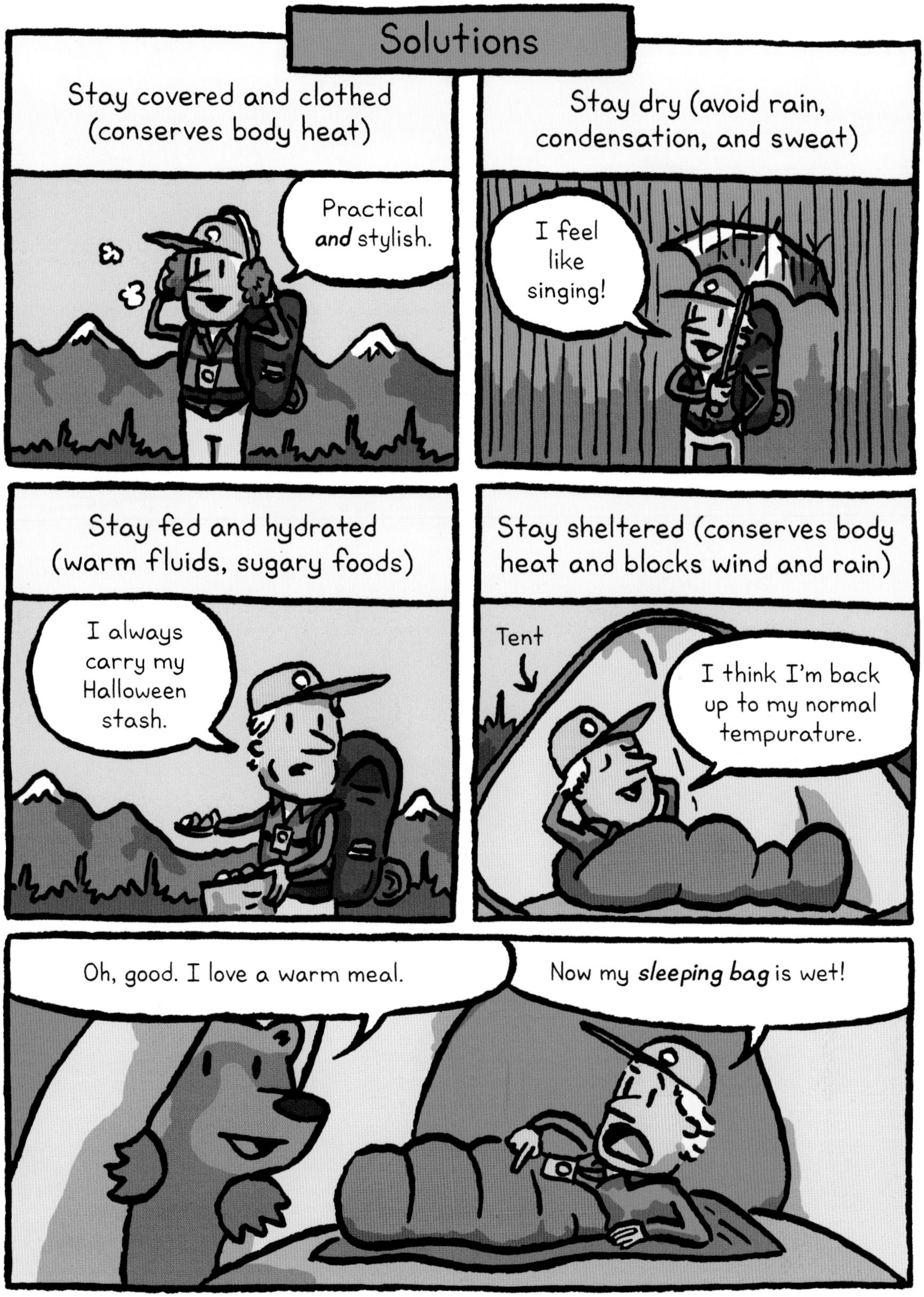
Solutions
Stay covered and clothed (conserves body heat)
Practical *and* stylish.
Stay dry (avoid rain, condensation, and sweat)
I feel like singing!
Stay fed and hydrated (warm fluids, sugary foods)
I always carry my Halloween stash.
Stay sheltered (conserves body heat and blocks wind and rain)
Tent
I think I'm back up to my normal tempurature.
Oh, good. I love a warm meal.
Now my *sleeping bag* is wet!

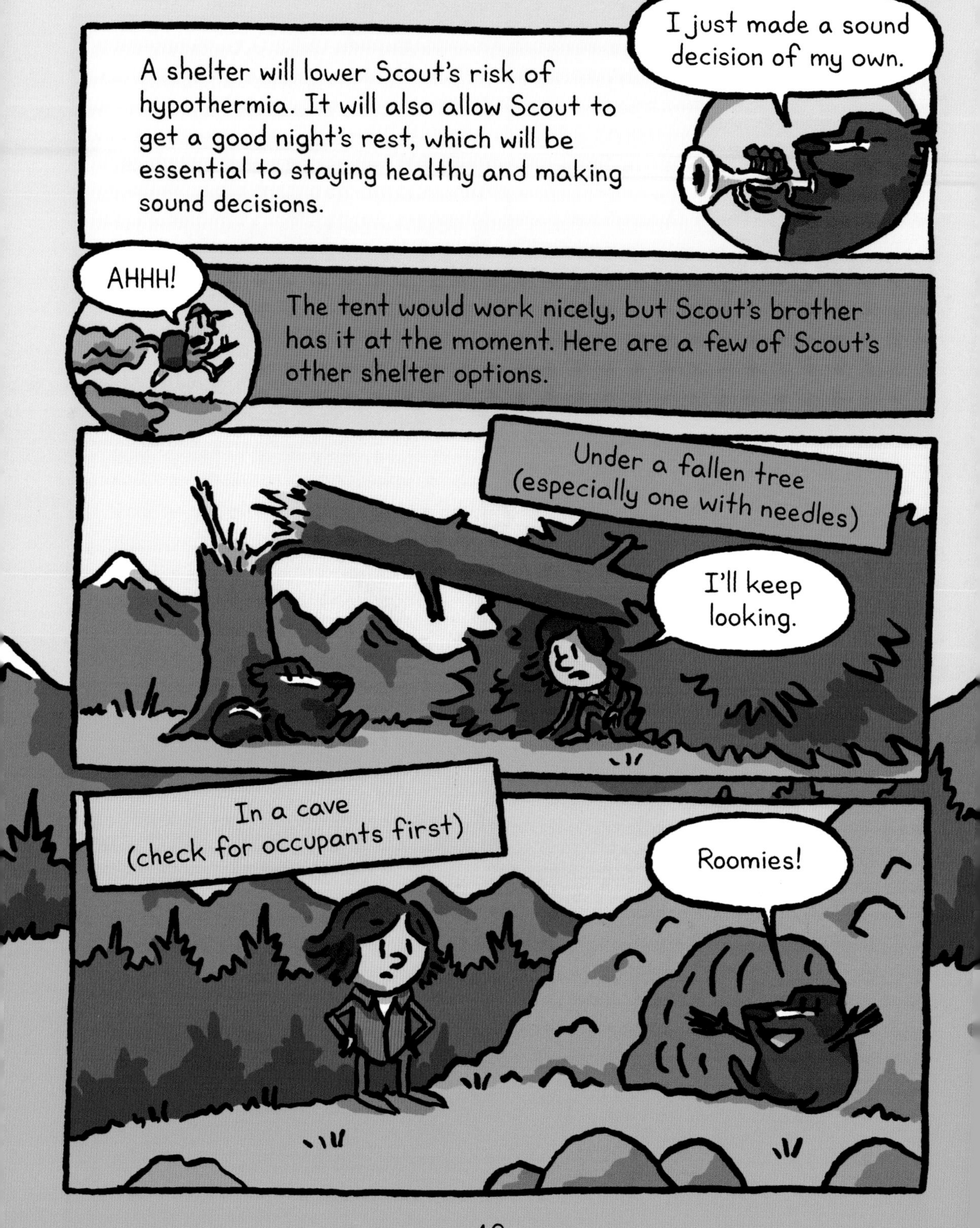

A shelter will lower Scout's risk of hypothermia. It will also allow Scout to get a good night's rest, which will be essential to staying healthy and making sound decisions.
I just made a sound decision of my own.
AHHH!
The tent would work nicely, but Scout's brother has it at the moment. Here are a few of Scout's other shelter options.
Under a fallen tree (especially one with needles)
I'll keep looking.
In a cave (check for occupants first)
Roomies!

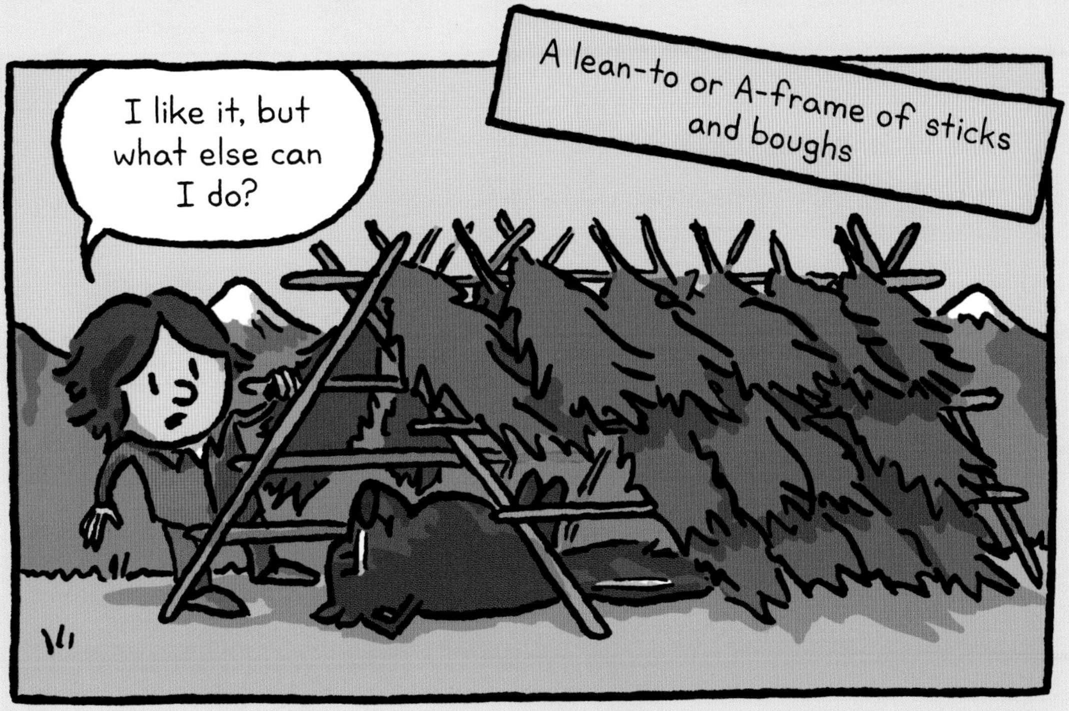
A lean-to or A-frame of sticks and boughs
I like it, but what else can I do?

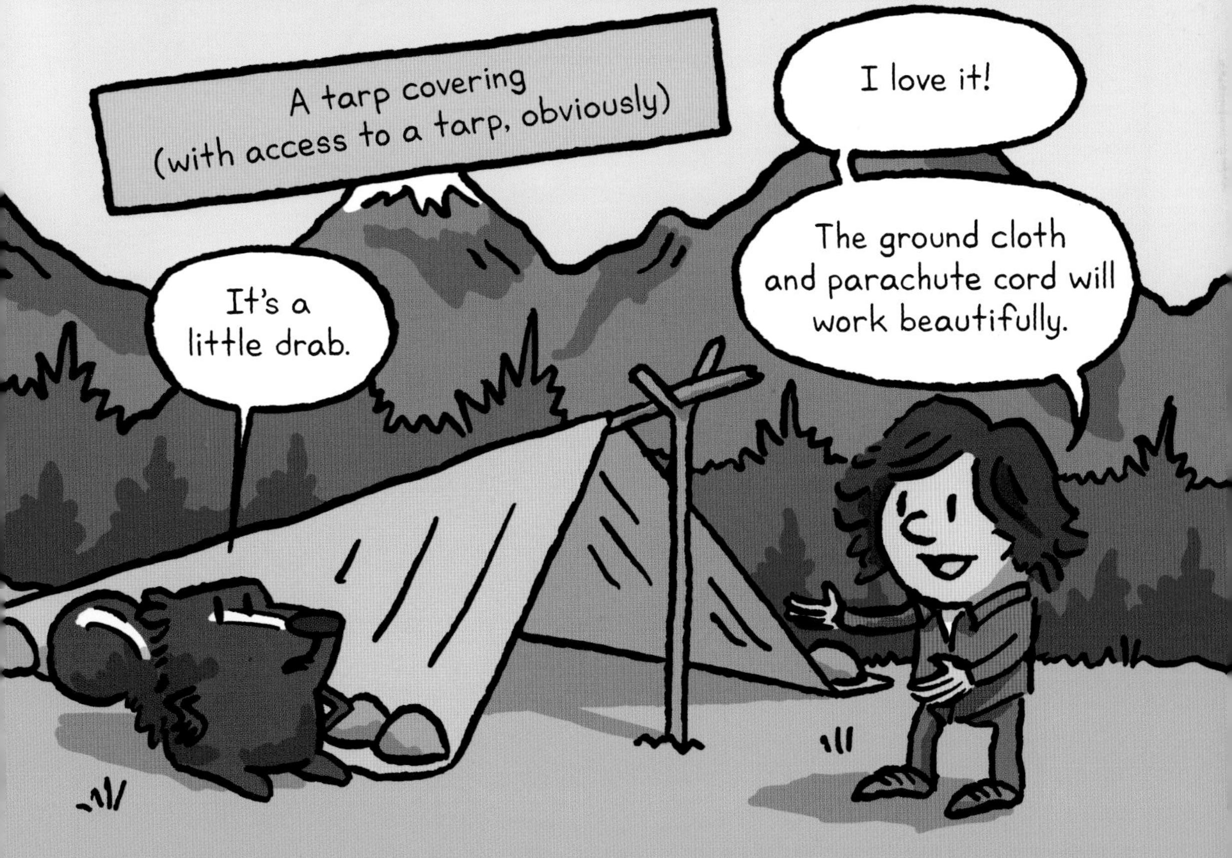
A tarp covering (with access to a tarp, obviously)
I love it!
The ground cloth and parachute cord will work beautifully.
It's a little drab.

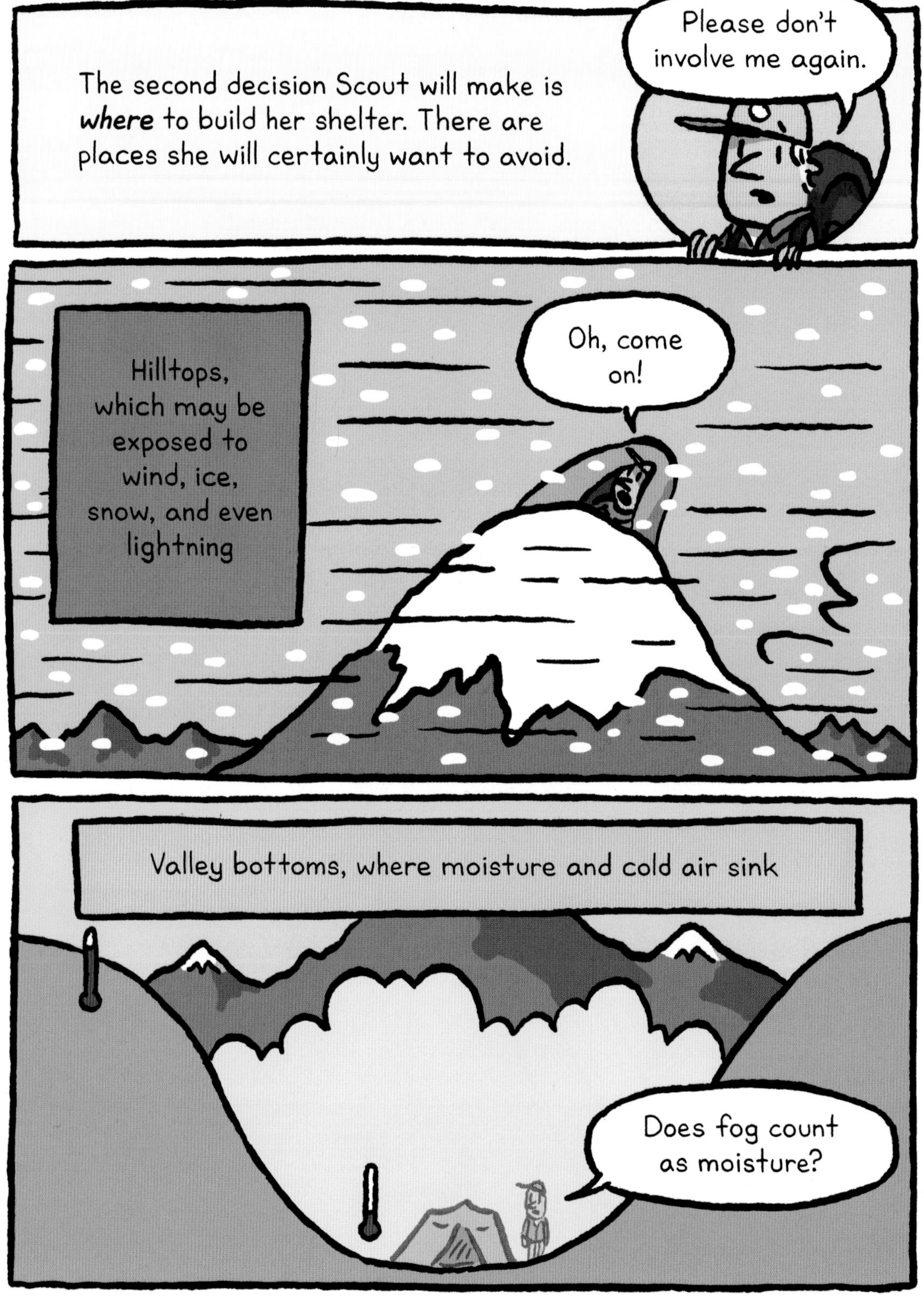

The second decision Scout will make is *where* to build her shelter. There are places she will certainly want to avoid.
Please don't involve me again.
Hilltops, which may be exposed to wind, ice, snow, and even lightning
Oh, come on!
Valley bottoms, where moisture and cold air sink
Does fog count as moisture?

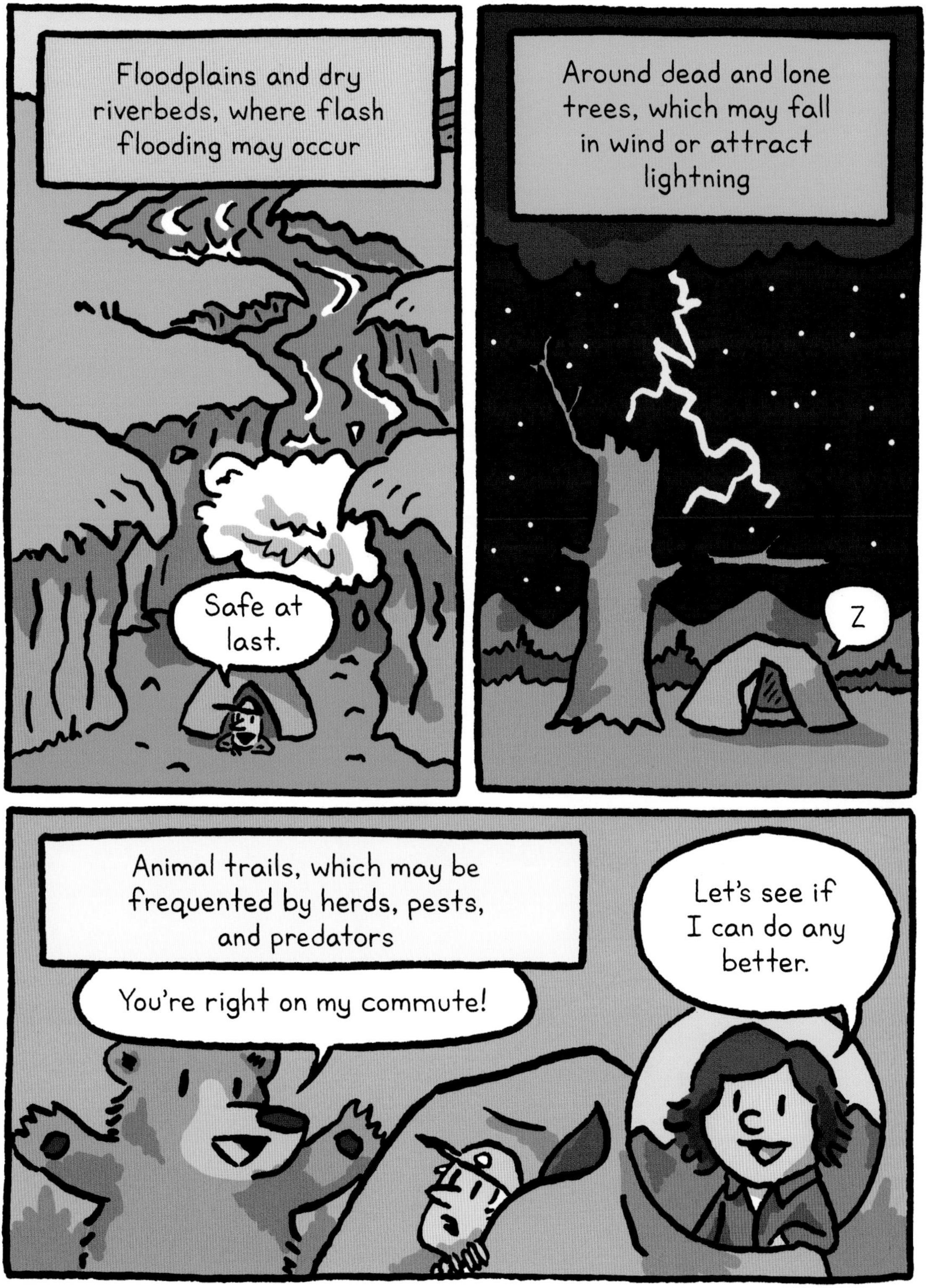
Floodplains and dry riverbeds, where flash flooding may occur
Safe at last.
Around dead and lone trees, which may fall in wind or attract lightning
Z
Animal trails, which may be frequented by herds, pests, and predators
You're right on my commute!
Let's see if I can do any better.

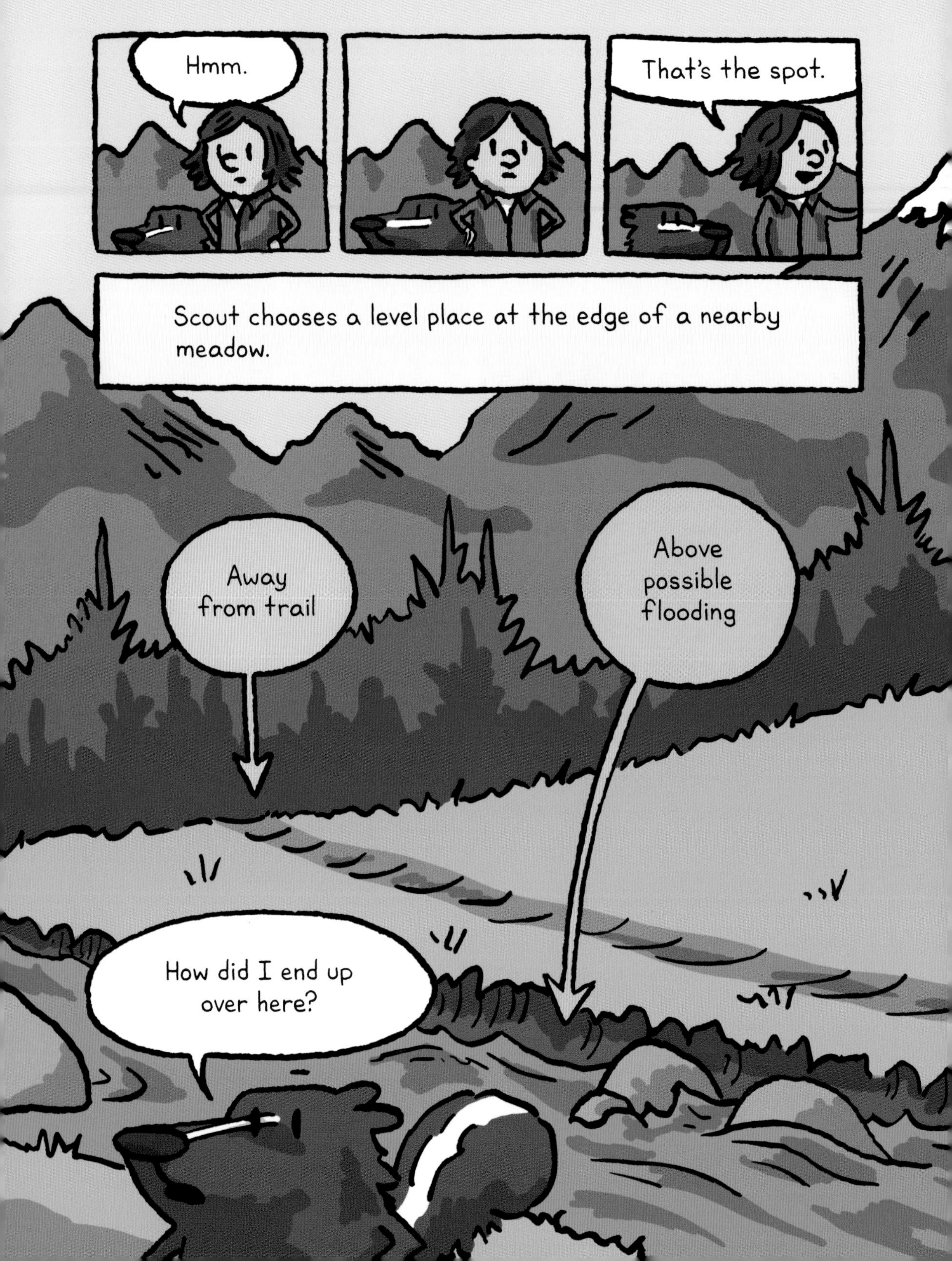
Hmm.
That's the spot.
Scout chooses a level place at the edge of a nearby meadow.
Away from trail
Above possible flooding
How did I end up over here?

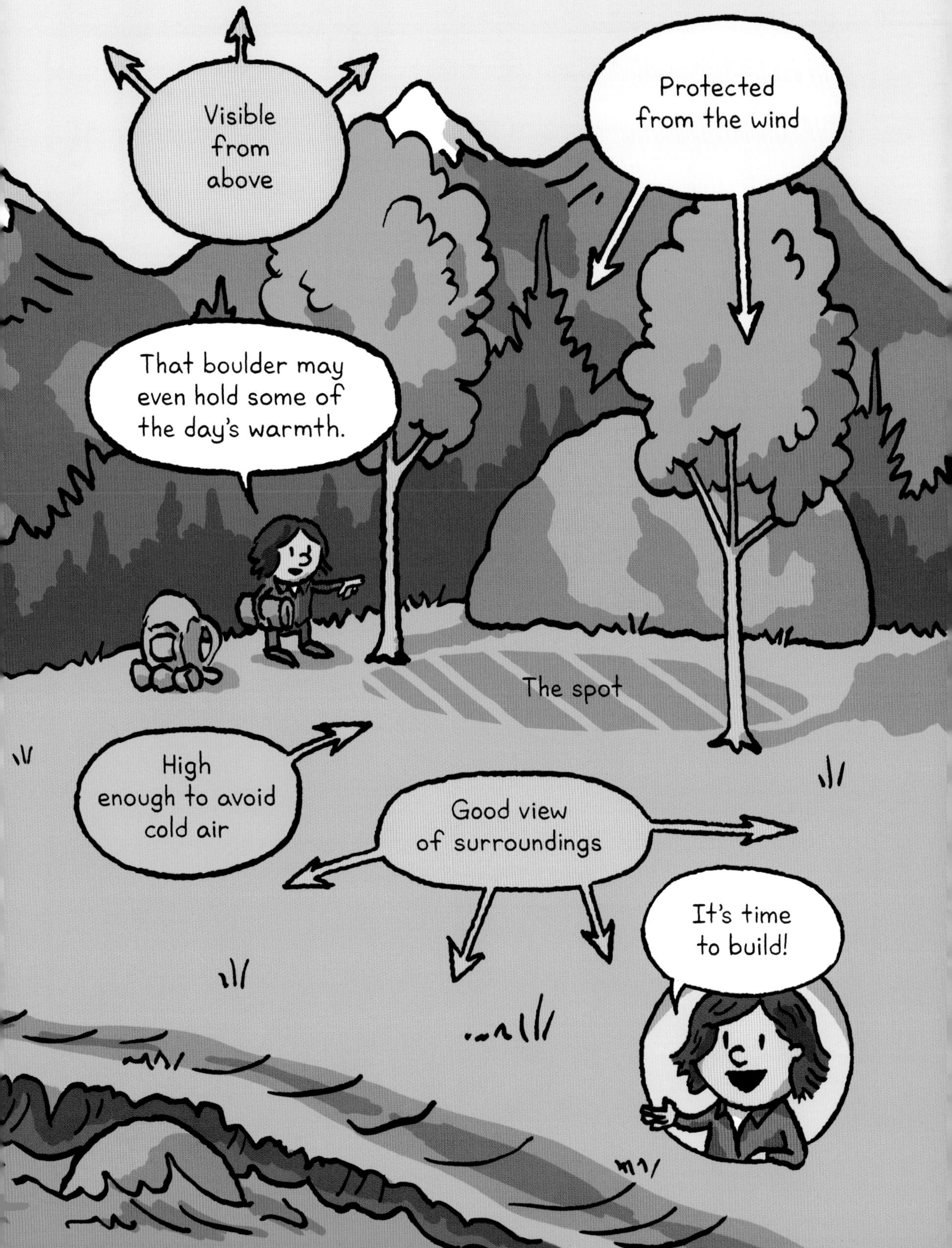
Visible from above
Protected from the wind
That boulder may even hold some of the day's warmth.
The spot
High enough to avoid cold air
Good view of surroundings
It's time to build!

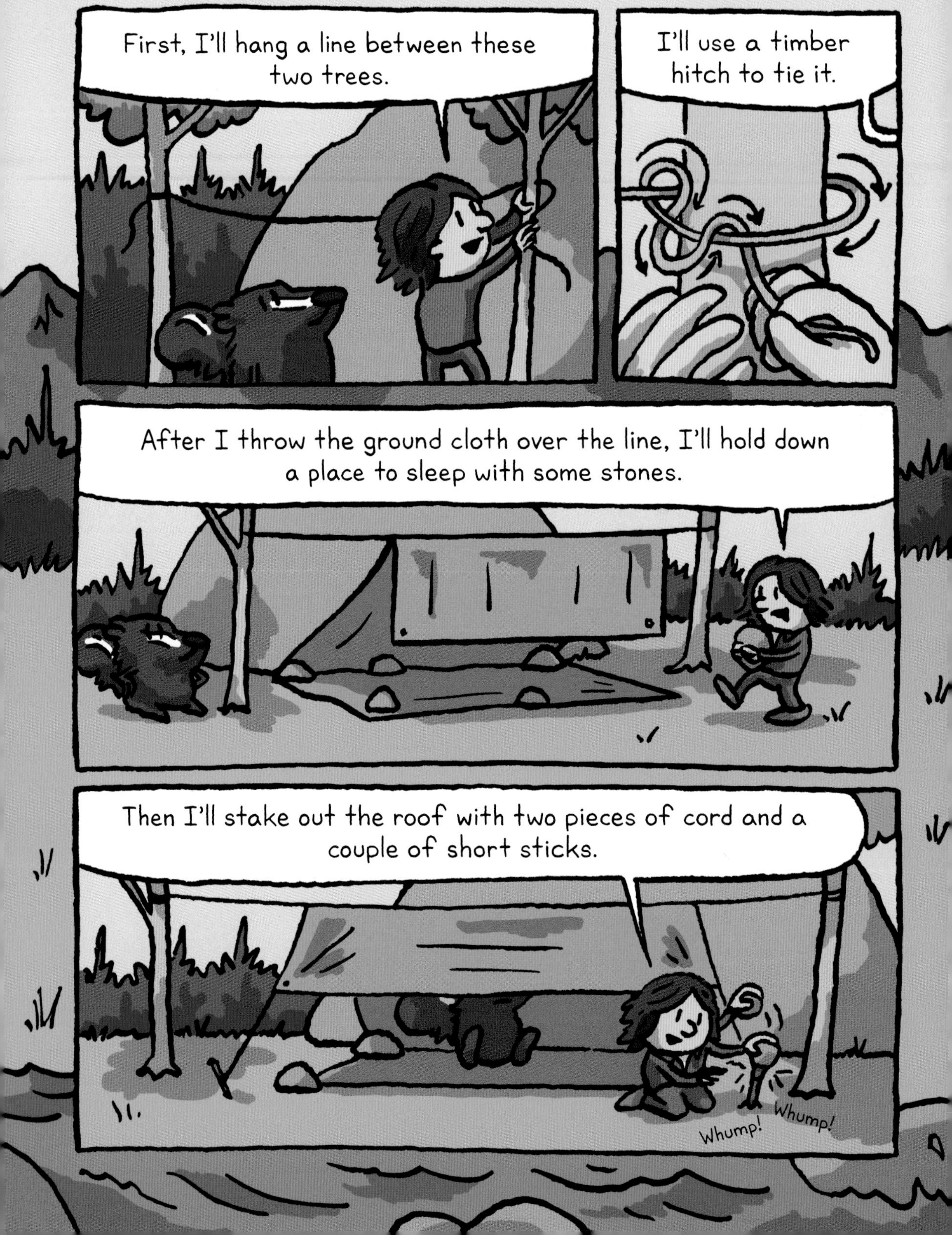
First, I'll hang a line between these two trees.
I'll use a timber hitch to tie it.
After I throw the ground cloth over the line, I'll hold down a place to sleep with some stones.
Then I'll stake out the roof with two pieces of cord and a couple of short sticks.
Whump!
Whump!

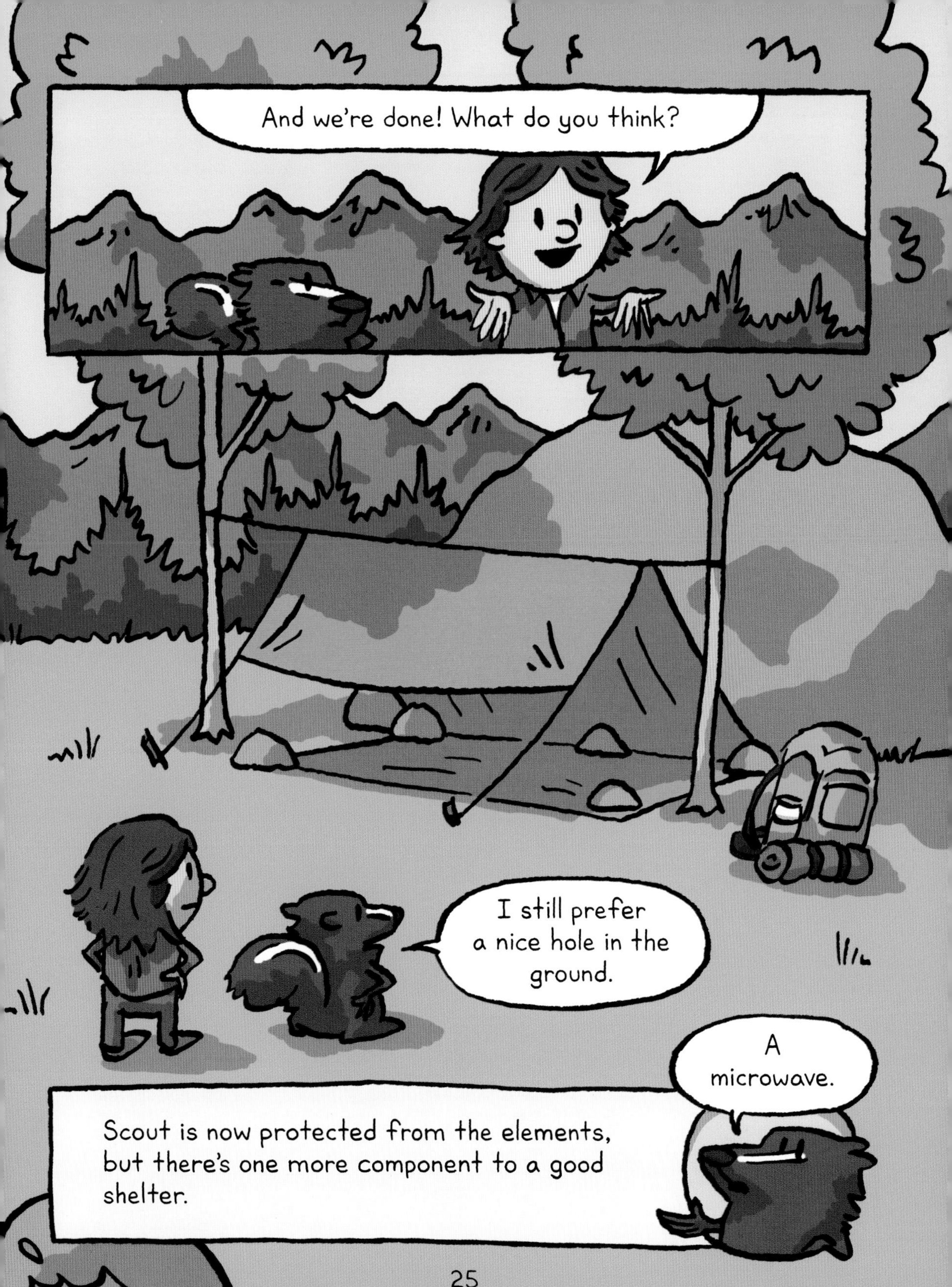
And we're done! What do you think?
I still prefer a nice hole in the ground.
A microwave.
Scout is now protected from the elements, but there's one more component to a good shelter.

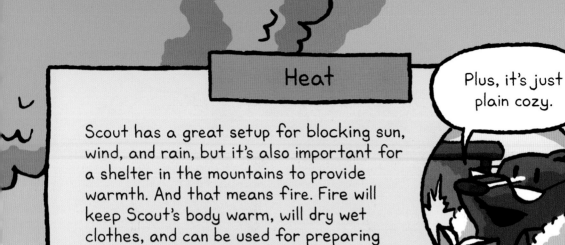

Heat

Scout has a great setup for blocking sun, wind, and rain, but it's also important for a shelter in the mountains to provide warmth. And that means fire. Fire will keep Scout's body warm, will dry wet clothes, and can be used for preparing water and food, as we will see.

Plus, it's just plain cozy.

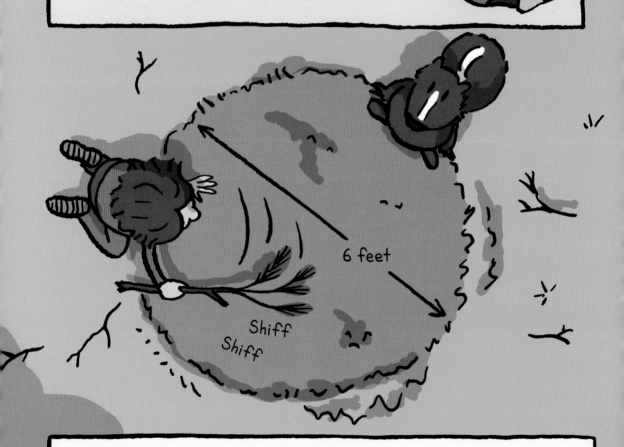

6 feet

Shiff
Shiff

Scout clears an area near her tent of anything that could catch fire, like dry grass, sticks, and pine needles.

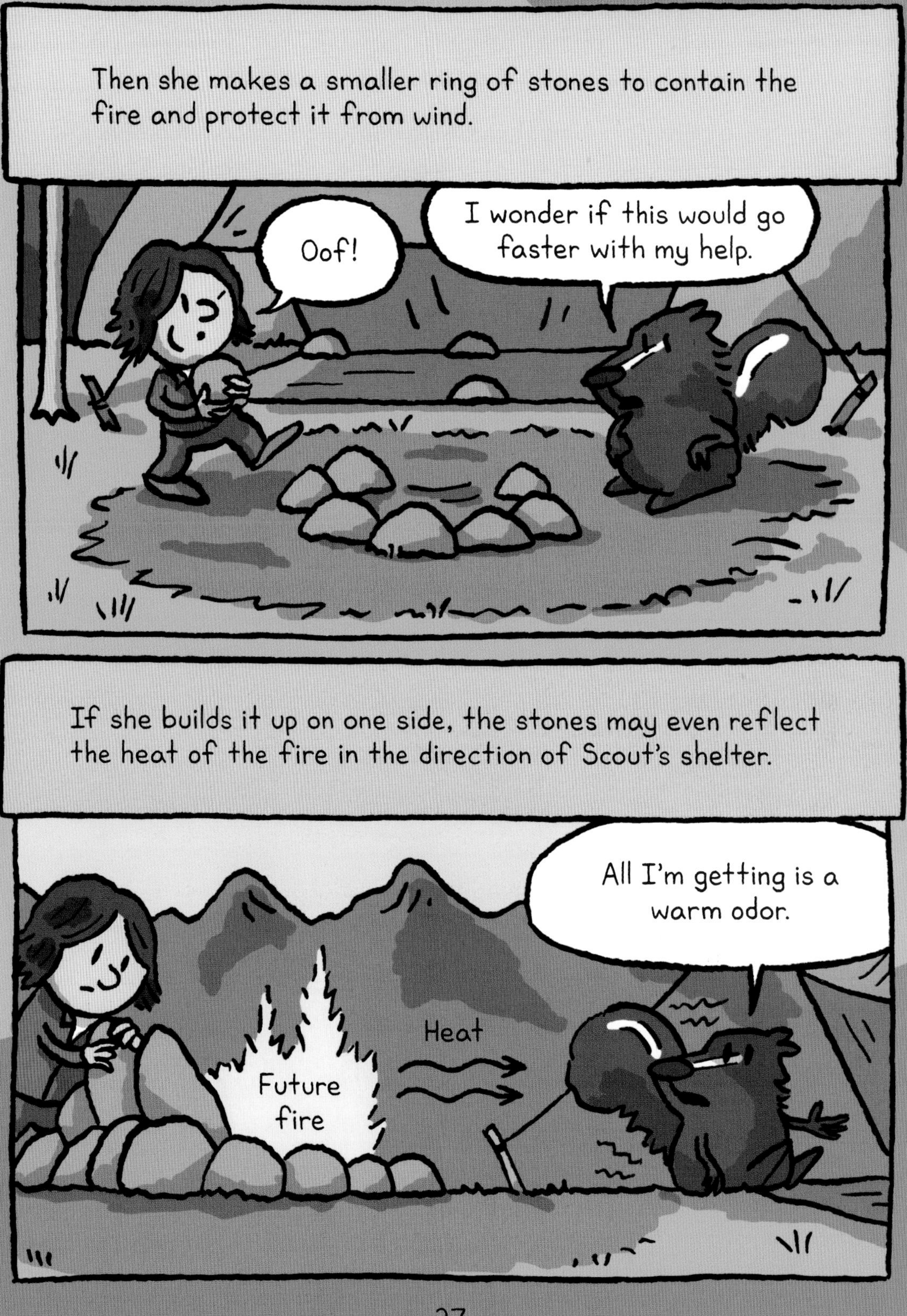
Then she makes a smaller ring of stones to contain the fire and protect it from wind.
Oof!
I wonder if this would go faster with my help.
If she builds it up on one side, the stones may even reflect the heat of the fire in the direction of Scout's shelter.
All I'm getting is a warm odor.
Heat
Future fire

Next, Scout gathers her three fire-making components. Here they are from smallest to largest, in the order they're lit.

Tinder

Tinder should require only a spark to light. The tinder will light the kindling.

Dry grass

Crumpled paper

Cotton balls

Wood shavings

Birch bark

Pine needles

It'll be a good idea for Scout to gather dry tinder as she finds it throughout her day. It's never a bad thing to have a pocketful of dry tinder at the ready!

No pants. No pockets.

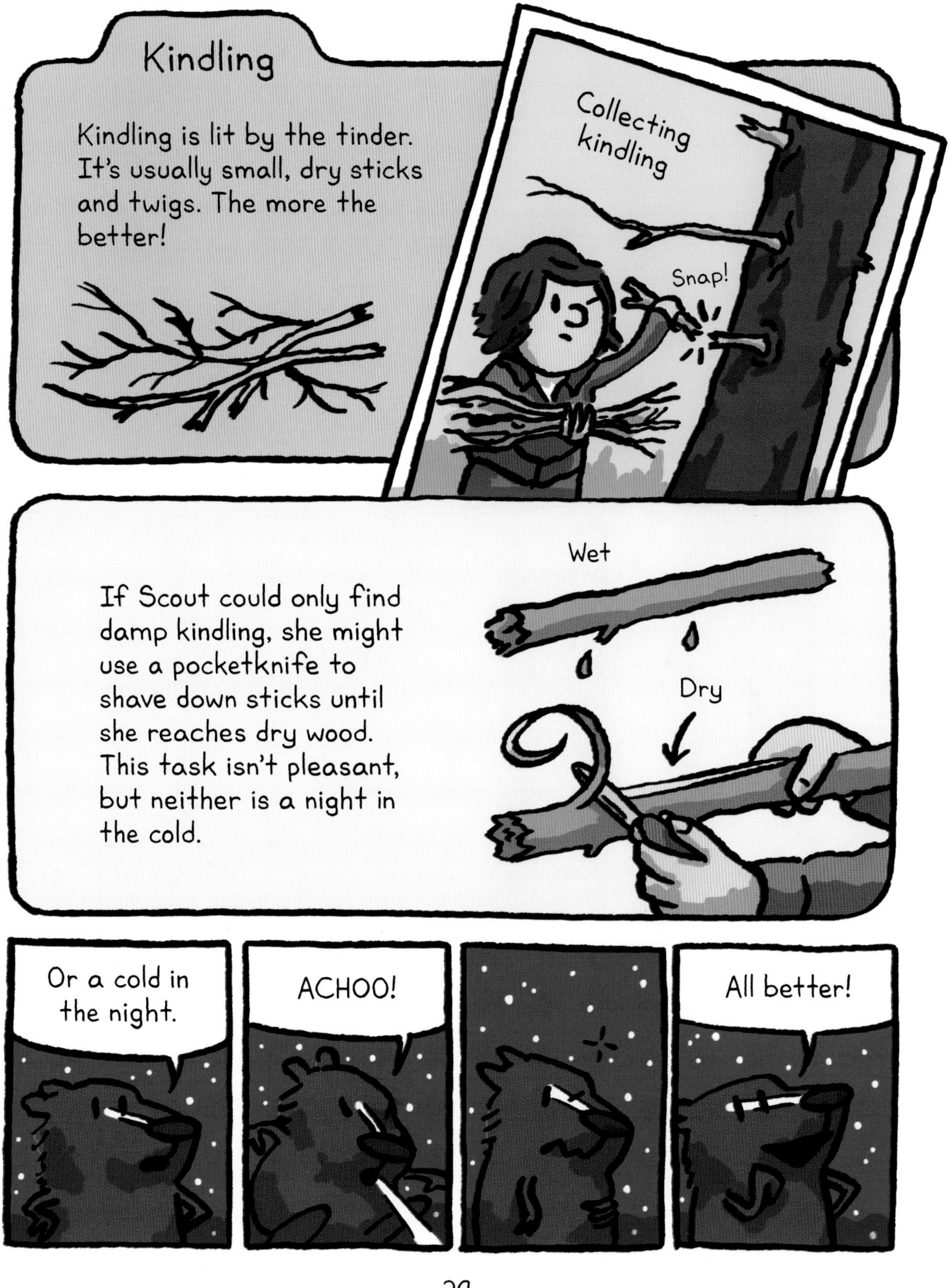
Kindling
Kindling is lit by the tinder. It's usually small, dry sticks and twigs. The more the better!
Collecting kindling
Snap!
If Scout could only find damp kindling, she might use a pocketknife to shave down sticks until she reaches dry wood. This task isn't pleasant, but neither is a night in the cold.
Wet
Dry
Or a cold in the night.
ACHOO!
All better!

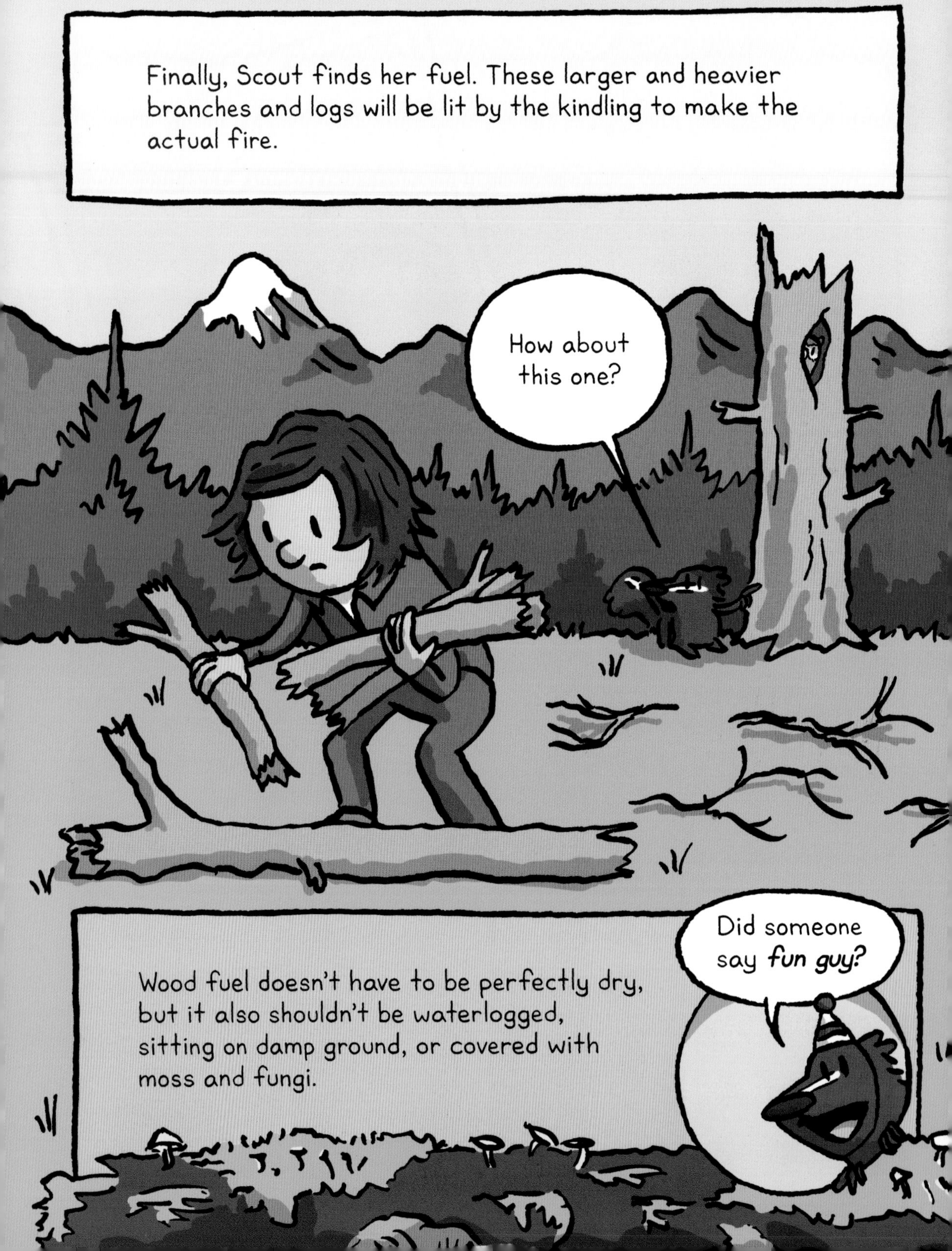
Finally, Scout finds her fuel. These larger and heavier branches and logs will be lit by the kindling to make the actual fire.
How about this one?
Wood fuel doesn't have to be perfectly dry, but it also shouldn't be waterlogged, sitting on damp ground, or covered with moss and fungi.
Did someone say *fun guy?*

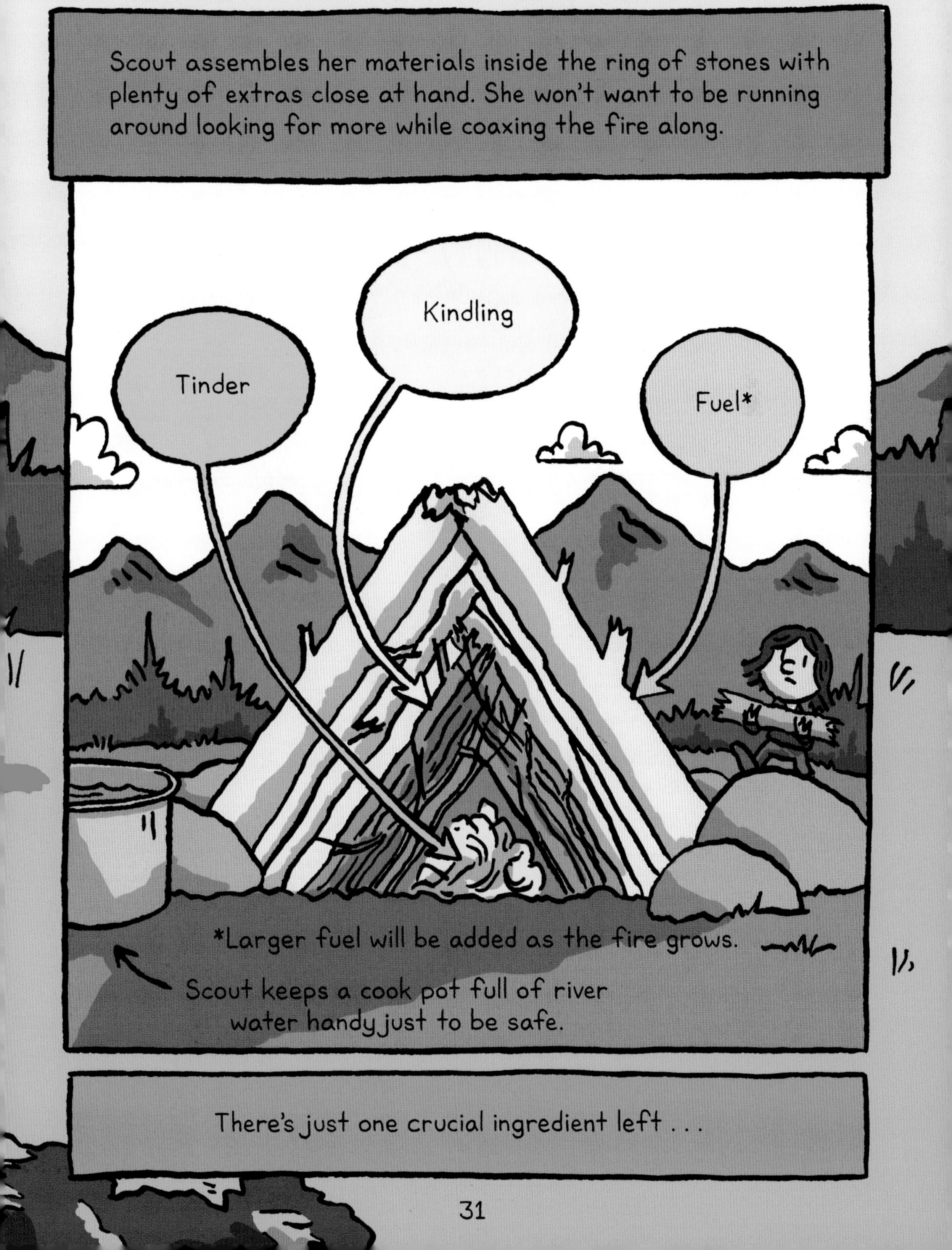
Scout assembles her materials inside the ring of stones with plenty of extras close at hand. She won't want to be running around looking for more while coaxing the fire along.
Kindling
Tinder
Fuel*
*Larger fuel will be added as the fire grows.
Scout keeps a cook pot full of river water handy just to be safe.
There's just one crucial ingredient left . . .

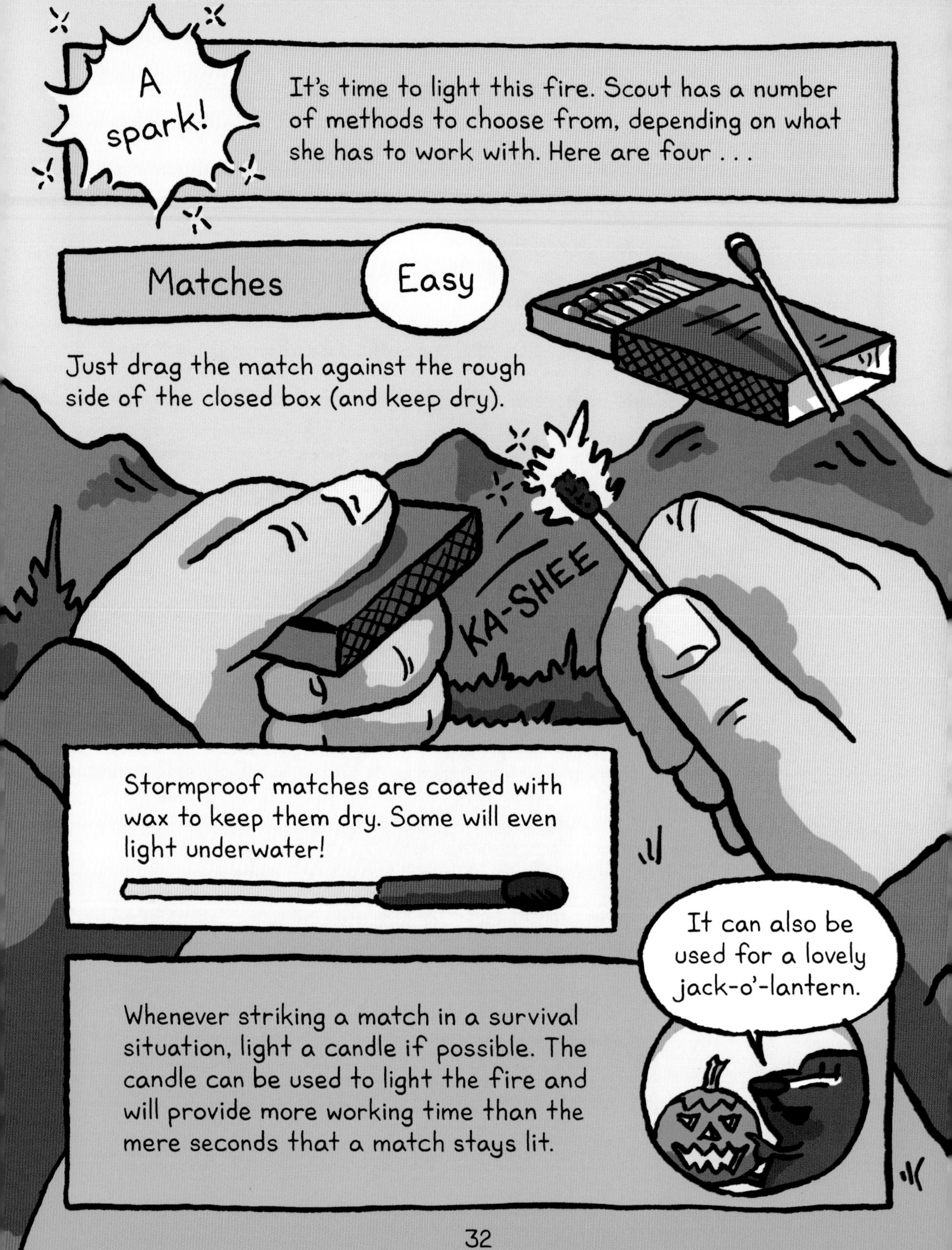
A spark!
It's time to light this fire. Scout has a number of methods to choose from, depending on what she has to work with. Here are four . . .
Matches
Easy
Just drag the match against the rough side of the closed box (and keep dry).
KA-SHEE
Stormproof matches are coated with wax to keep them dry. Some will even light underwater!
It can also be used for a lovely jack-o'-lantern.
Whenever striking a match in a survival situation, light a candle if possible. The candle can be used to light the fire and will provide more working time than the mere seconds that a match stays lit.

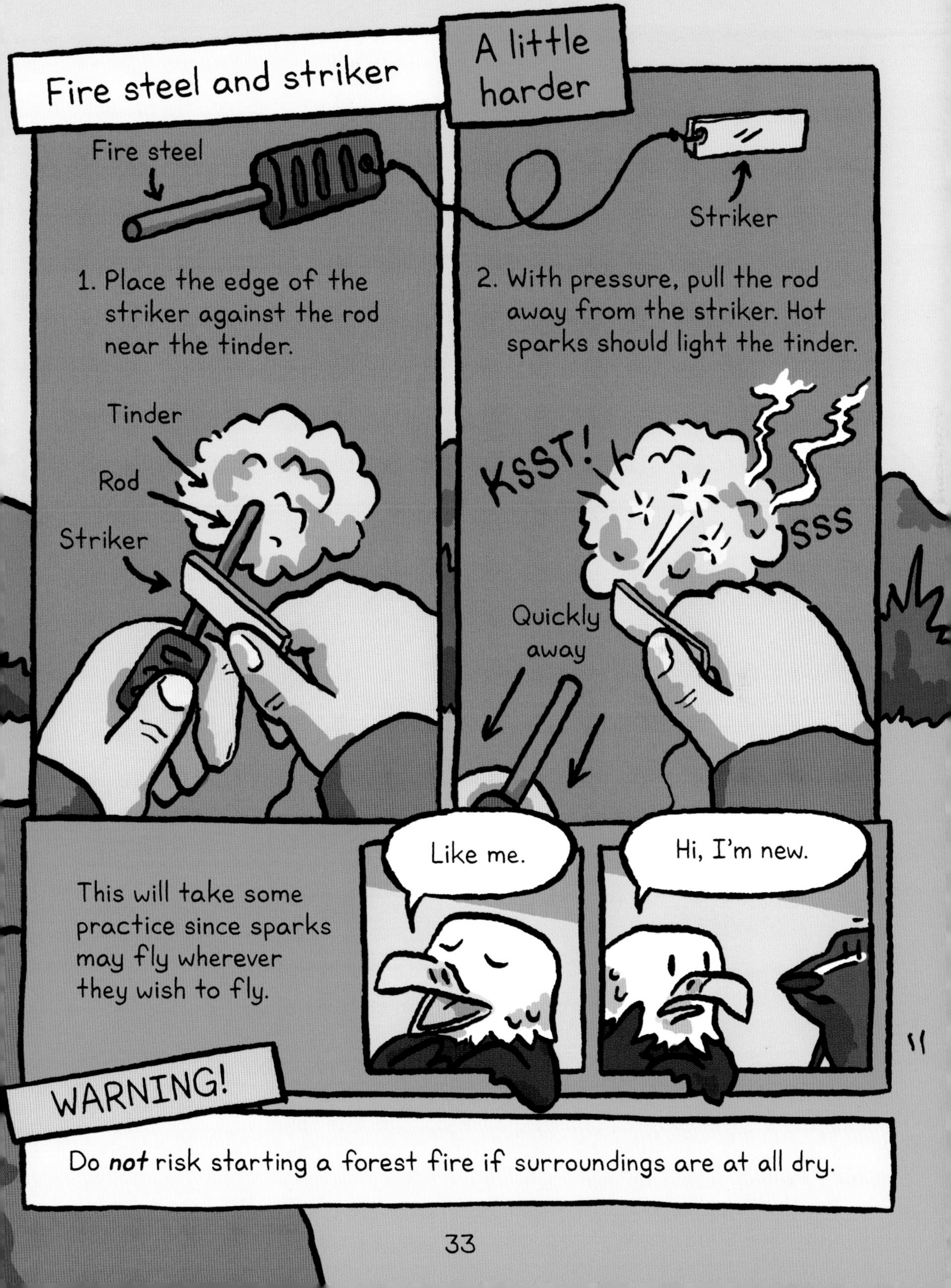

Fire steel and striker
A little harder
Fire steel
Striker
1. Place the edge of the striker against the rod near the tinder.
Tinder
Rod
Striker
2. With pressure, pull the rod away from the striker. Hot sparks should light the tinder.
KSST!
SSS
Quickly away
This will take some practice since sparks may fly wherever they wish to fly.
Like me.
Hi, I'm new.
WARNING!
Do **not** risk starting a forest fire if surroundings are at all dry.

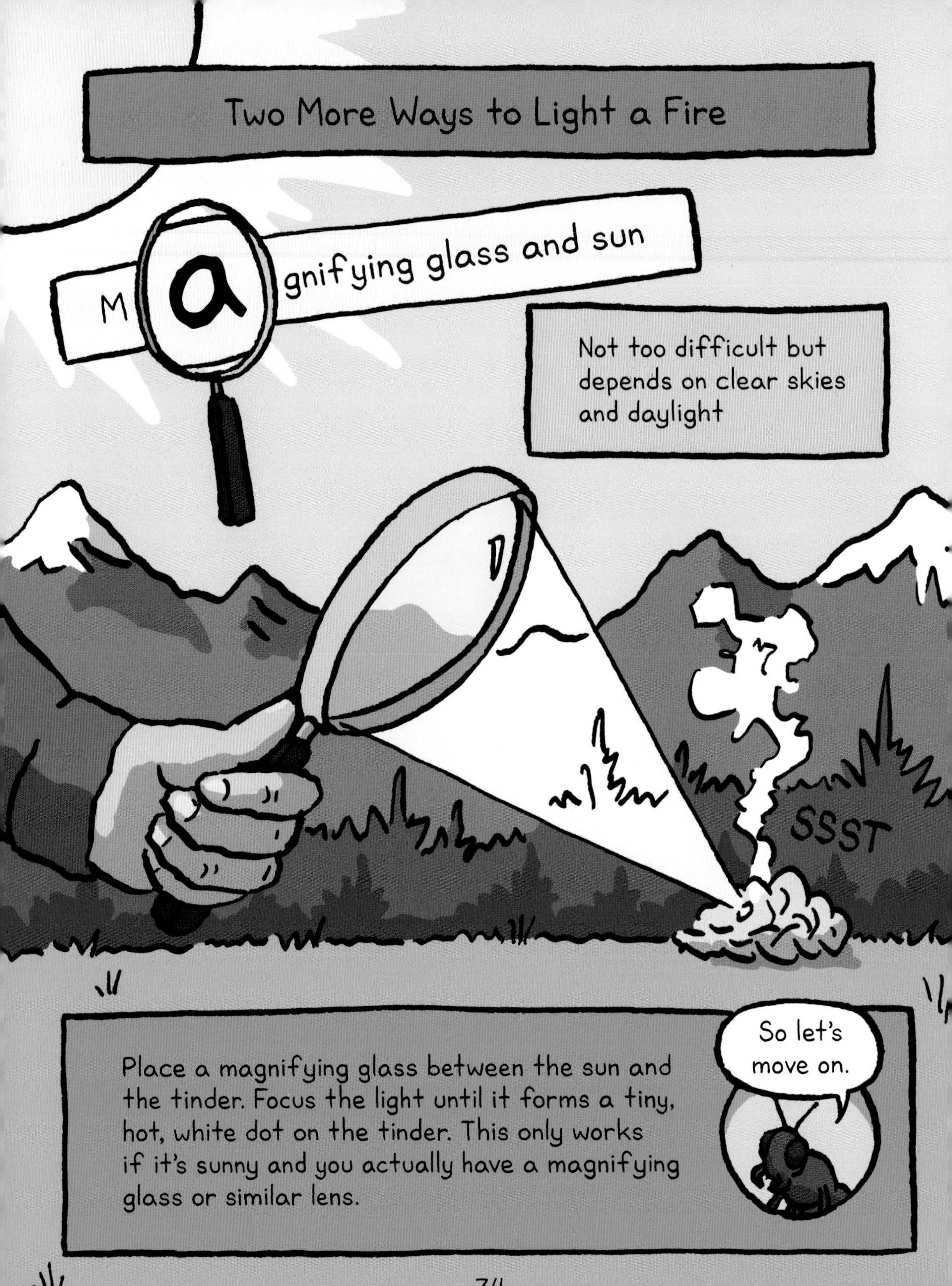
Two More Ways to Light a Fire
Magnifying glass and sun
Not too difficult but depends on clear skies and daylight
SSST
Place a magnifying glass between the sun and the tinder. Focus the light until it forms a tiny, hot, white dot on the tinder. This only works if it's sunny and you actually have a magnifying glass or similar lens.
So let's move on.

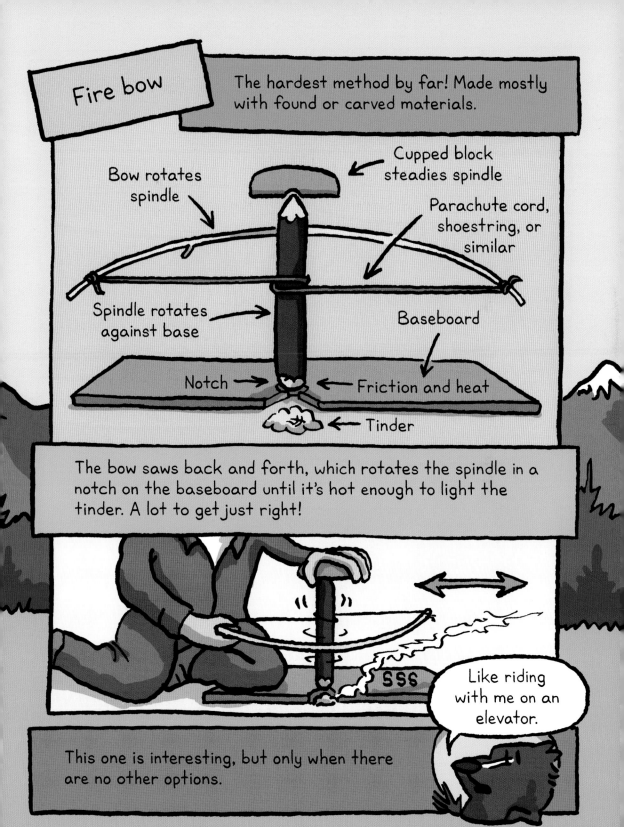

Fire bow

The hardest method by far! Made mostly with found or carved materials.

Bow rotates spindle

Cupped block steadies spindle

Parachute cord, shoestring, or similar

Spindle rotates against base

Baseboard

Notch → ← Friction and heat

← Tinder

The bow saws back and forth, which rotates the spindle in a notch on the baseboard until it's hot enough to light the tinder. A lot to get just right!

SSS

Like riding with me on an elevator.

This one is interesting, but only when there are no other options.

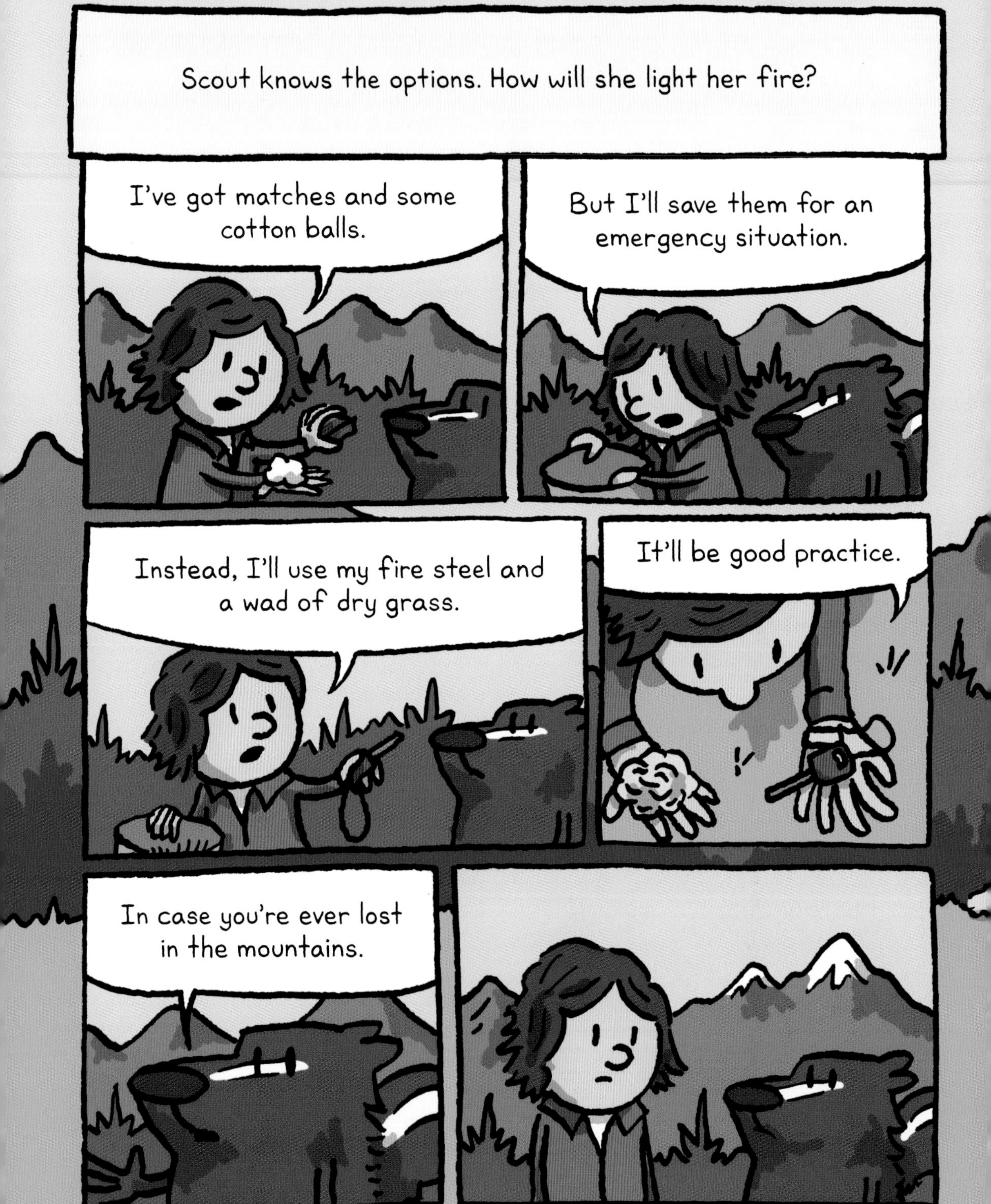
Scout knows the options. How will she light her fire?
I've got matches and some cotton balls.
But I'll save them for an emergency situation.
Instead, I'll use my fire steel and a wad of dry grass.
It'll be good practice.
In case you're ever lost in the mountains.

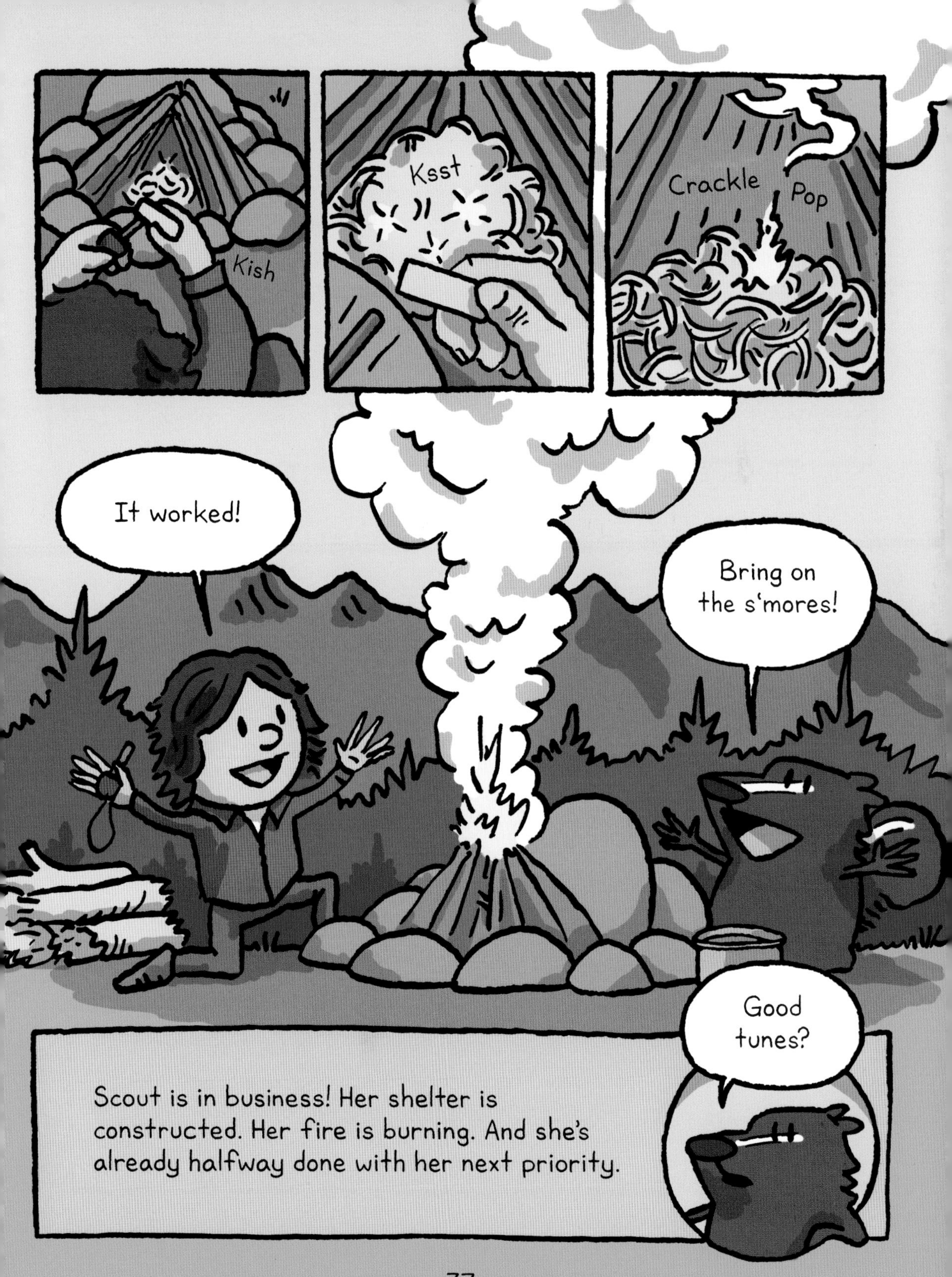
Kish
Ksst
Crackle
Pop
It worked!
Bring on the s'mores!
Good tunes?
Scout is in business! Her shelter is constructed. Her fire is burning. And she's already halfway done with her next priority.

Priority 2: Signals

At some point, someone is going to realize that Scout and her brother are missing. And soon after, people will begin to search. Often, this will mean search parties on the ground.

Did I hear *party?*

Because of the size and remoteness of this area, as well as Scout's age, this search will likely involve planes or helicopters.*

*But *NEVER* count on planes and helicopters to come rescue you.

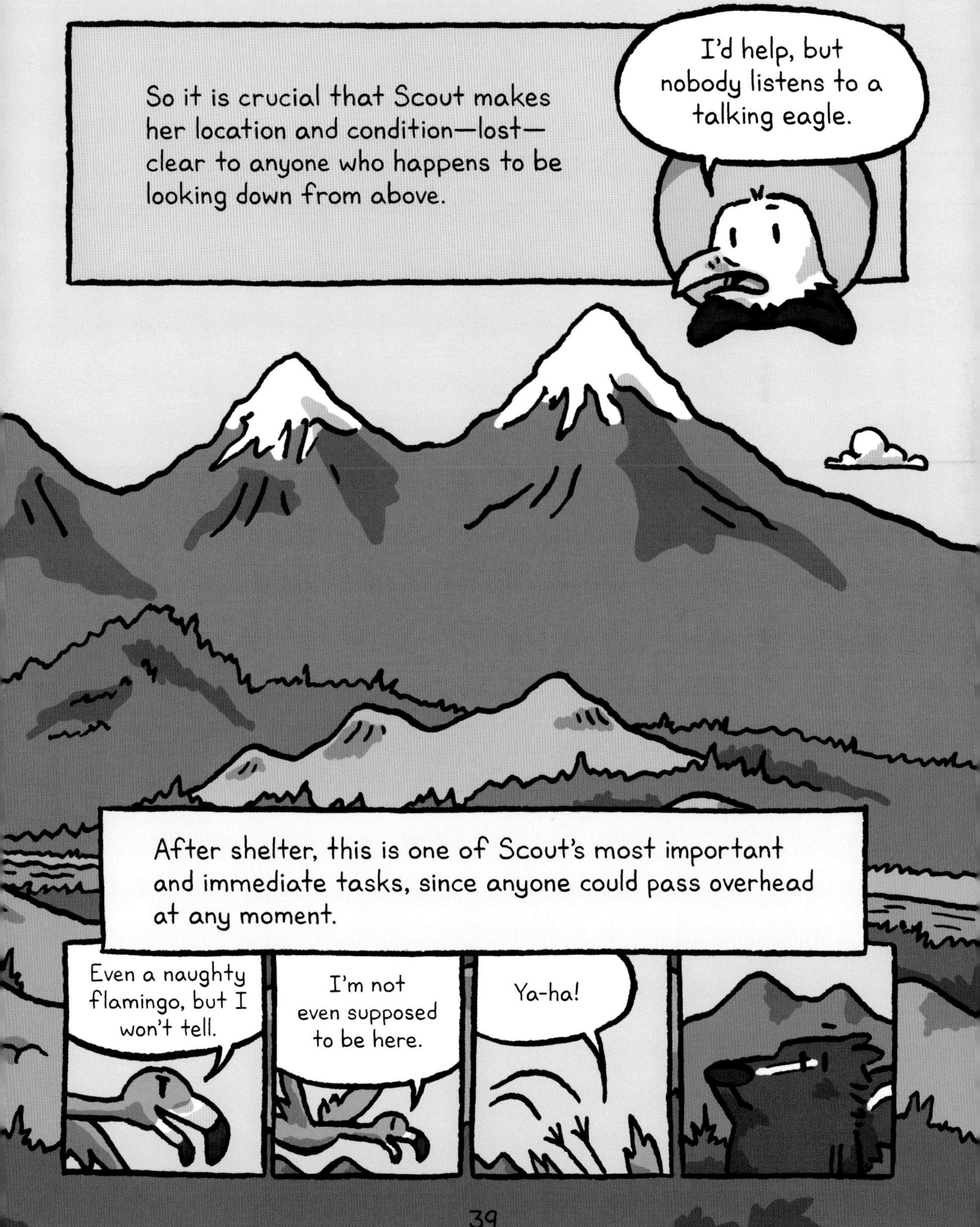
So it is crucial that Scout makes her location and condition—lost—clear to anyone who happens to be looking down from above.
I'd help, but nobody listens to a talking eagle.
After shelter, this is one of Scout's most important and immediate tasks, since anyone could pass overhead at any moment.
Even a naughty flamingo, but I won't tell.
I'm not even supposed to be here.
Ya-ha!

Scout starts with the basics and lays out an unmistakable message with rocks from the river.
SOS stands for *save our ship* and is universally recognized as a call for help. Even on dry land.
It could also mean *super outstanding skunk.*

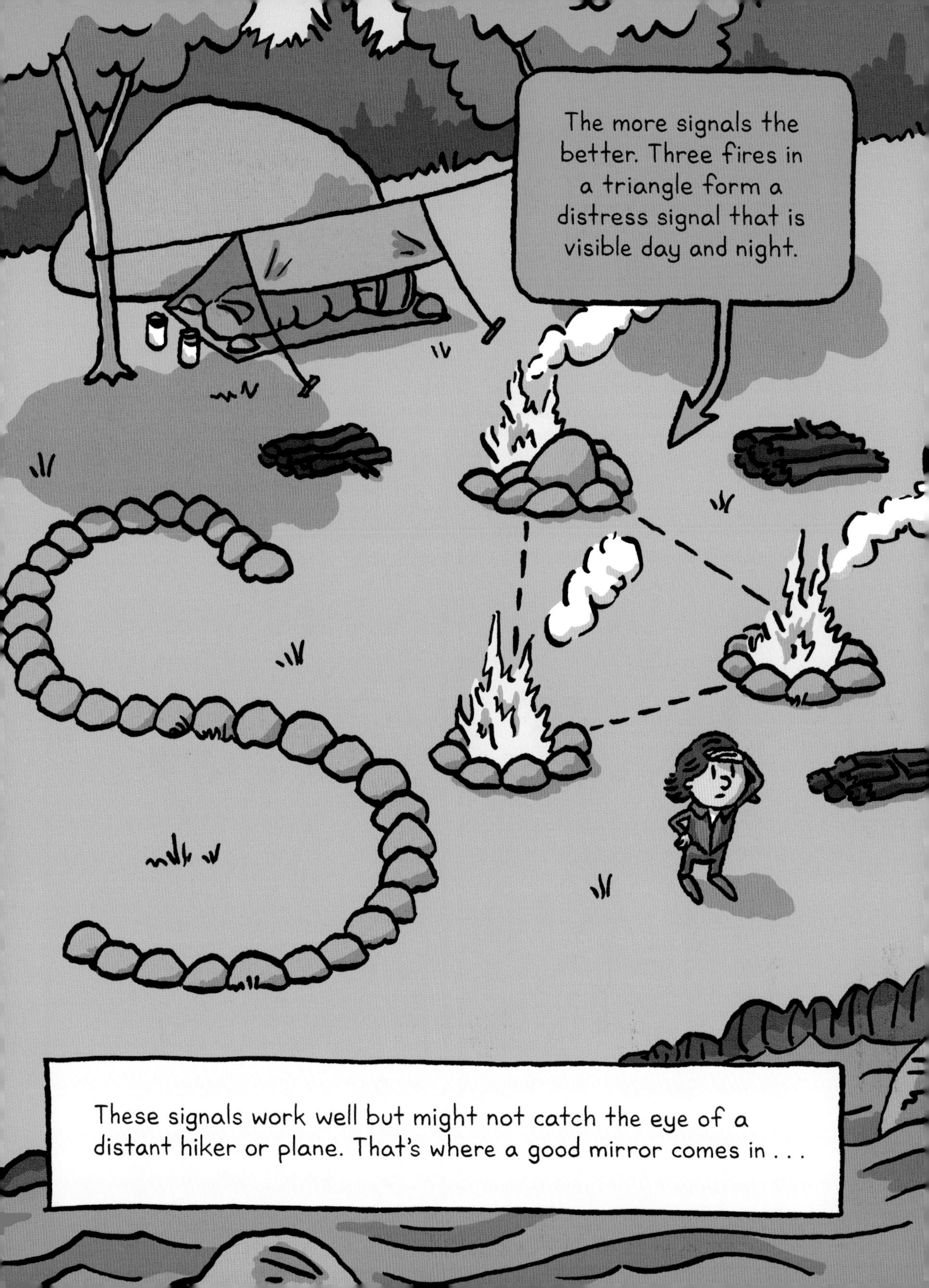
The more signals the better. Three fires in a triangle form a distress signal that is visible day and night.
These signals work well but might not catch the eye of a distant hiker or plane. That's where a good mirror comes in . . .

A signal mirror—or heliograph—is a double-sided mirror with a hole in the middle used to flash signals using sunlight. It can be visible for miles, assuming clear daytime skies.

Front faces target

Back faces user

Instructions

This plane will see a flash of light when the mirror is angled exactly halfway between it and the sun.

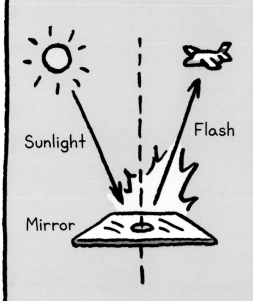

Sunlight

Flash

Mirror

But how do you figure out that angle?

Spot the plane through the hole. Then find the dot of sunlight that passes through the hole in the signal mirror.

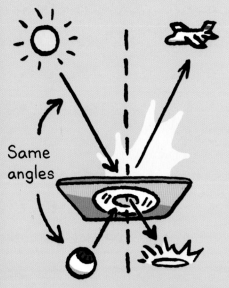

Same angles

If the eye can see the plane *and* the spot, then the plane can see the flash of light.

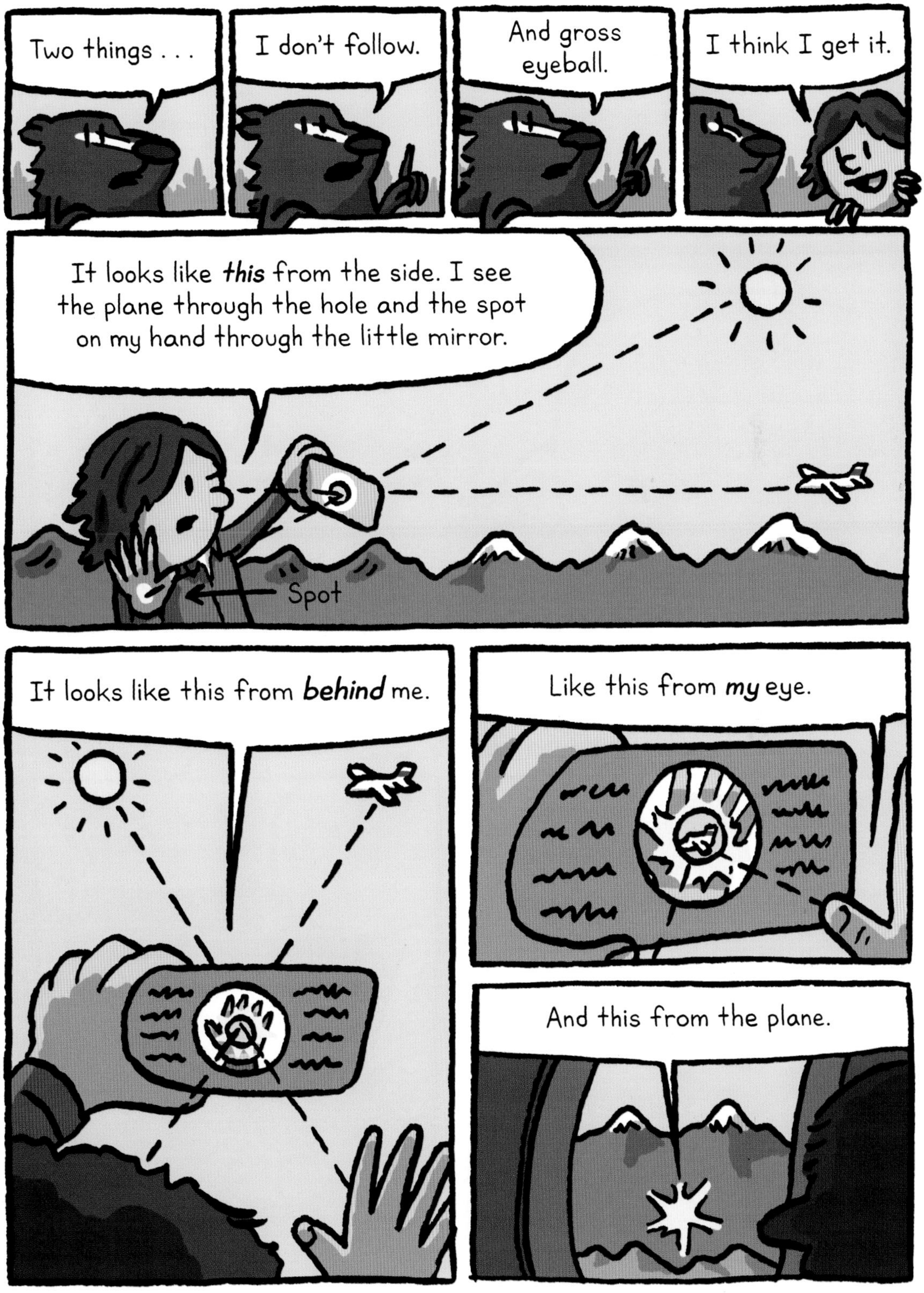
Two things . . .
I don't follow.
And gross eyeball.
I think I get it.
It looks like *this* from the side. I see the plane through the hole and the spot on my hand through the little mirror.
Spot
It looks like this from *behind* me.
Like this from *my* eye.
And this from the plane.

(By the way, please don't look directly at the sun. You know this.)

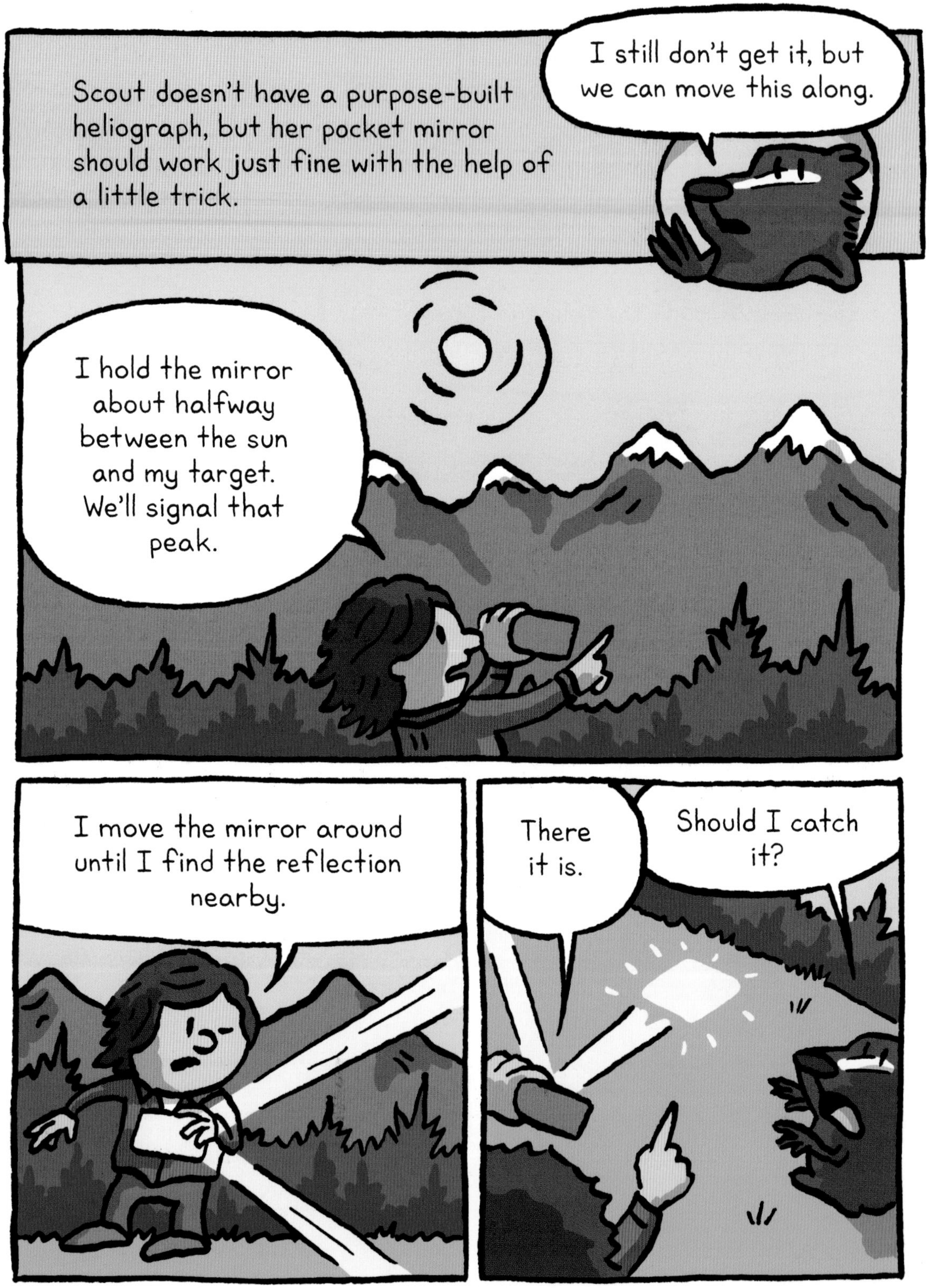
Scout doesn't have a purpose-built heliograph, but her pocket mirror should work just fine with the help of a little trick.
I still don't get it, but we can move this along.
I hold the mirror about halfway between the sun and my target. We'll signal that peak.
I move the mirror around until I find the reflection nearby.
There it is.
Should I catch it?

With the mirror held next to my face, I slowly move the light up my arm.

Then I make a V with my fingers.

I put the peak inside the V and flash the light between my fingers.

Using **Morse code,** a language of dots and dashes (or short and long flashes), Scout can now send messages.

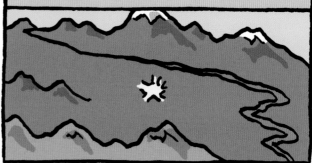

S = dot dot dot / O = dash dash dash / S = dot dot dot

Scout will keep the mirror ready in her pocket at all times and can even use it to sweep the horizon when not busy. You never know who may be out there.

Me! *I* am! Help!

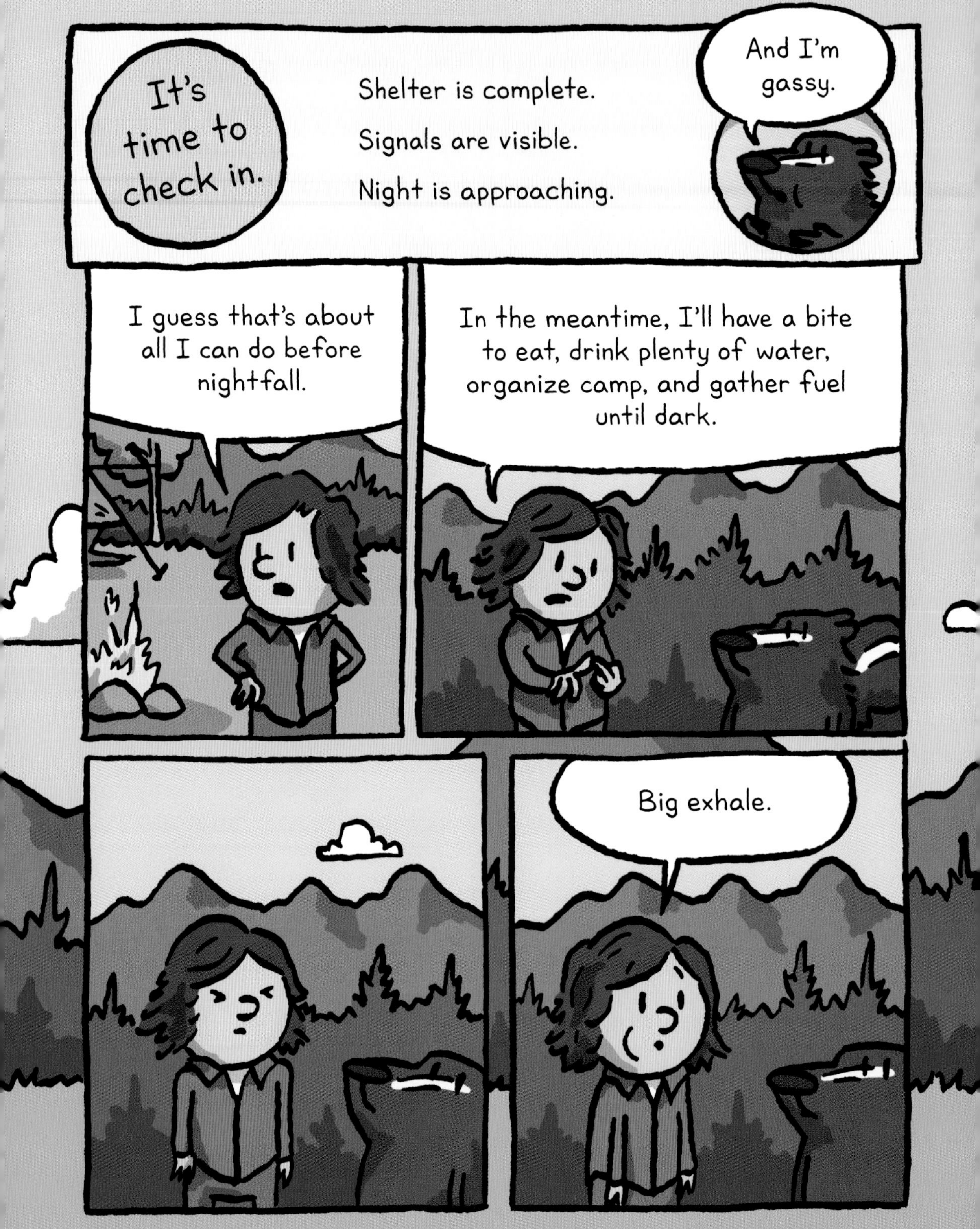
It's time to check in.
Shelter is complete.
Signals are visible.
Night is approaching.
And I'm gassy.
I guess that's about all I can do before nightfall.
In the meantime, I'll have a bite to eat, drink plenty of water, organize camp, and gather fuel until dark.
Big exhale.

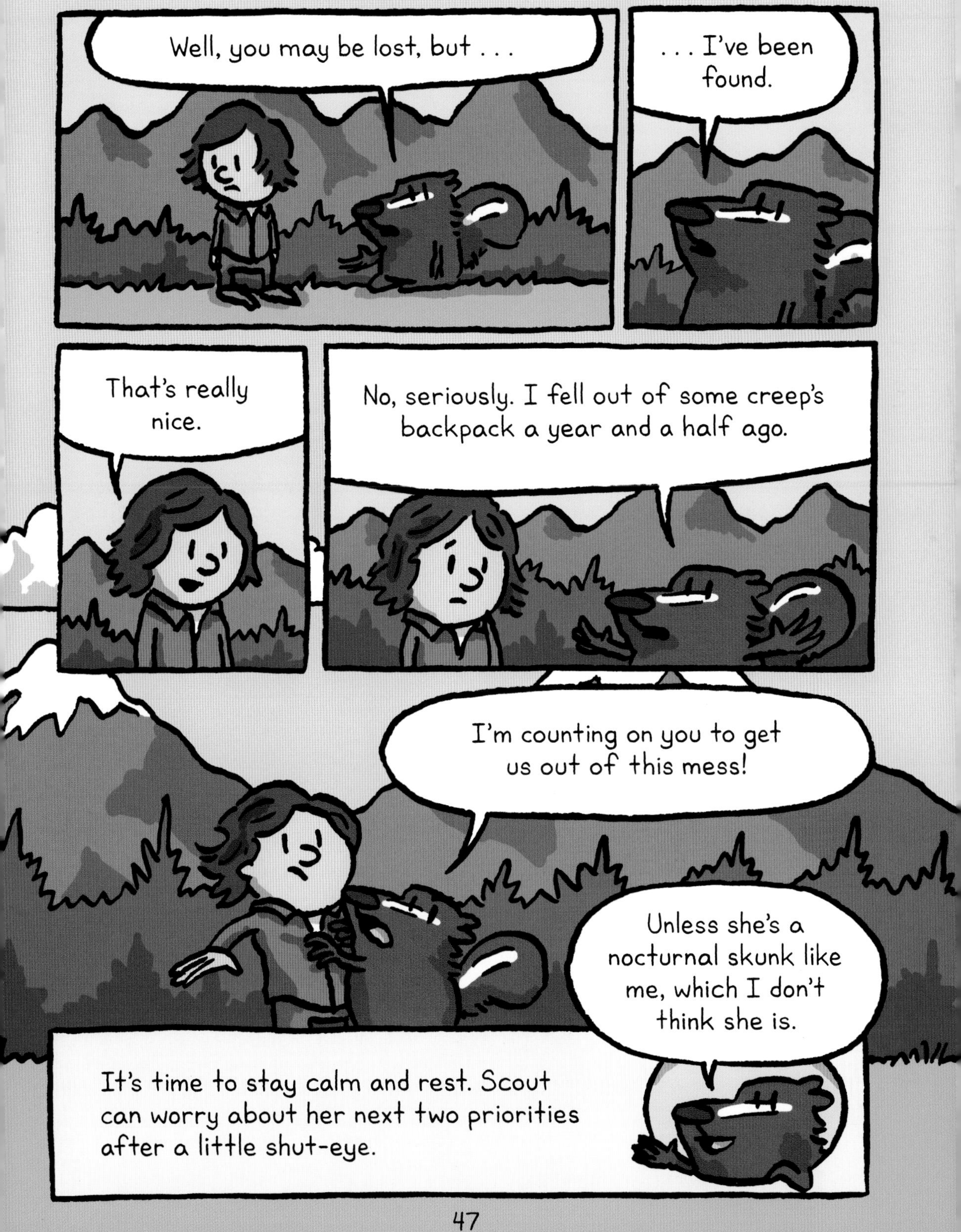
Well, you may be lost, but . . .
. . . I've been found.
That's really nice.
No, seriously. I fell out of some creep's backpack a year and a half ago.
I'm counting on you to get us out of this mess!
Unless she's a nocturnal skunk like me, which I don't think she is.
It's time to stay calm and rest. Scout can worry about her next two priorities after a little shut-eye.

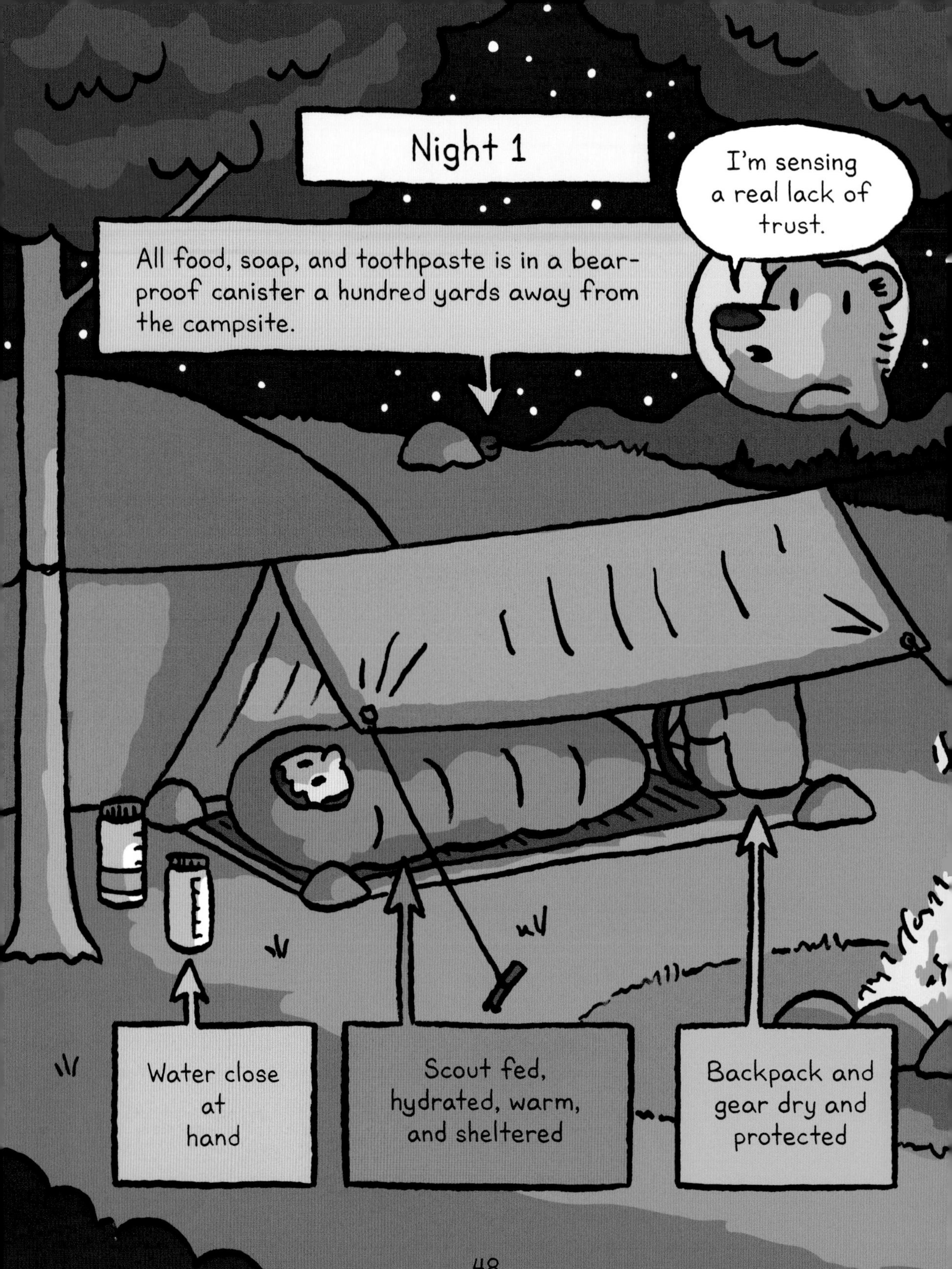
Night 1
All food, soap, and toothpaste is in a bear-proof canister a hundred yards away from the campsite.
I'm sensing a real lack of trust.
Water close at hand
Scout fed, hydrated, warm, and sheltered
Backpack and gear dry and protected

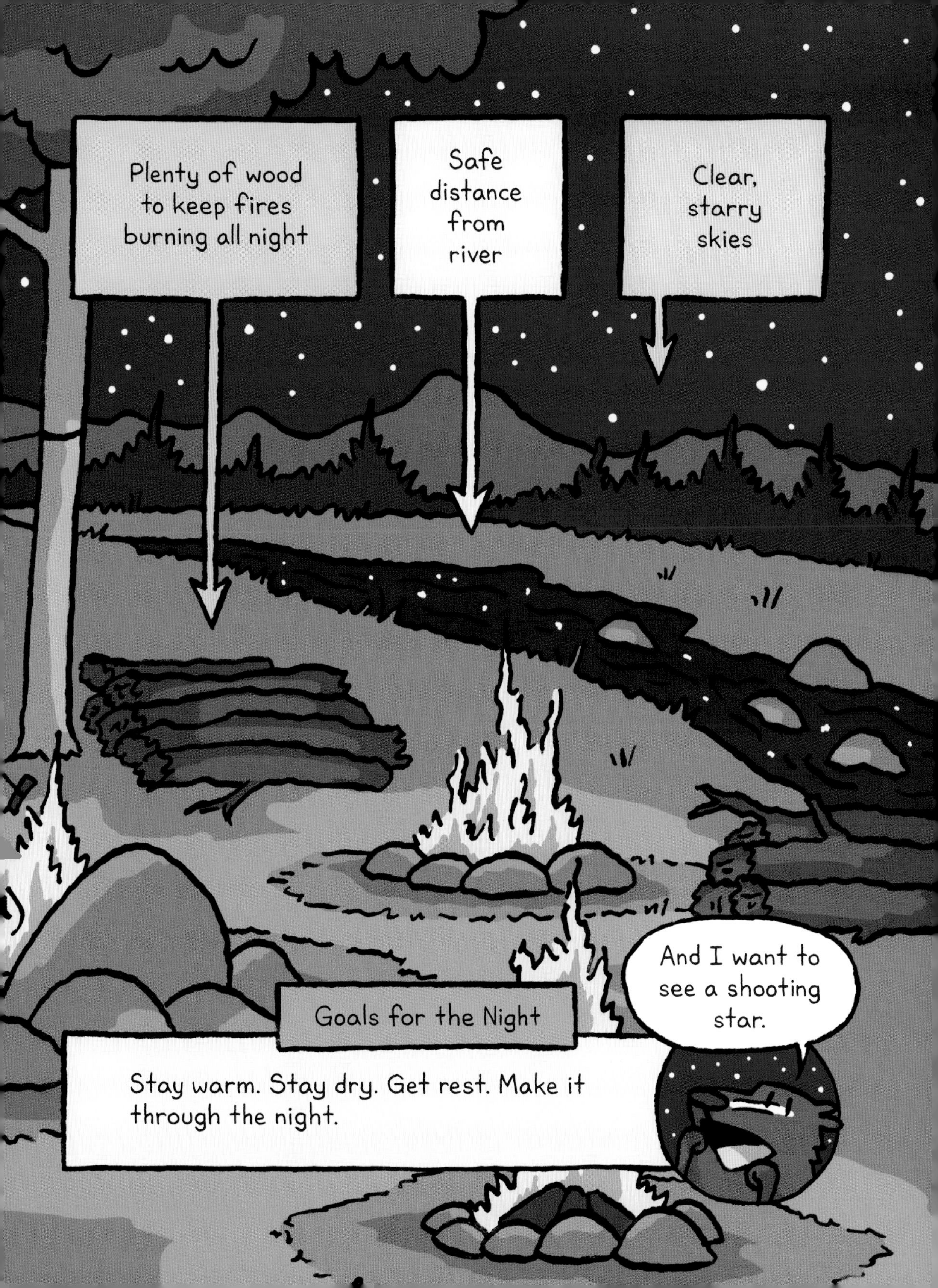
Plenty of wood to keep fires burning all night
Safe distance from river
Clear, starry skies
Goals for the Night
Stay warm. Stay dry. Get rest. Make it through the night.
And I want to see a shooting star.

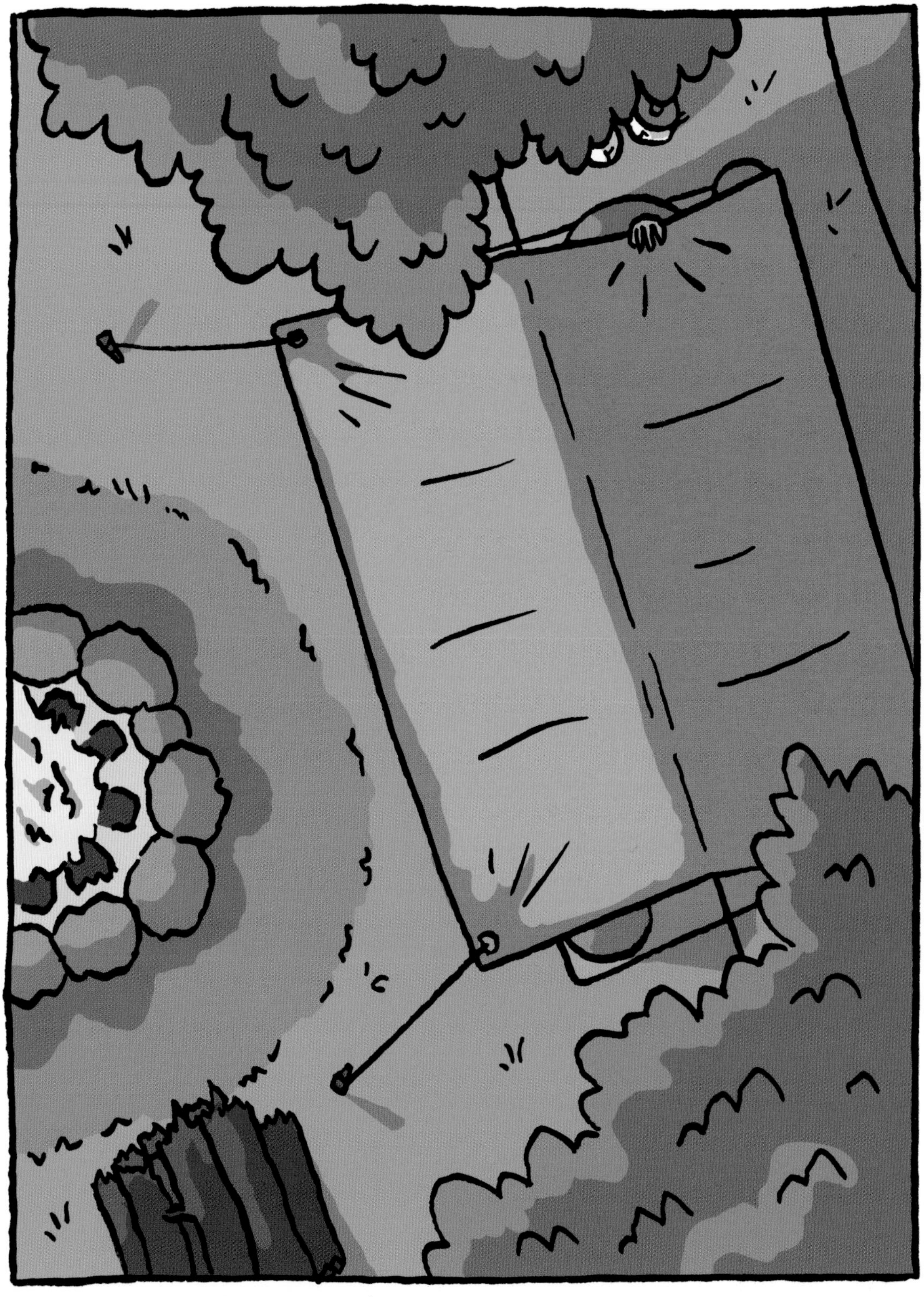

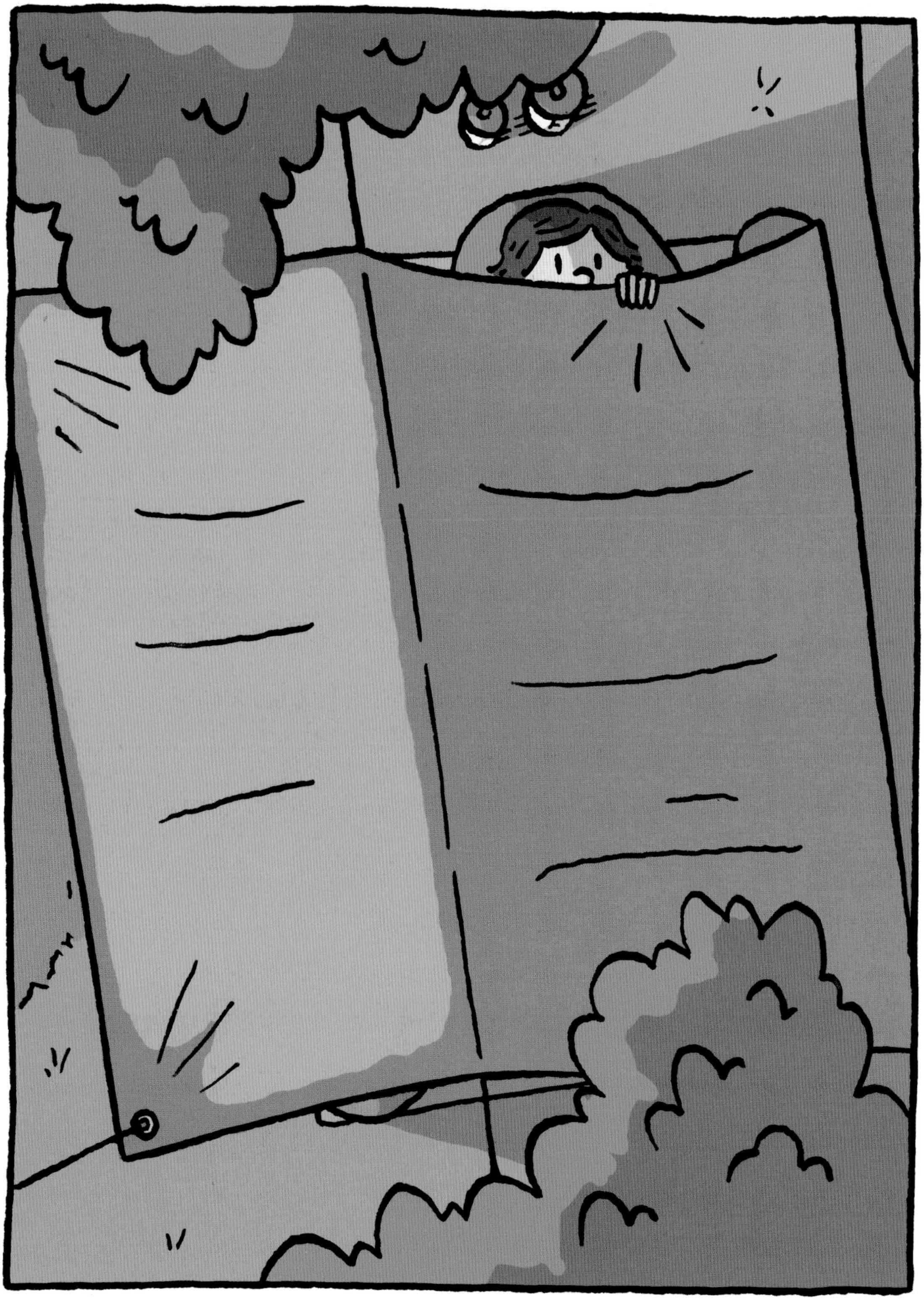

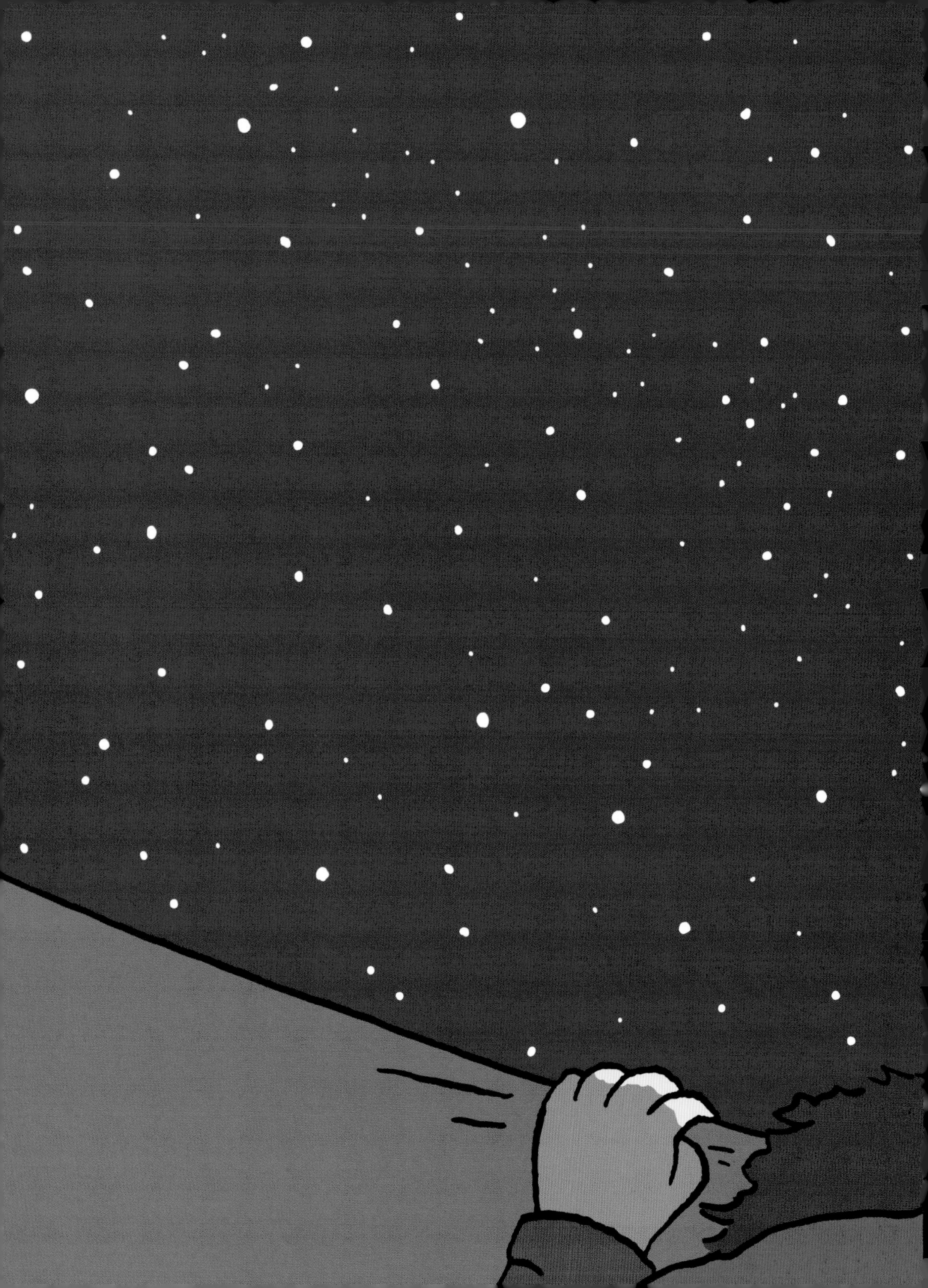

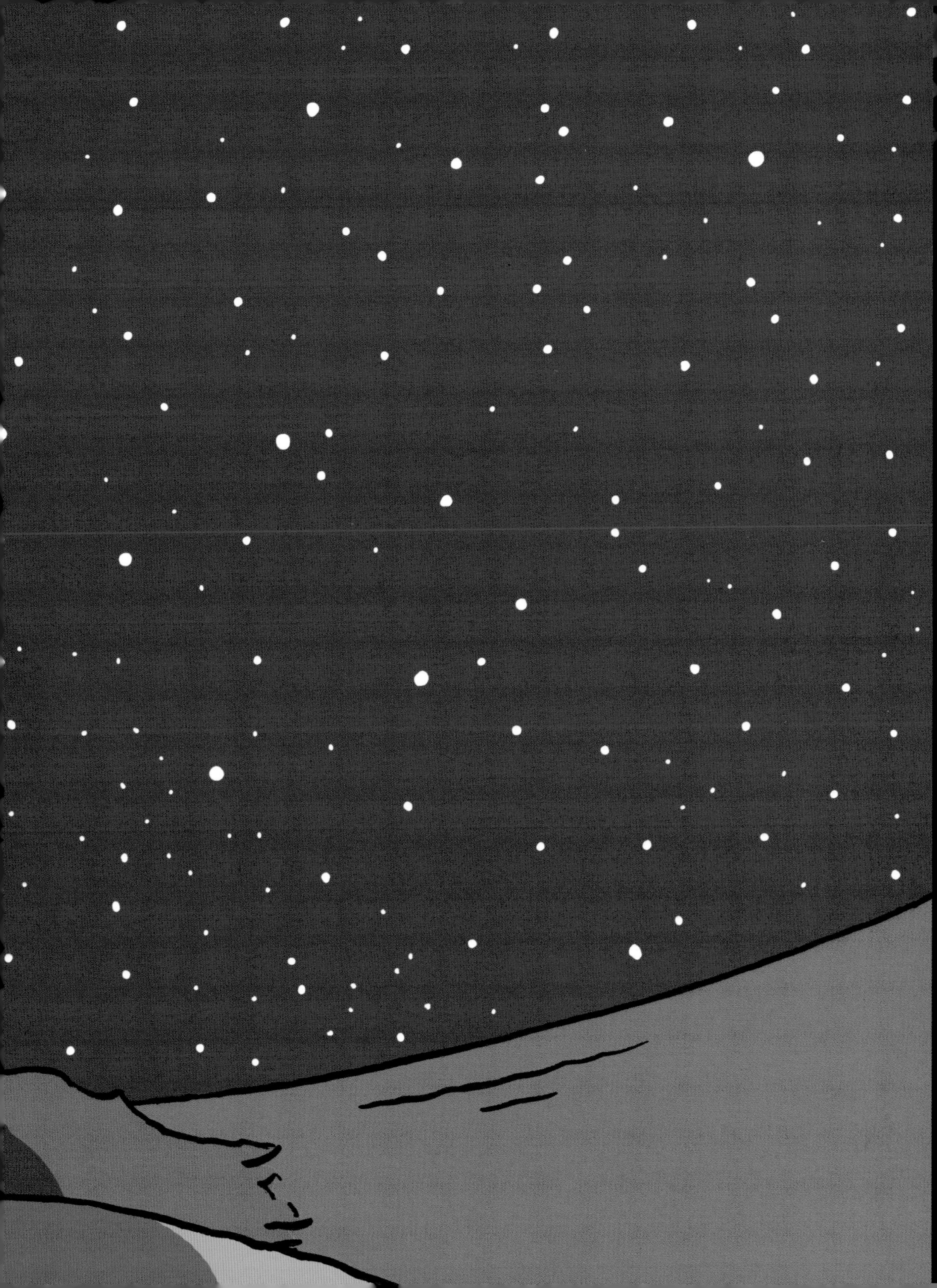

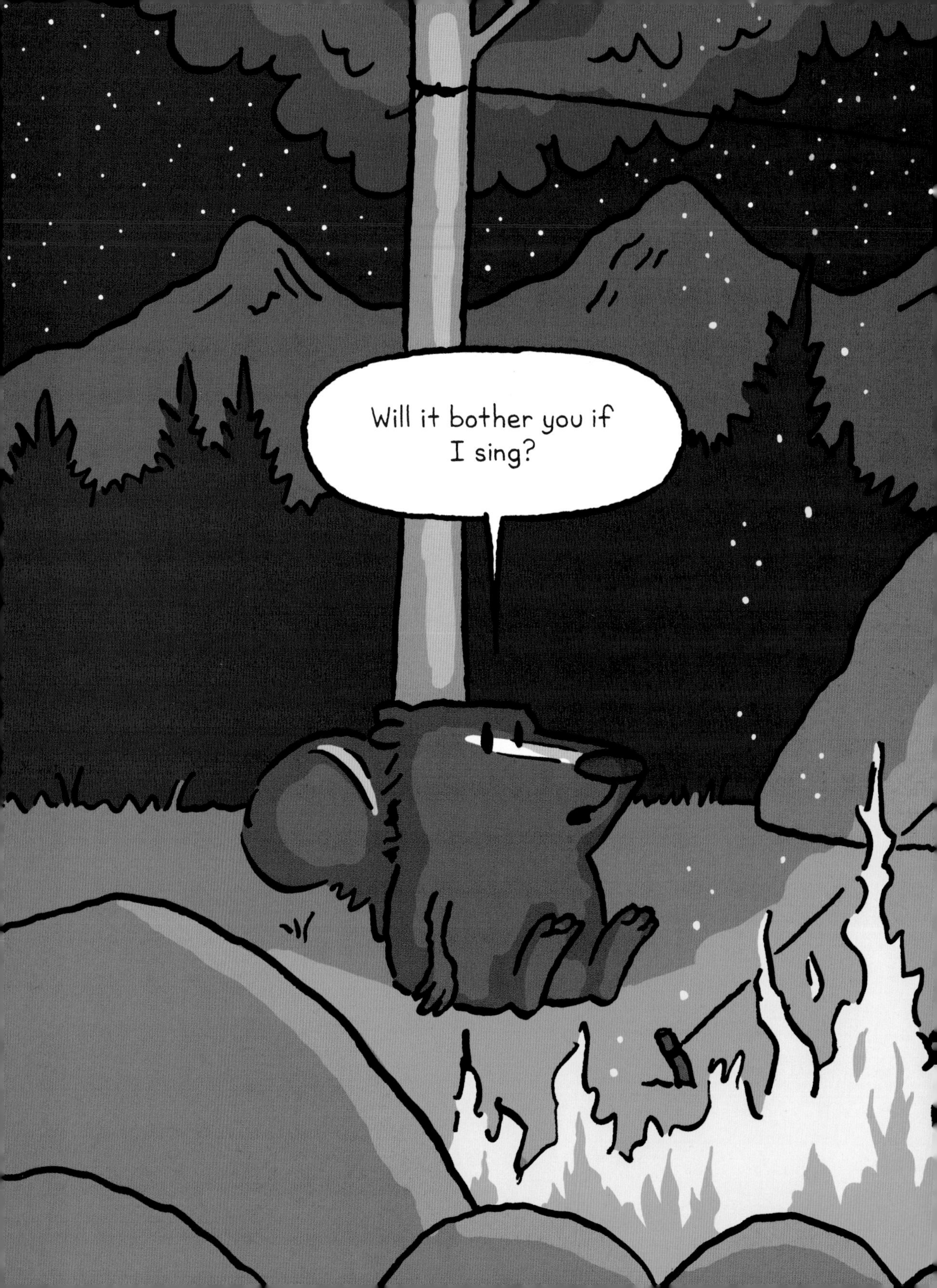
Will it bother you if I sing?

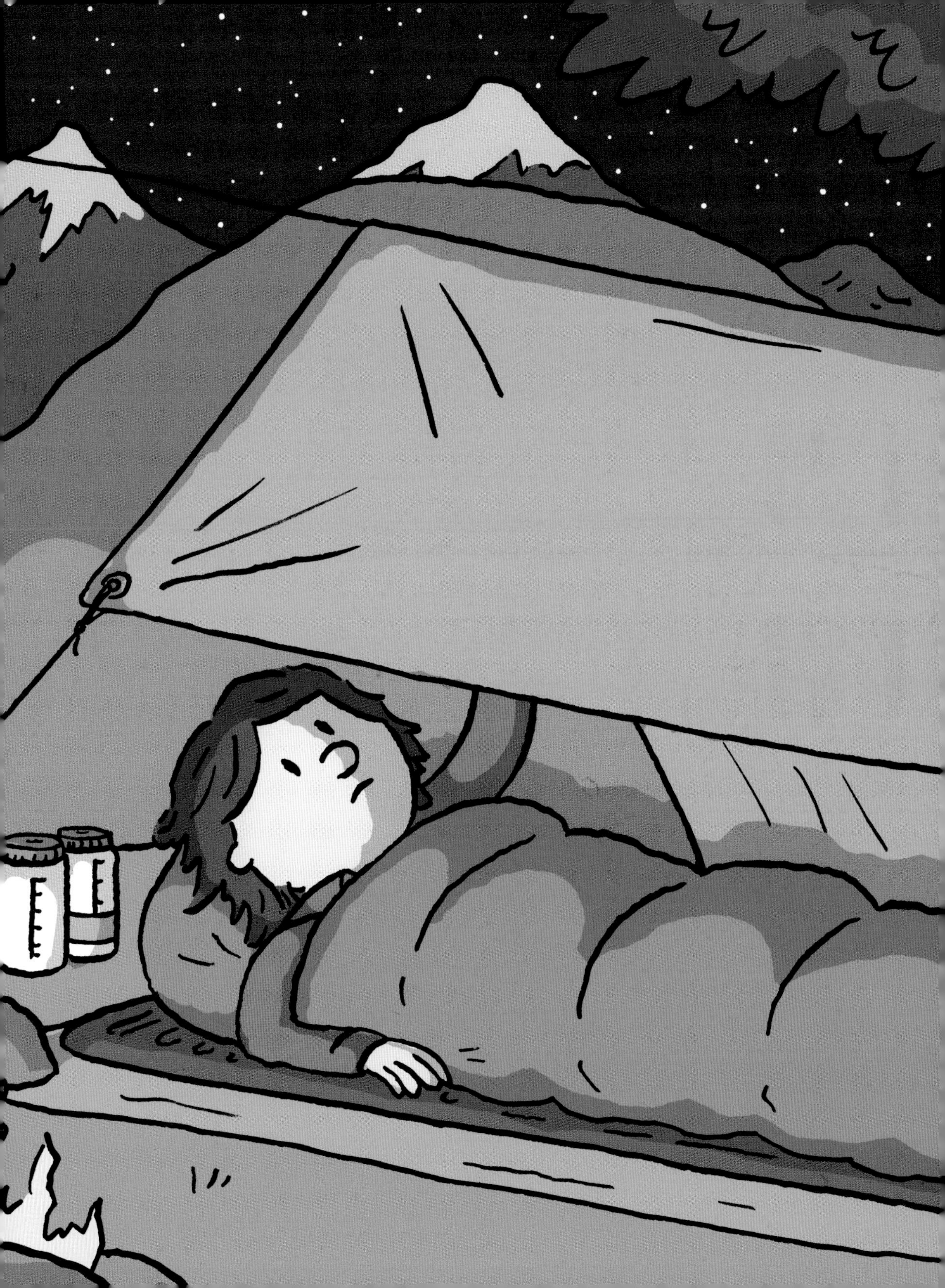

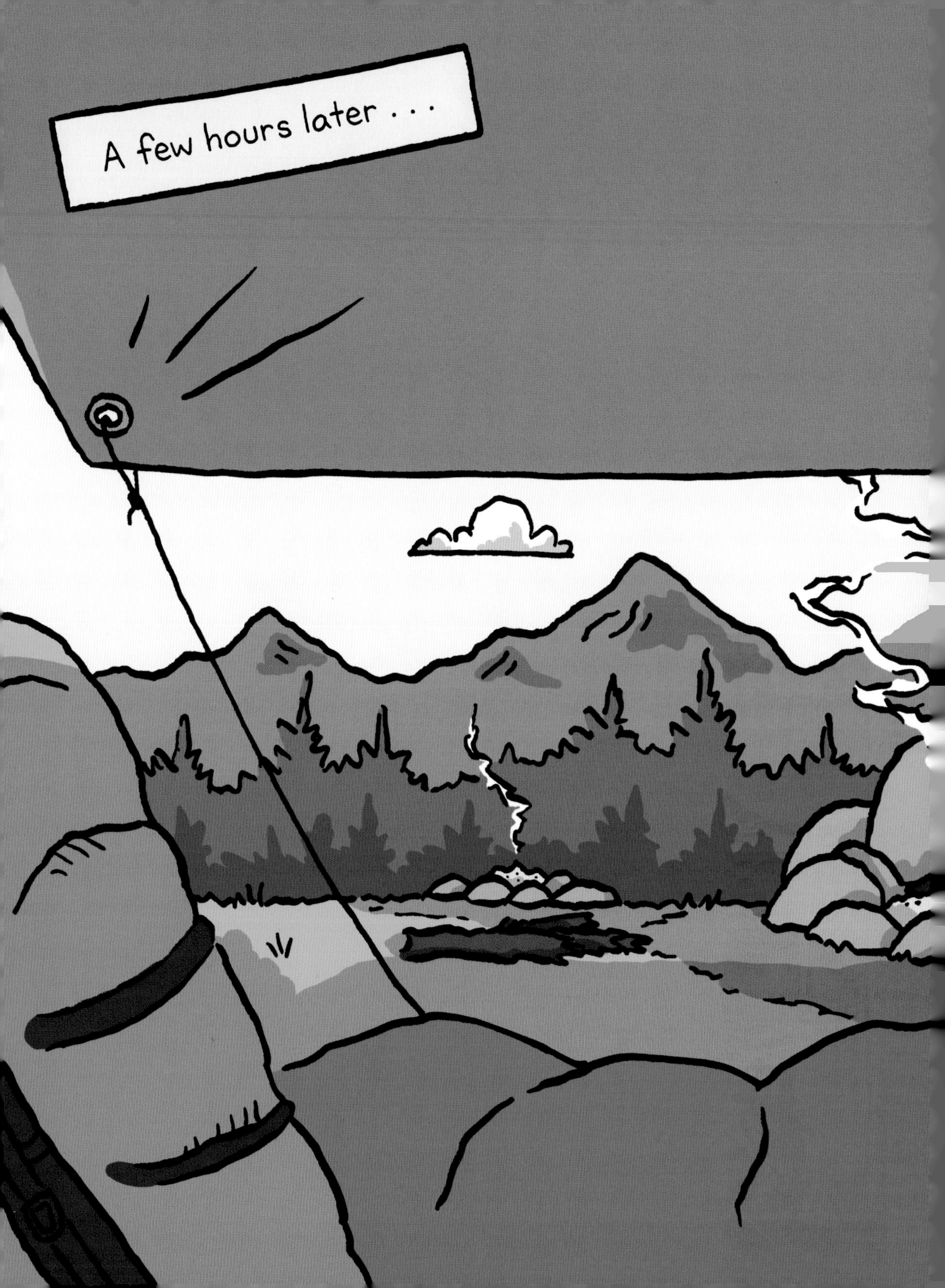
A few hours later . . .

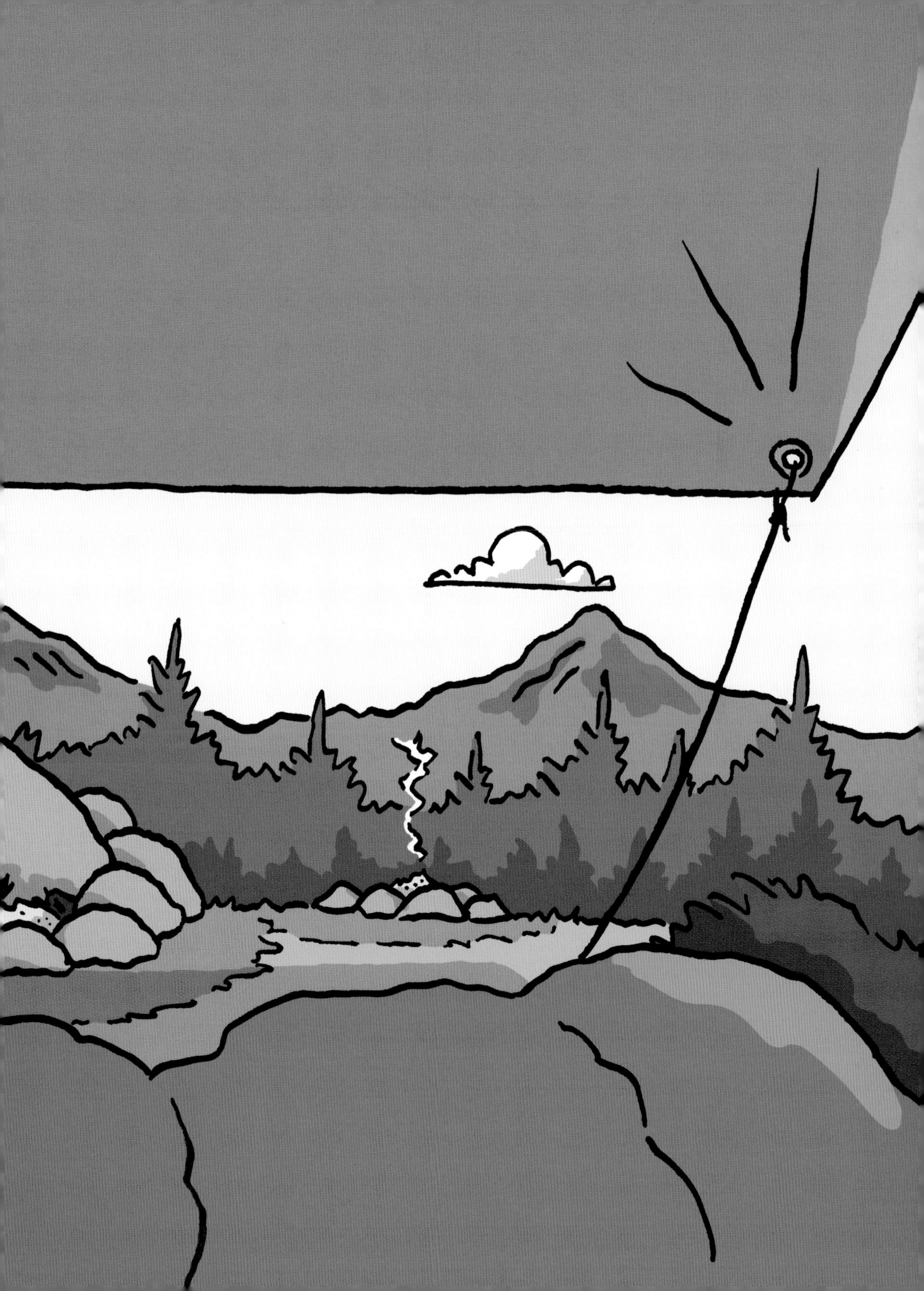

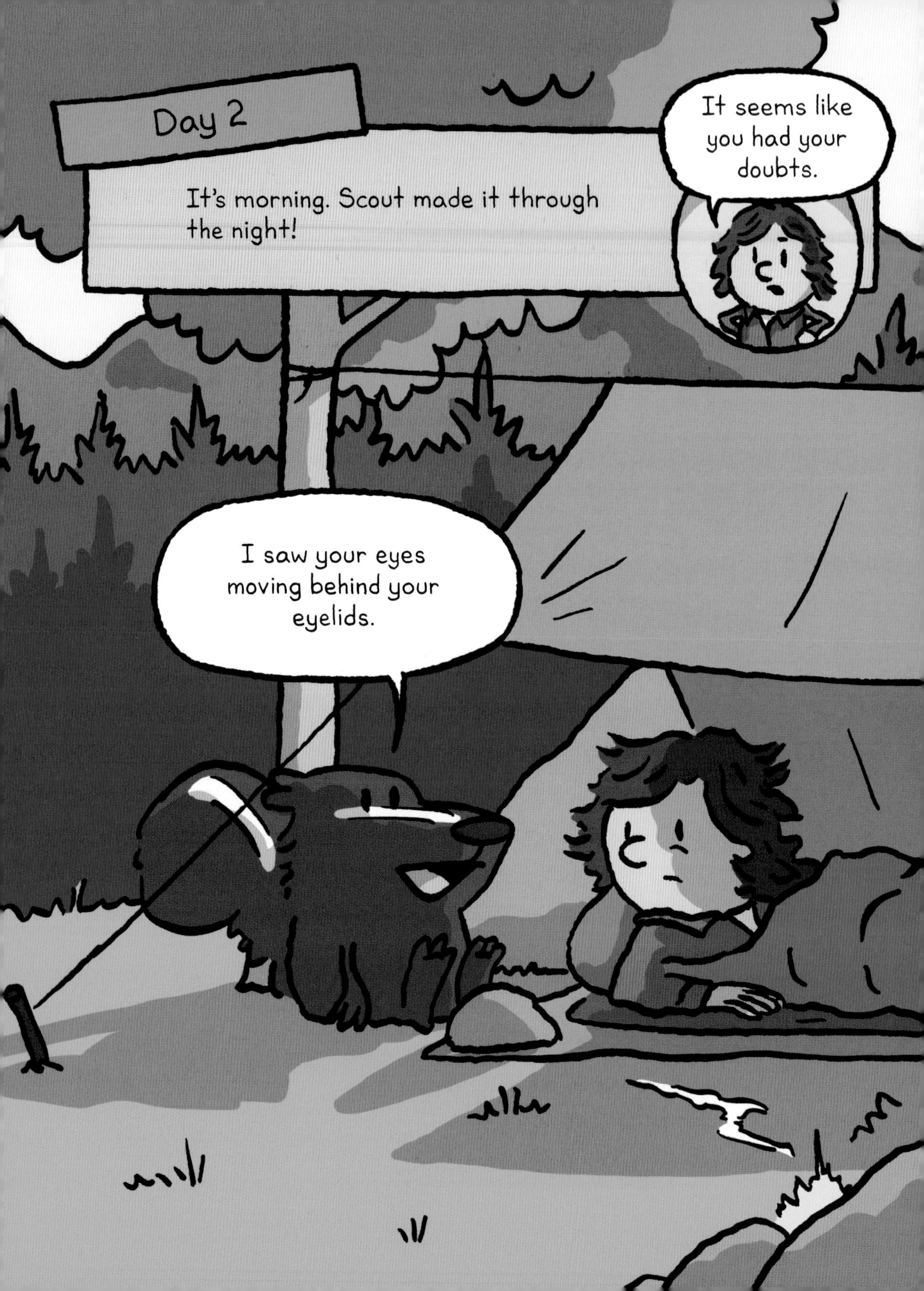
Day 2
It's morning. Scout made it through the night!
It seems like you had your doubts.
I saw your eyes moving behind your eyelids.

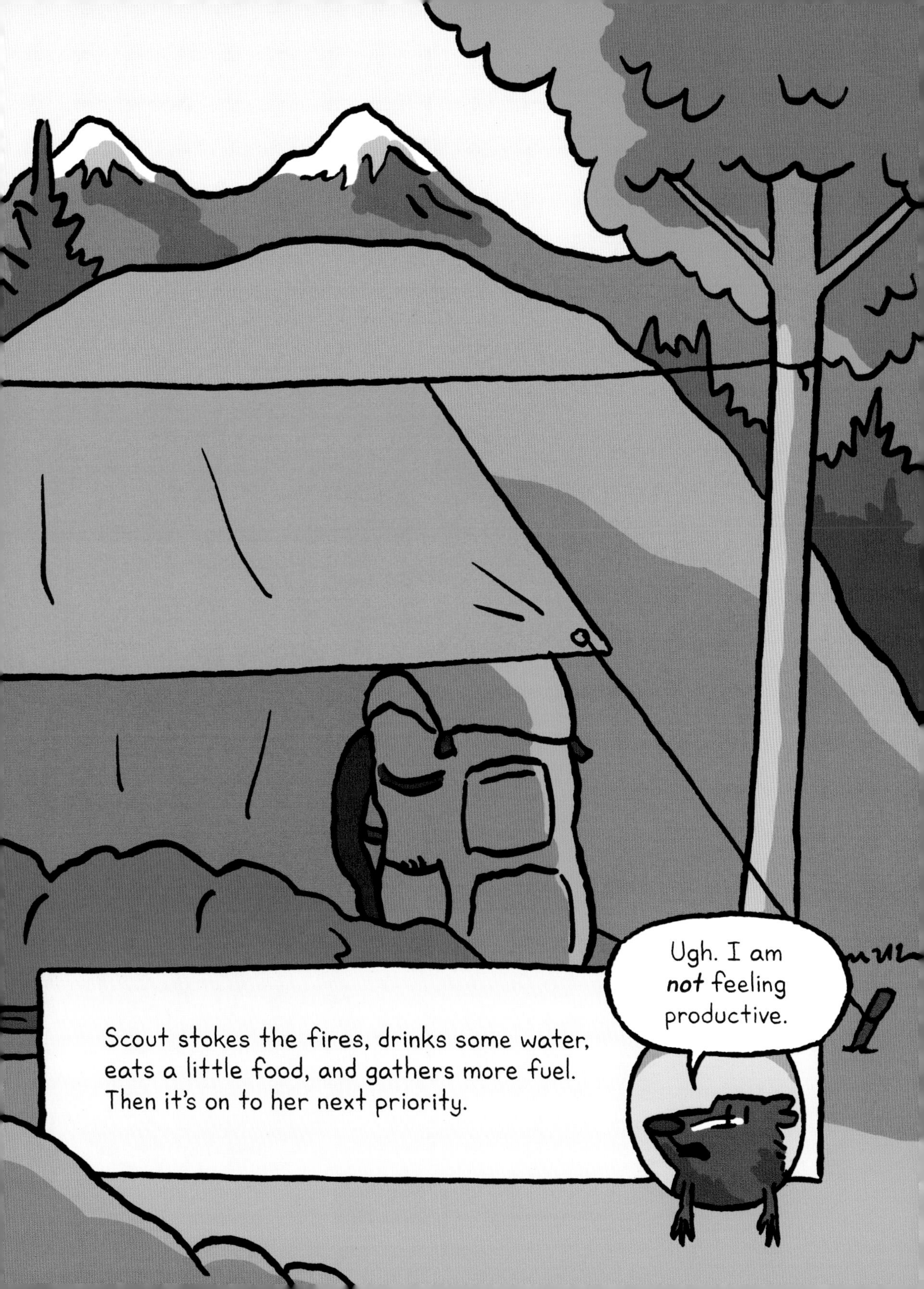
Scout stokes the fires, drinks some water, eats a little food, and gathers more fuel. Then it's on to her next priority.
Ugh. I am *not* feeling productive.

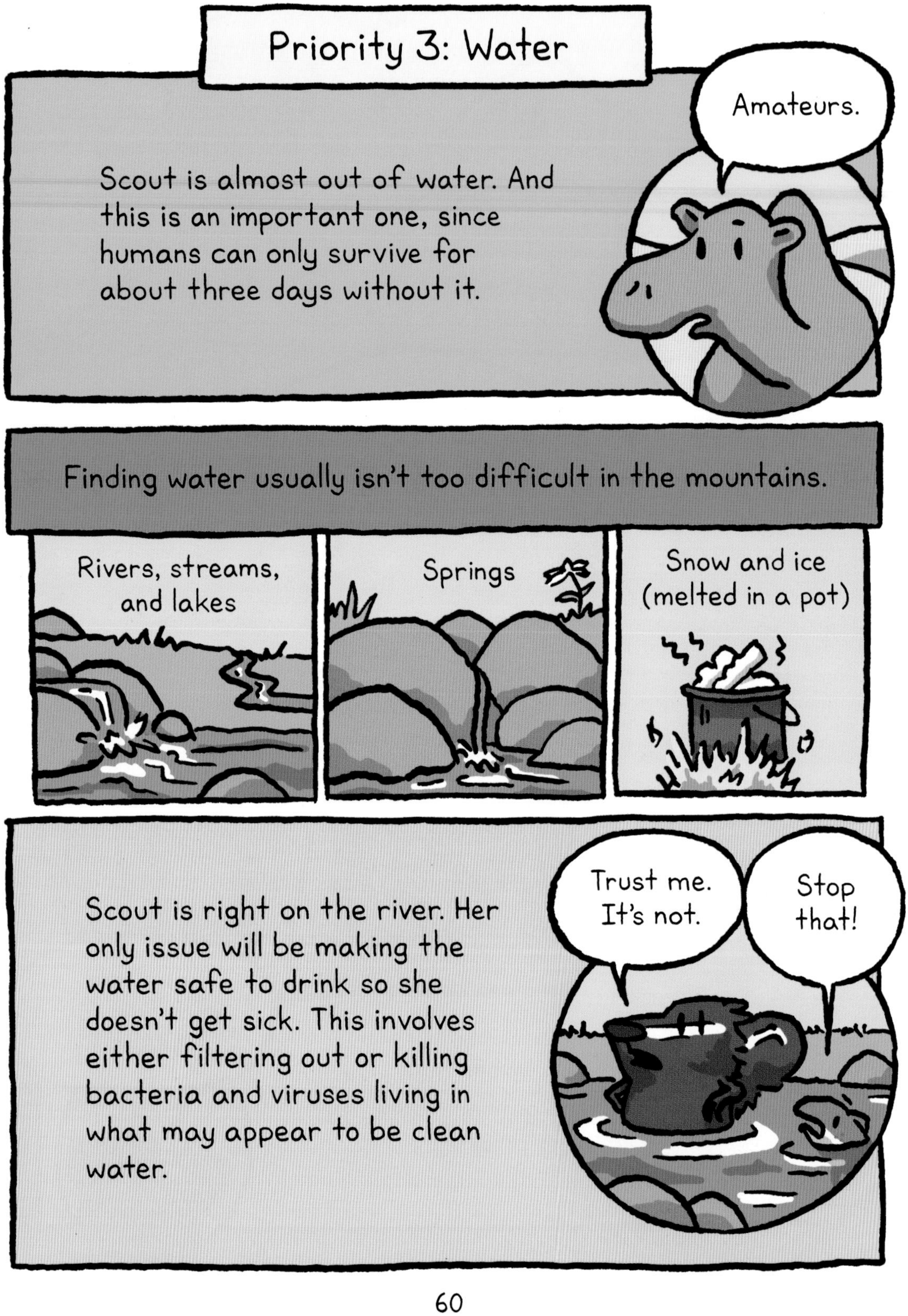

Priority 3: Water

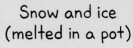

Amateurs.

Scout is almost out of water. And this is an important one, since humans can only survive for about three days without it.

Finding water usually isn't too difficult in the mountains.

Rivers, streams, and lakes

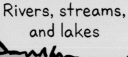

Springs

Snow and ice (melted in a pot)

Scout is right on the river. Her only issue will be making the water safe to drink so she doesn't get sick. This involves either filtering out or killing bacteria and viruses living in what may appear to be clean water.

Trust me. It's not.

Stop that!

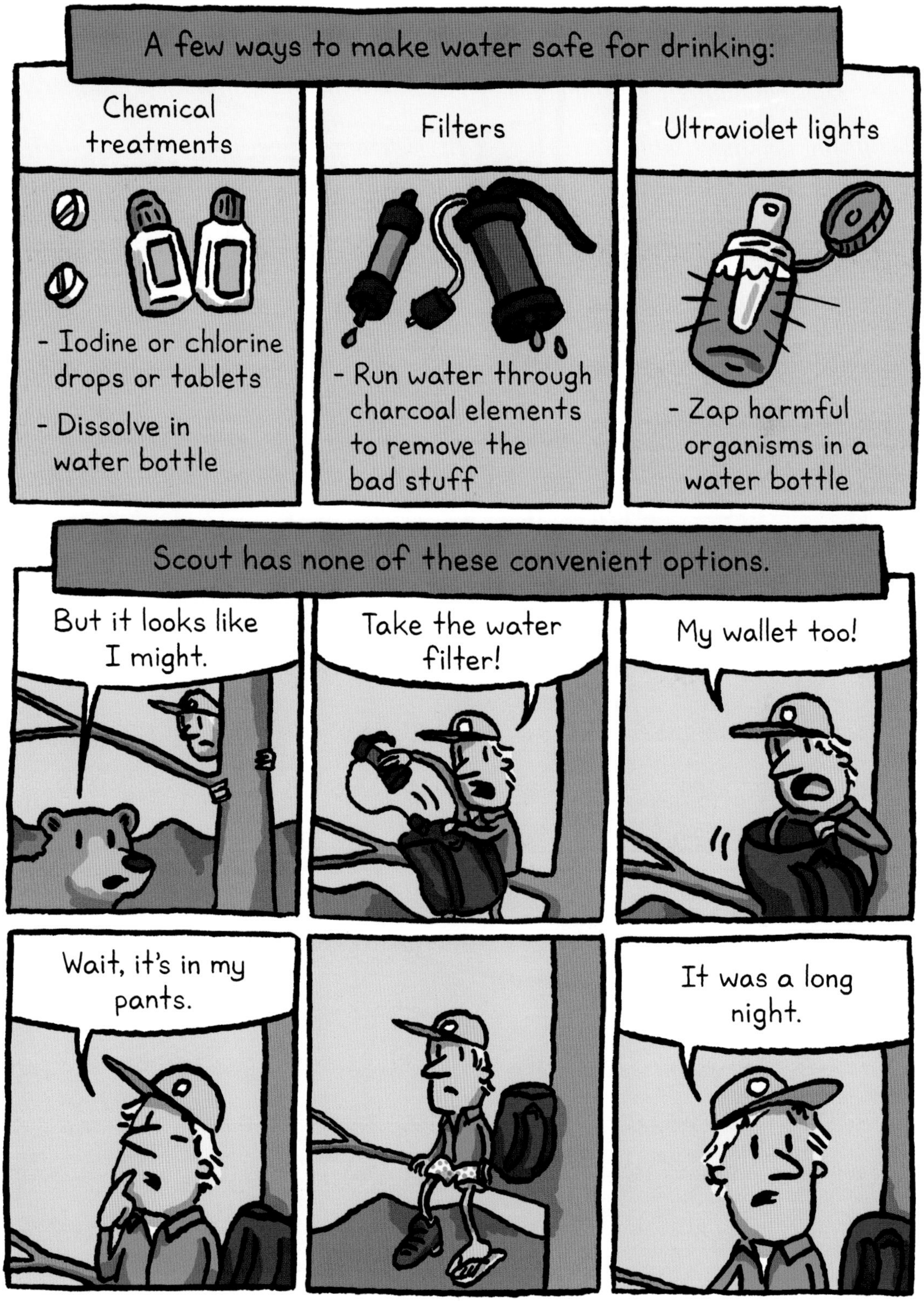
A few ways to make water safe for drinking:
Chemical treatments
- Iodine or chlorine drops or tablets
- Dissolve in water bottle
Filters
- Run water through charcoal elements to remove the bad stuff
Ultraviolet lights
- Zap harmful organisms in a water bottle
Scout has none of these convenient options.
But it looks like I might.
Take the water filter!
My wallet too!
Wait, it's in my pants.
It was a long night.

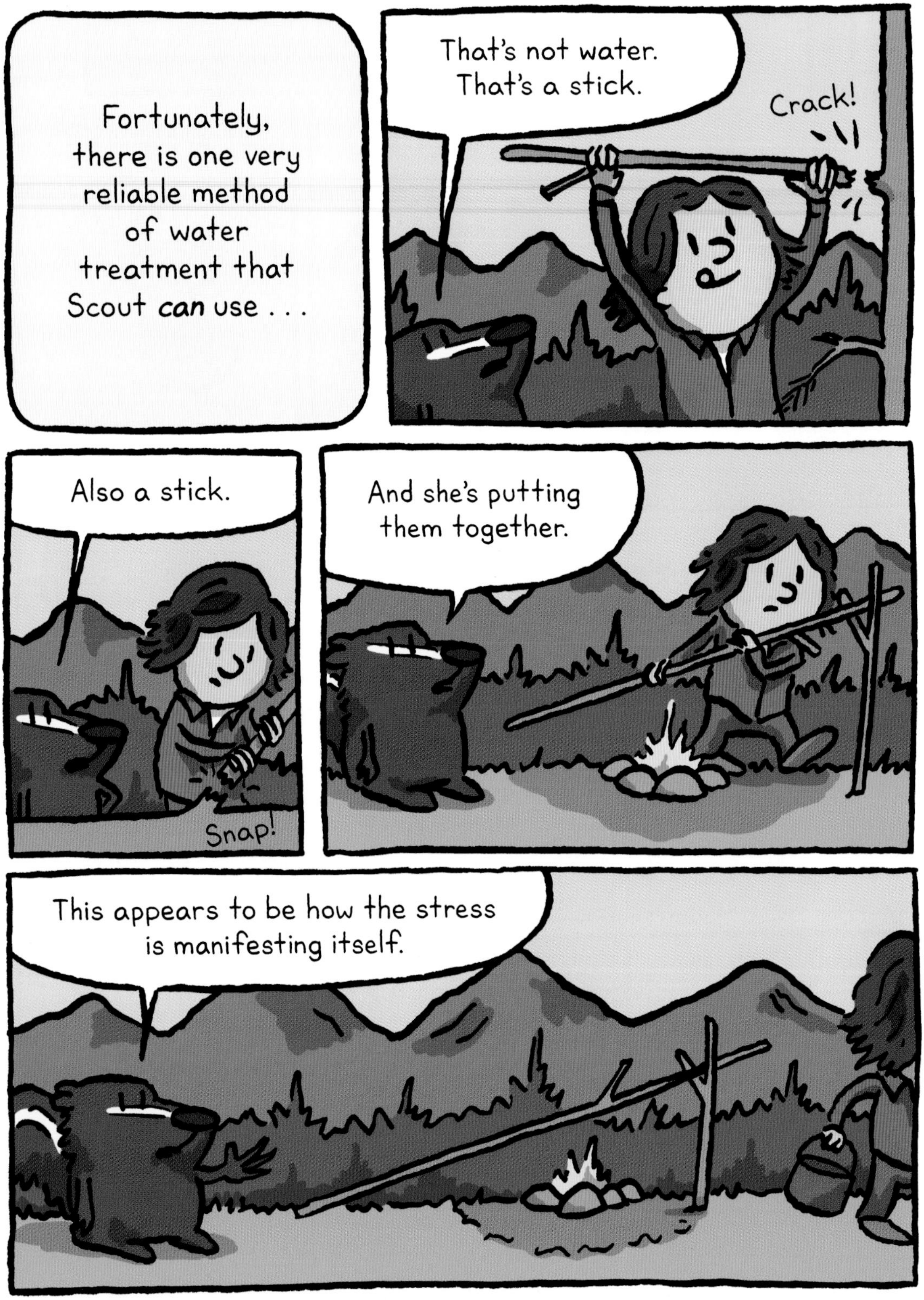
Fortunately, there is one very reliable method of water treatment that Scout **can** use . . .
That's not water. That's a stick.
Crack!
Also a stick.
Snap!
And she's putting them together.
This appears to be how the stress is manifesting itself.

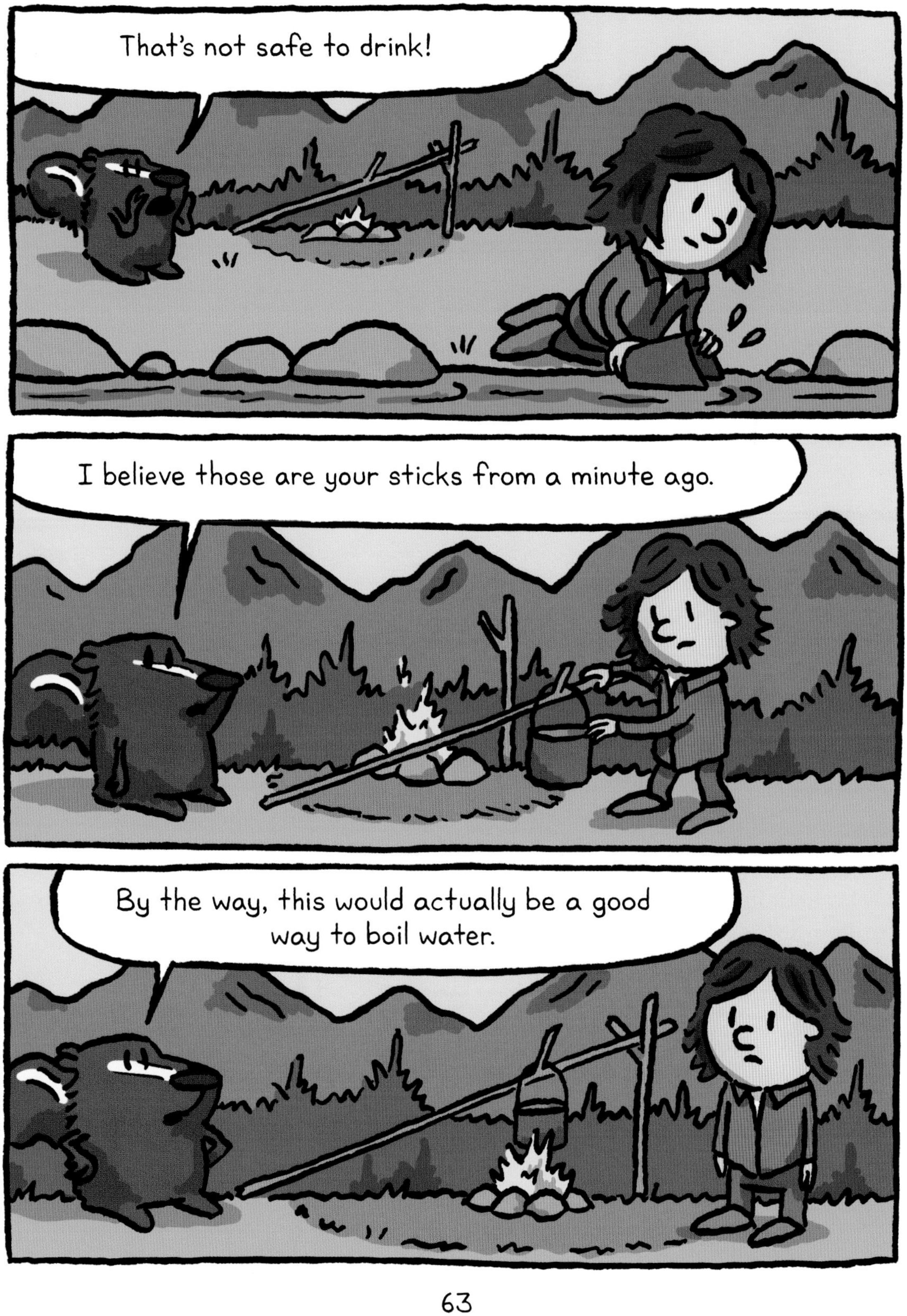
That's not safe to drink!
I believe those are your sticks from a minute ago.
By the way, this would actually be a good way to boil water.

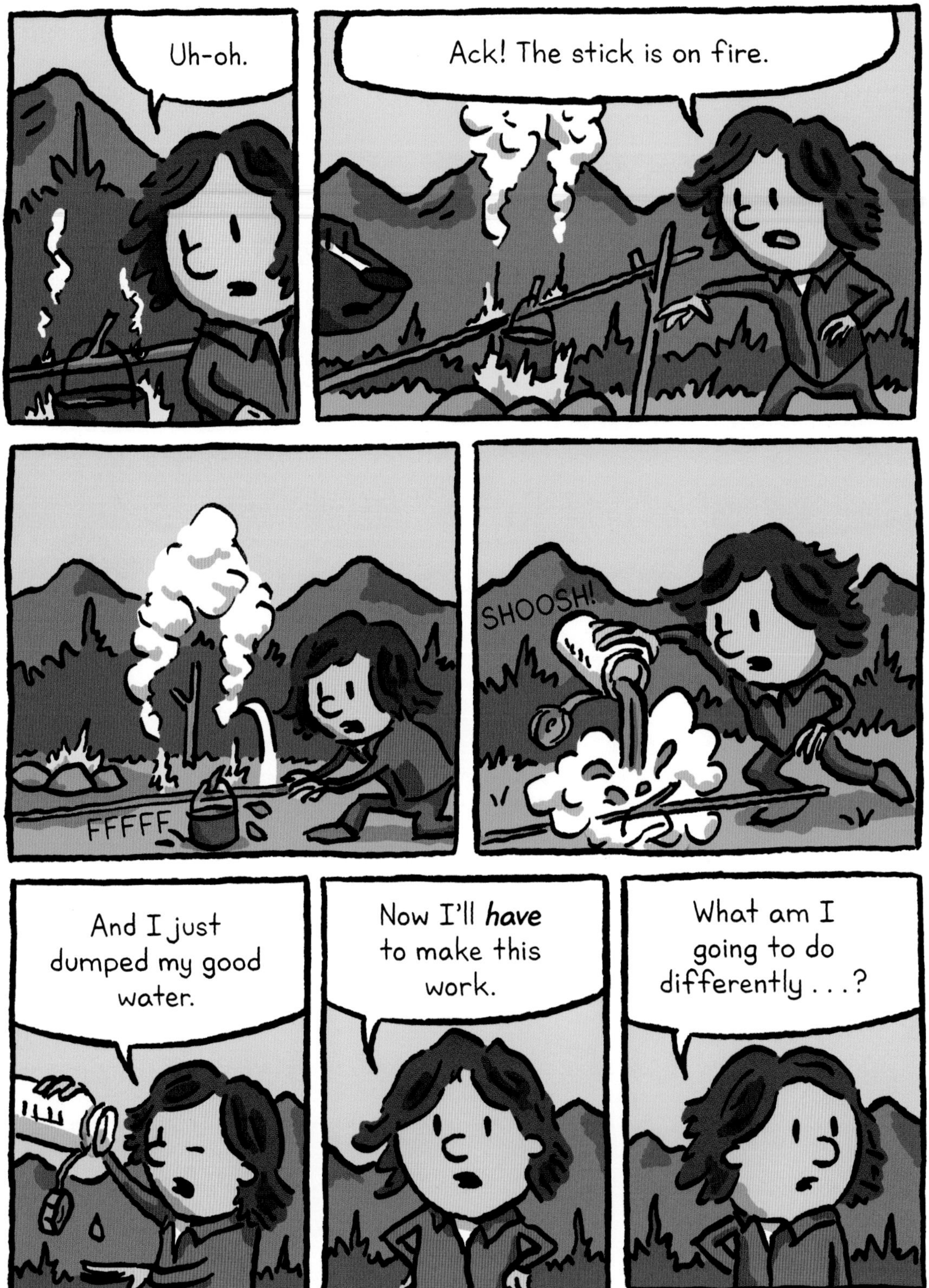
Uh-oh.
Ack! The stick is on fire.
FFFFF
SHOOSH!
And I just dumped my good water.
Now I'll *have* to make this work.
What am I going to do differently . . . ?

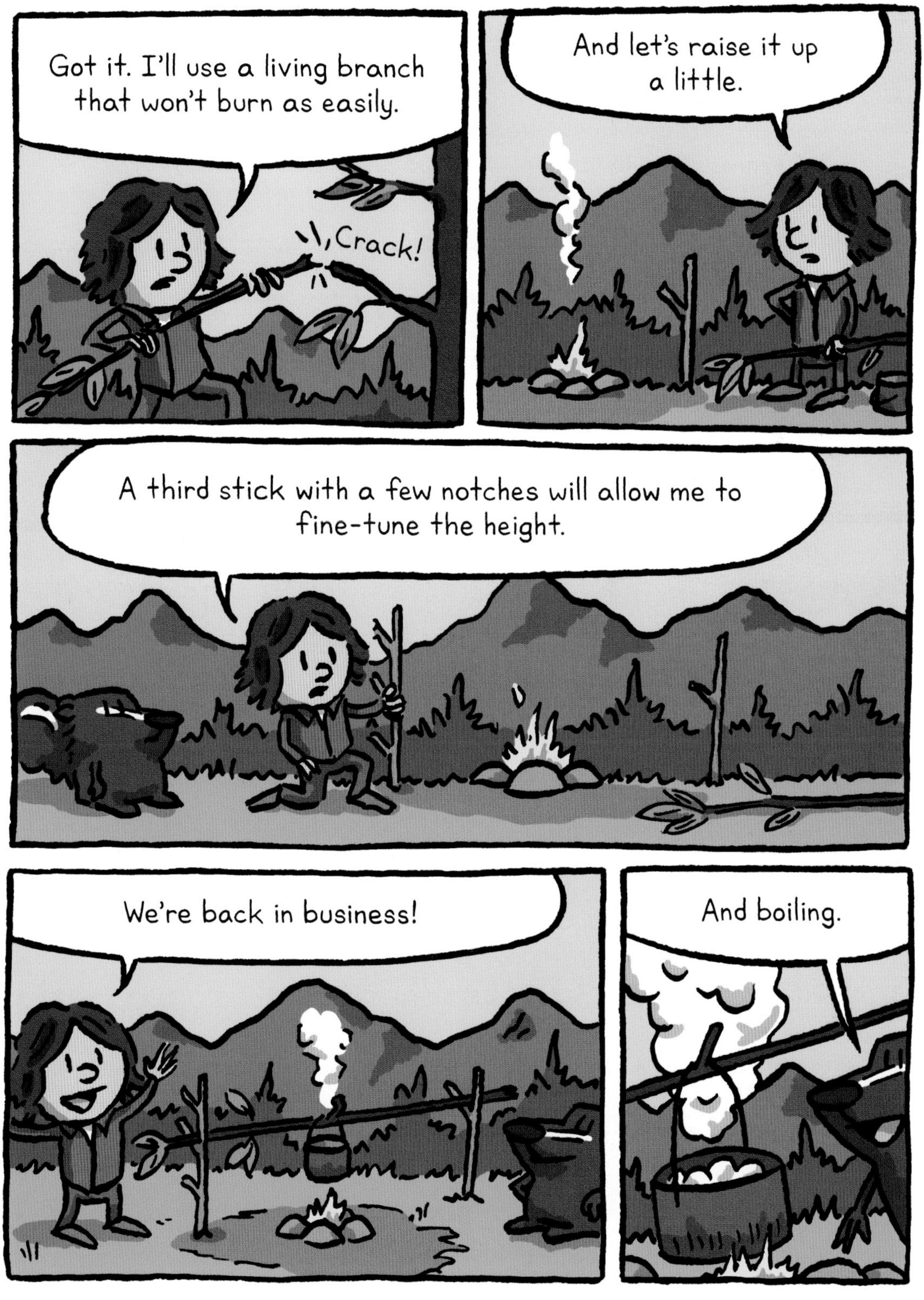

Got it. I'll use a living branch that won't burn as easily.
Crack!
And let's raise it up a little.
A third stick with a few notches will allow me to fine-tune the height.
We're back in business!
And boiling.

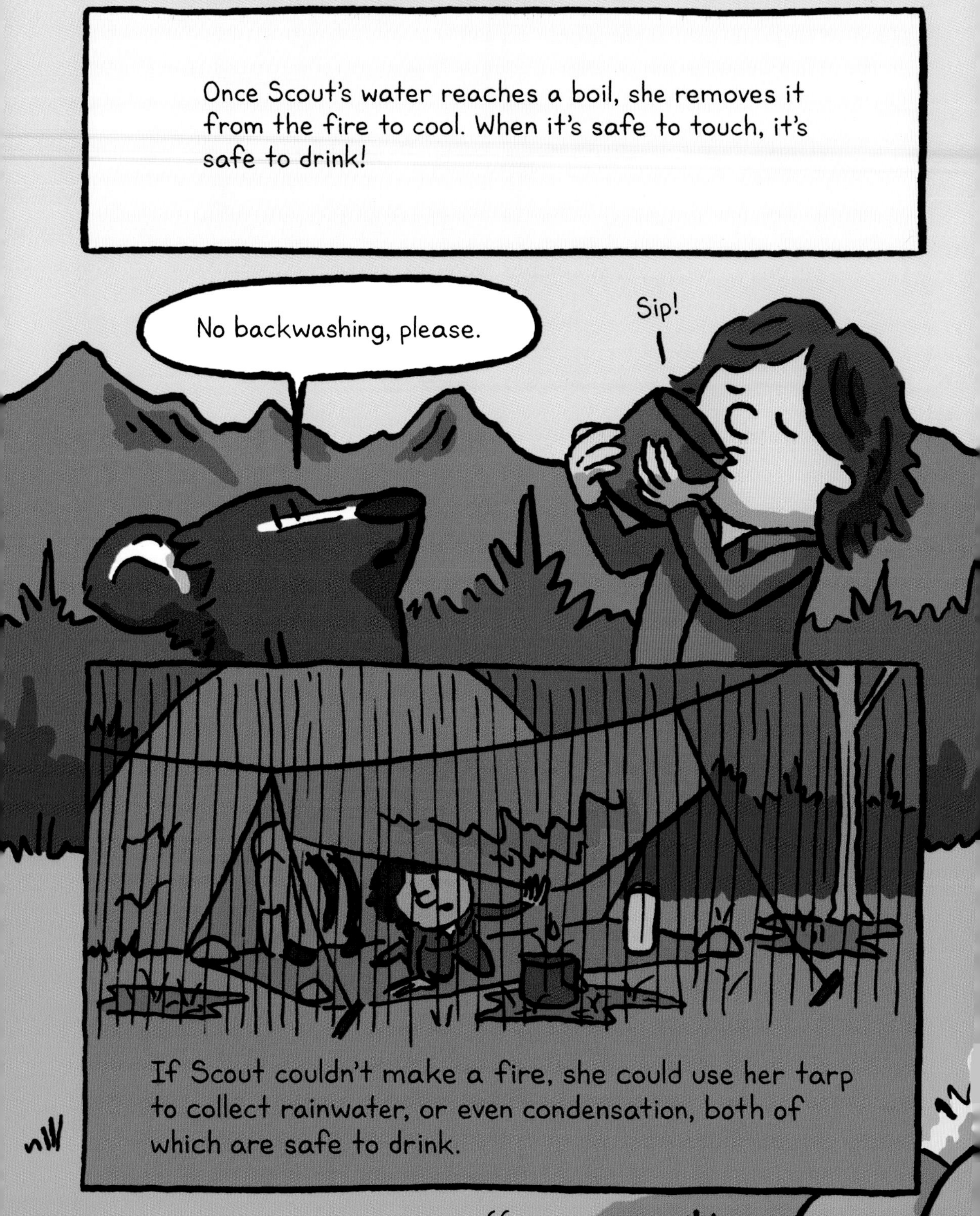
Once Scout's water reaches a boil, she removes it from the fire to cool. When it's safe to touch, it's safe to drink!
No backwashing, please.
Sip!
If Scout couldn't make a fire, she could use her tarp to collect rainwater, or even condensation, both of which are safe to drink.

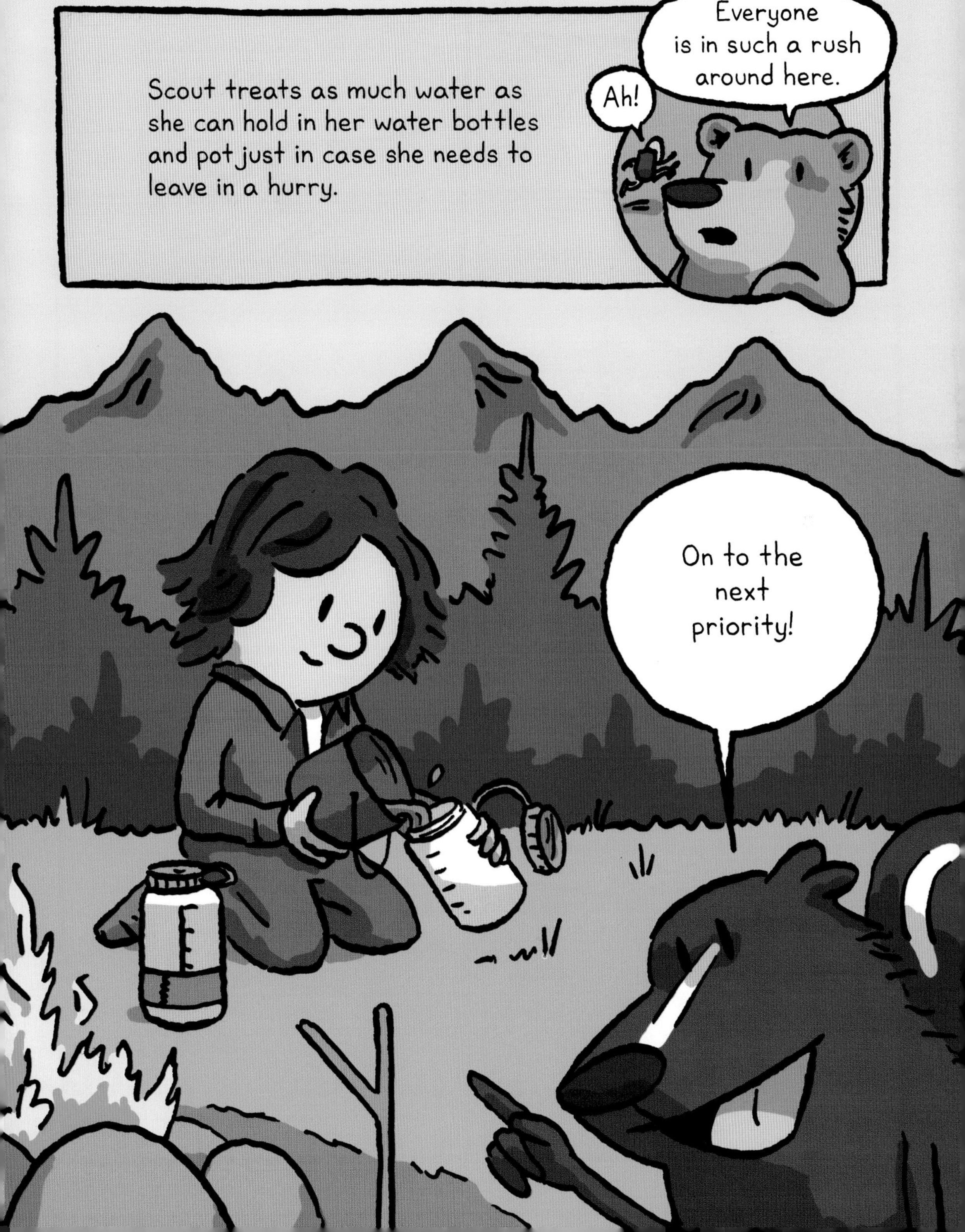

Scout treats as much water as she can hold in her water bottles and pot just in case she needs to leave in a hurry.
Ah!
Everyone is in such a rush around here.
On to the next priority!

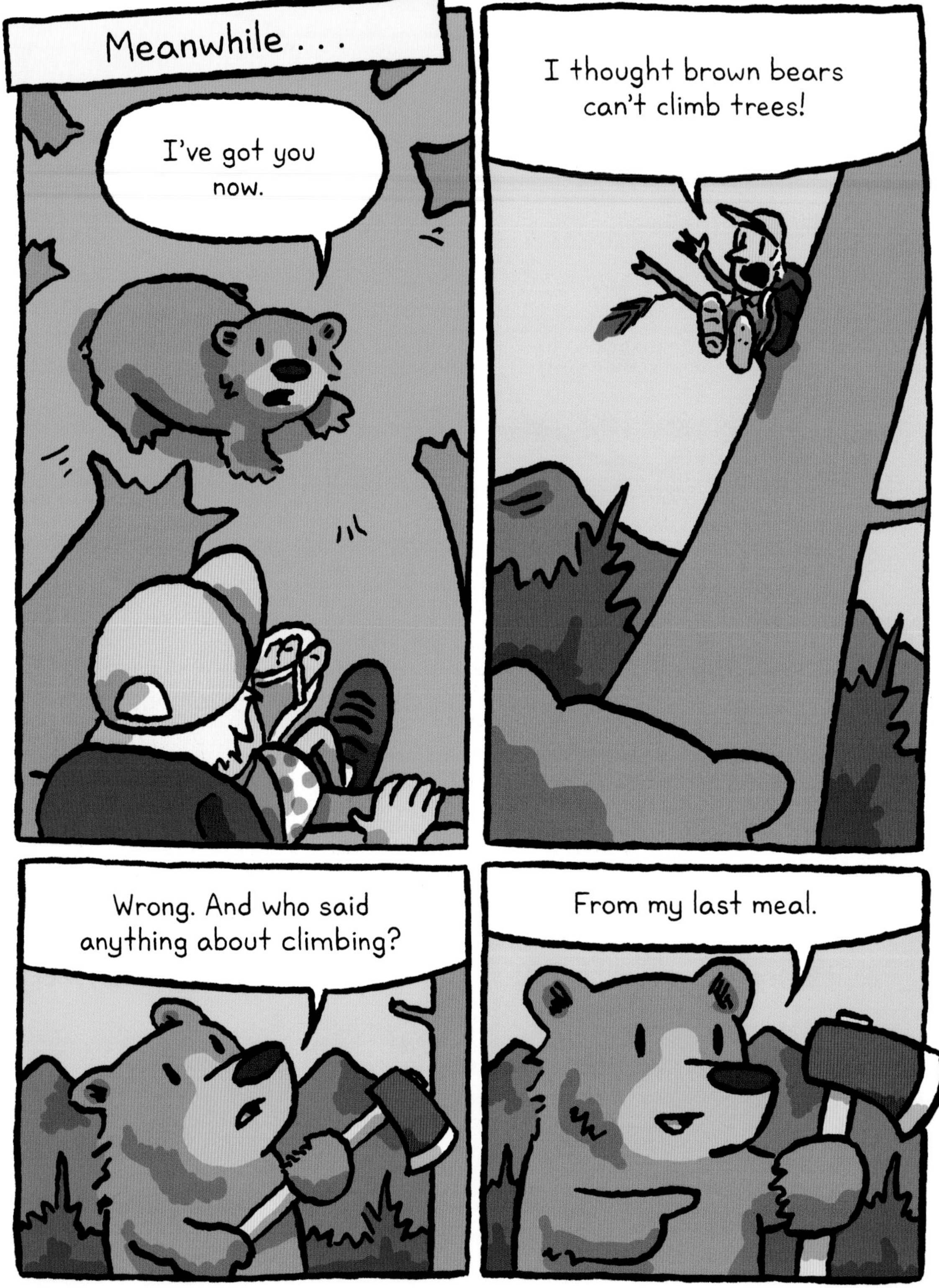
Meanwhile . . .
I've got you now.
I thought brown bears can't climb trees!
Wrong. And who said anything about climbing?
From my last meal.

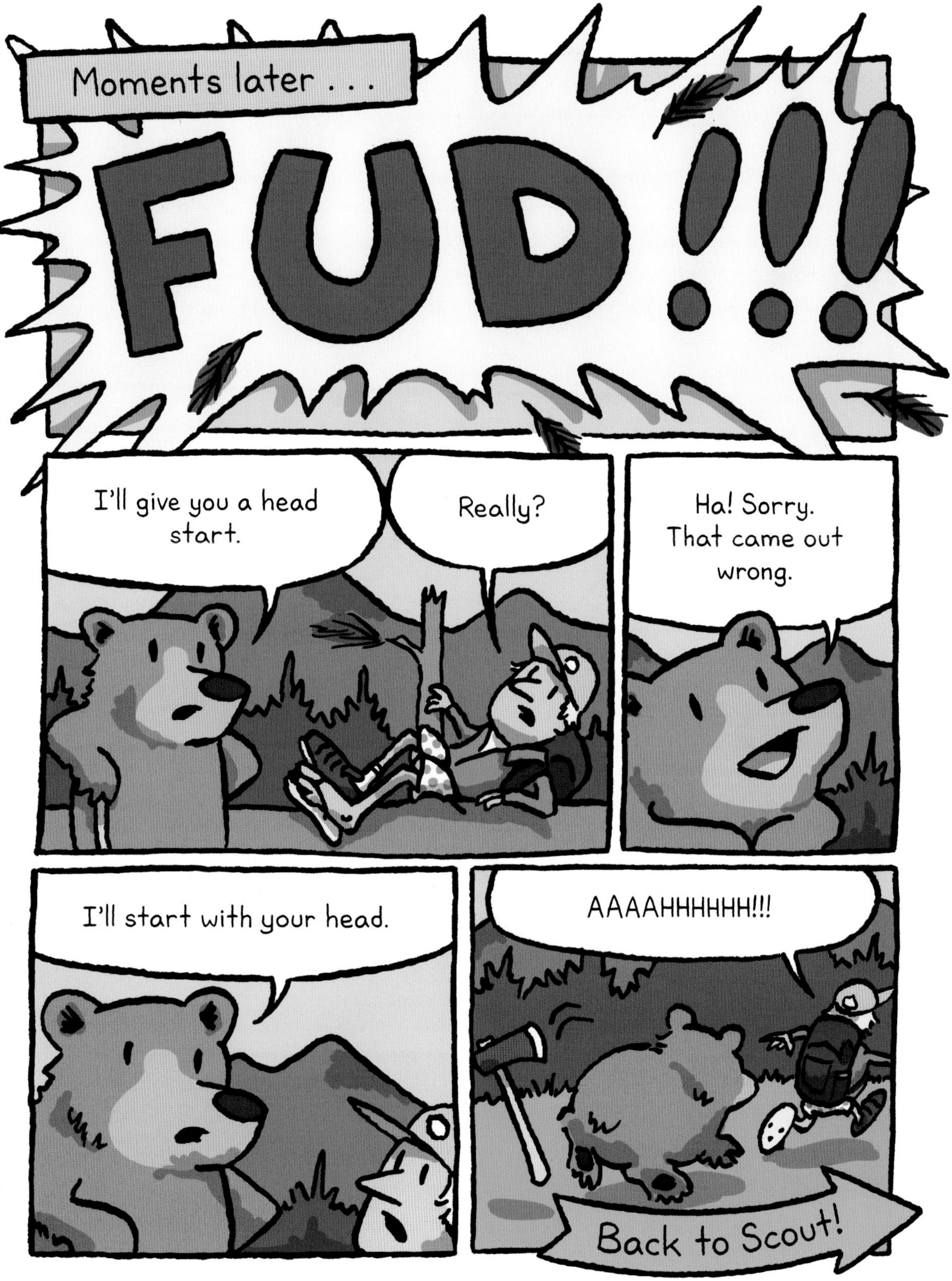
Moments later . . .
FUD!!!
I'll give you a head start.
Really?
Ha! Sorry. That came out wrong.
I'll start with your head.
AAAAHHHHHH!!!
Back to Scout!

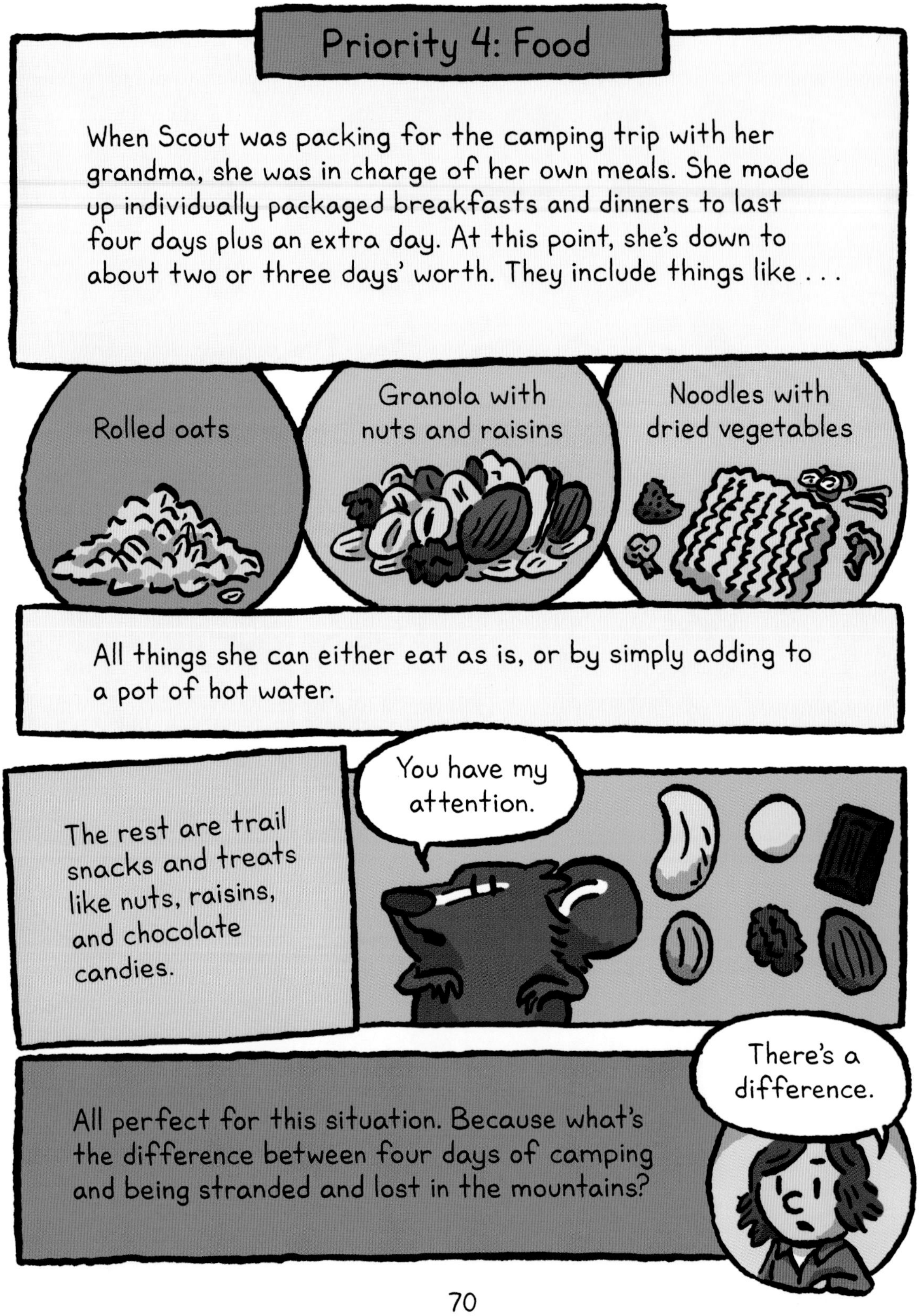
Priority 4: Food
When Scout was packing for the camping trip with her grandma, she was in charge of her own meals. She made up individually packaged breakfasts and dinners to last four days plus an extra day. At this point, she's down to about two or three days' worth. They include things like . . .
Rolled oats
Granola with nuts and raisins
Noodles with dried vegetables
All things she can either eat as is, or by simply adding to a pot of hot water.
The rest are trail snacks and treats like nuts, raisins, and chocolate candies.
You have my attention.
All perfect for this situation. Because what's the difference between four days of camping and being stranded and lost in the mountains?
There's a difference.

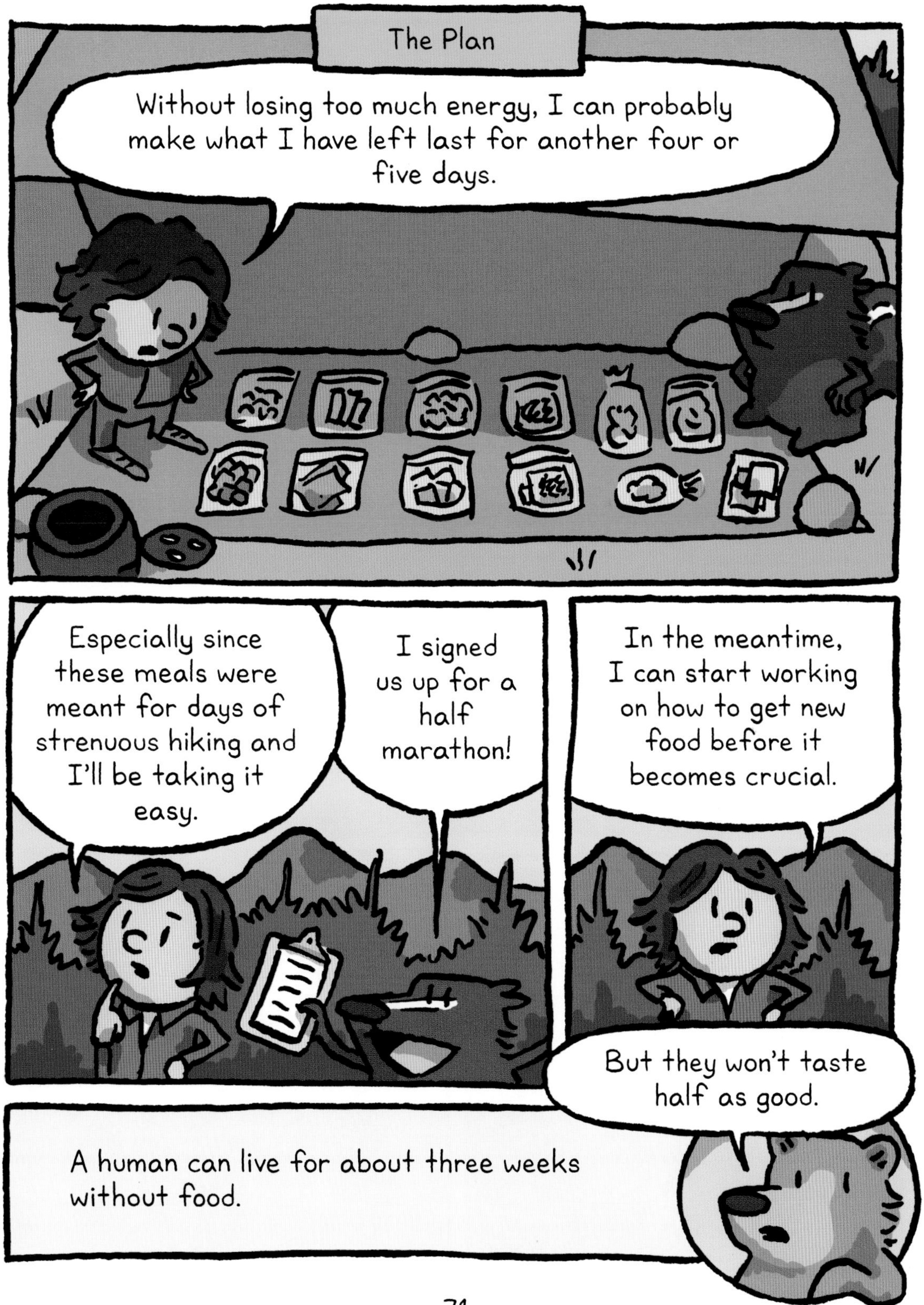
The Plan
Without losing too much energy, I can probably make what I have left last for another four or five days.
Especially since these meals were meant for days of strenuous hiking and I'll be taking it easy.
I signed us up for a half marathon!
In the meantime, I can start working on how to get new food before it becomes crucial.
But they won't taste half as good.
A human can live for about three weeks without food.

Scout is in an area with an abundance of food options, from squirrels and larger mammals to roots and tubers. Even bird eggs and earthworms! But the most bang for Scout's buck is probably fish. And she's got just the thing.

Someone else can eat worms.

For once, my brother was prepared.

Line

Hooks

It's my training.

First, I'll tie the hook to the fishing line.

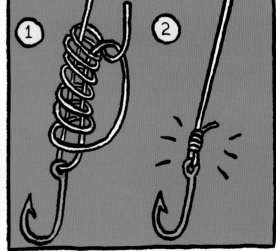

1

2

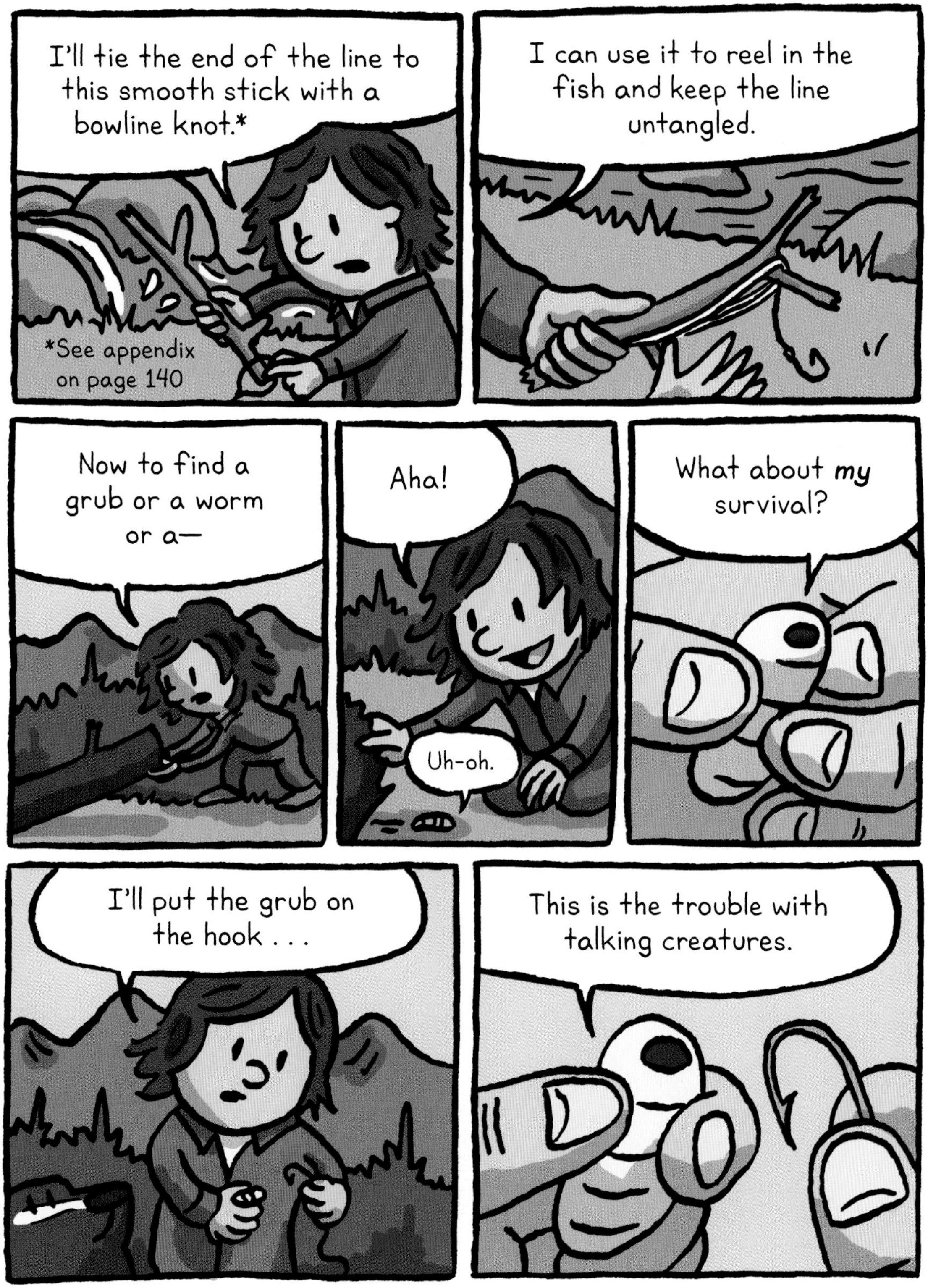
I'll tie the end of the line to this smooth stick with a bowline knot.*
*See appendix on page 140
I can use it to reel in the fish and keep the line untangled.
Now to find a grub or a worm or a—
Aha!
Uh-oh.
What about *my* survival?
I'll put the grub on the hook . . .
This is the trouble with talking creatures.

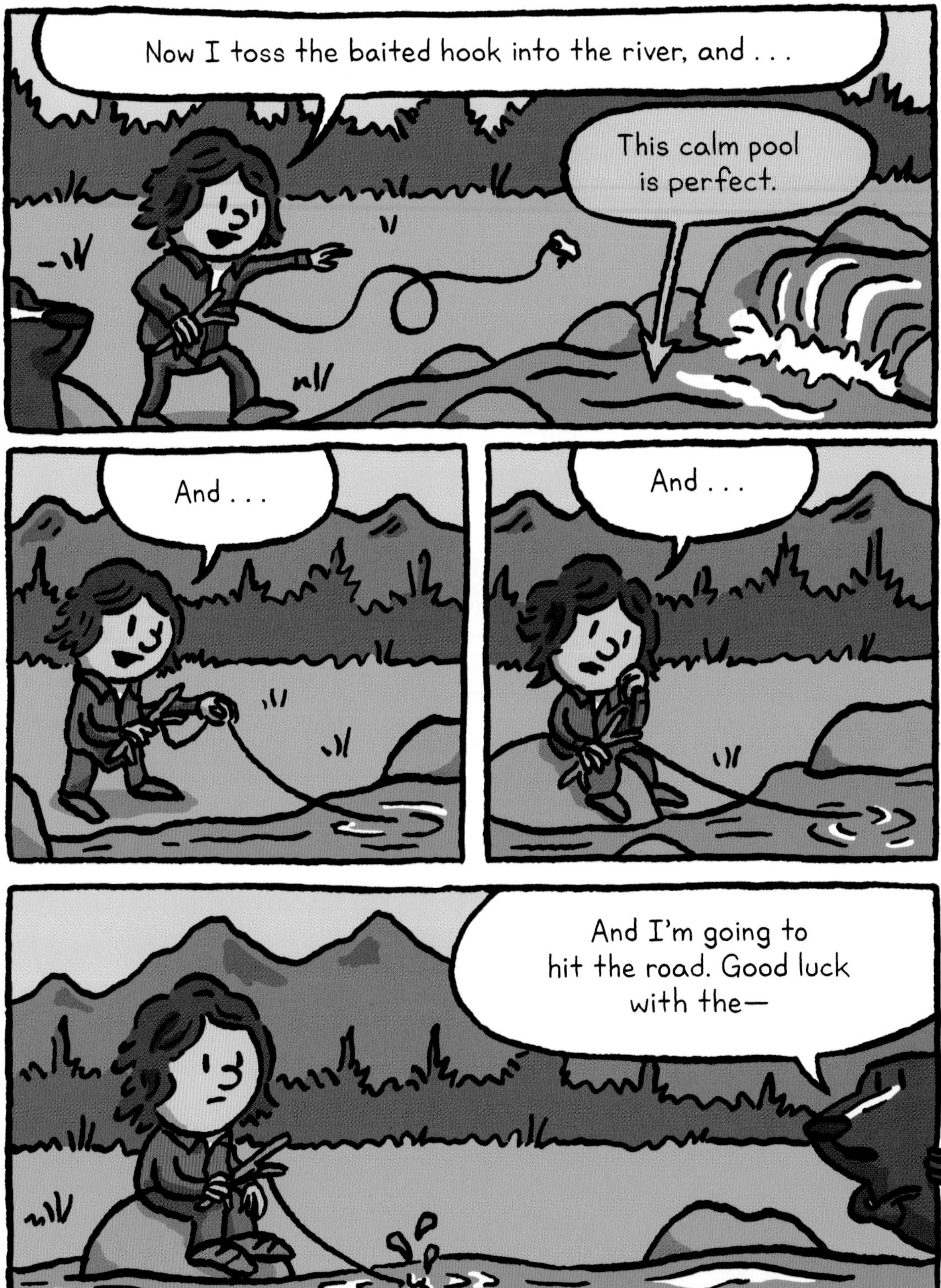
Now I toss the baited hook into the river, and . . .
This calm pool is perfect.
And . . .
And . . .
And I'm going to hit the road. Good luck with the—

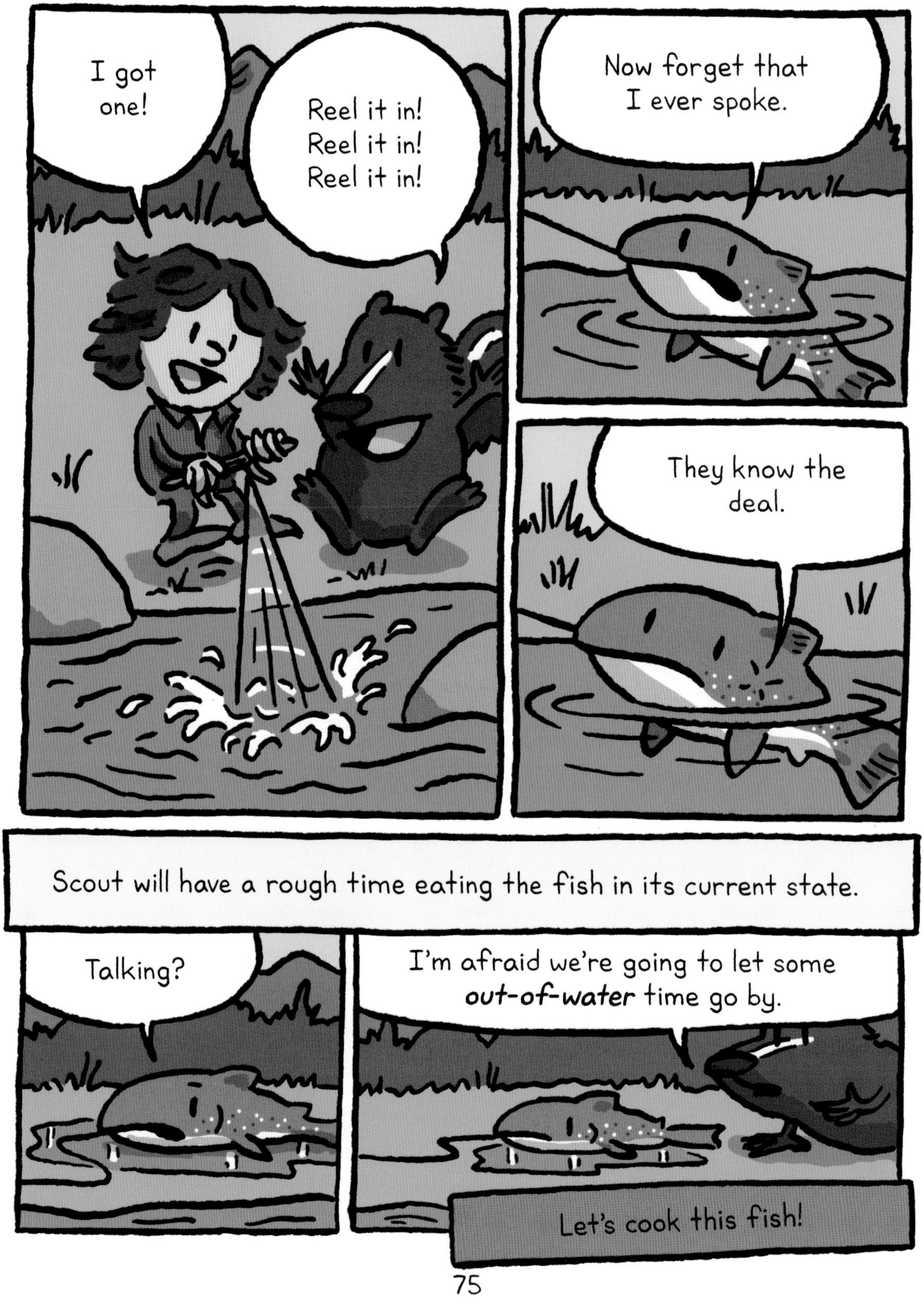

I got one!
Reel it in! Reel it in! Reel it in!
Now forget that I ever spoke.
They know the deal.
Scout will have a rough time eating the fish in its current state.
Talking?
I'm afraid we're going to let some ***out-of-water*** time go by.
Let's cook this fish!

One Way to Clean and Cook a Fish

First of all, any handling or consuming of fish should be done at least a hundred yards from camp. Care should also be taken to keep fish smells off of clothes and skin. Nothing attracts bears like fish scent.

I love them almost as much as wannabe guides.

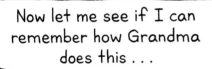

Now let me see if I can remember how Grandma does this . . .

I start with a shallow cut along the belly of the fish and up to the chin.

Squick!

76

Then I insert my knife and cut the gills away from the bottom jaw.

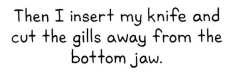

Shuck!

Rip out the gills and guts altogether.

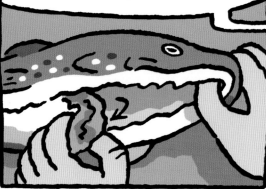

I'll let the river wash those away so they don't attract any bears.

Wait, *I* can eat them!

I've actually got bigger fish to fry.

I'm getting dizzy.

Now, I'll scrape off the kidney along the spine.

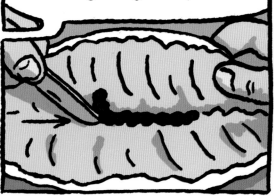

Into the river with that.

I'm going in.

Sploip!

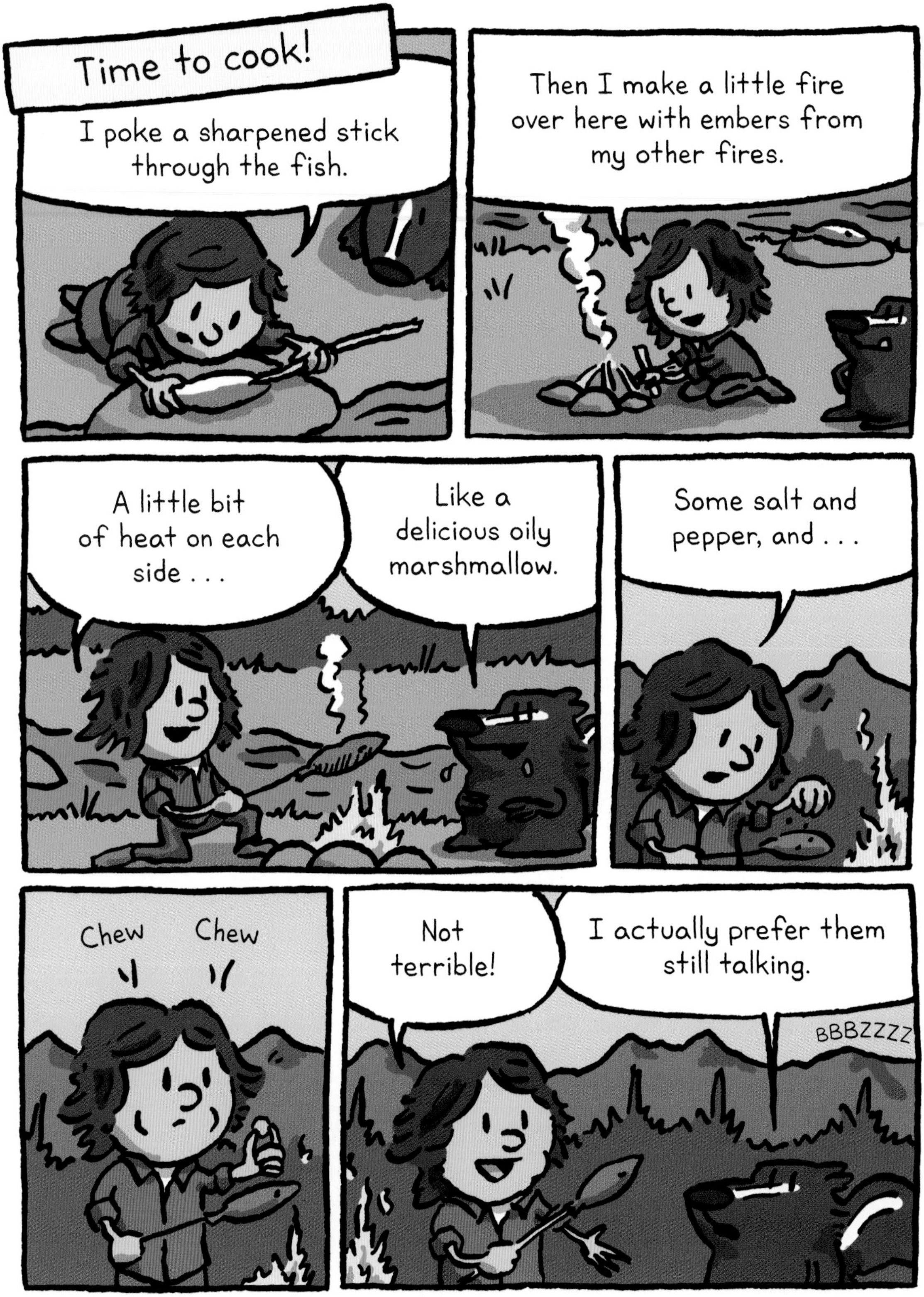
Time to cook!
I poke a sharpened stick through the fish.
Then I make a little fire over here with embers from my other fires.
A little bit of heat on each side . . .
Like a delicious oily marshmallow.
Some salt and pepper, and . . .
Chew Chew
Not terrible!
I actually prefer them still talking.
BBBZZZZ

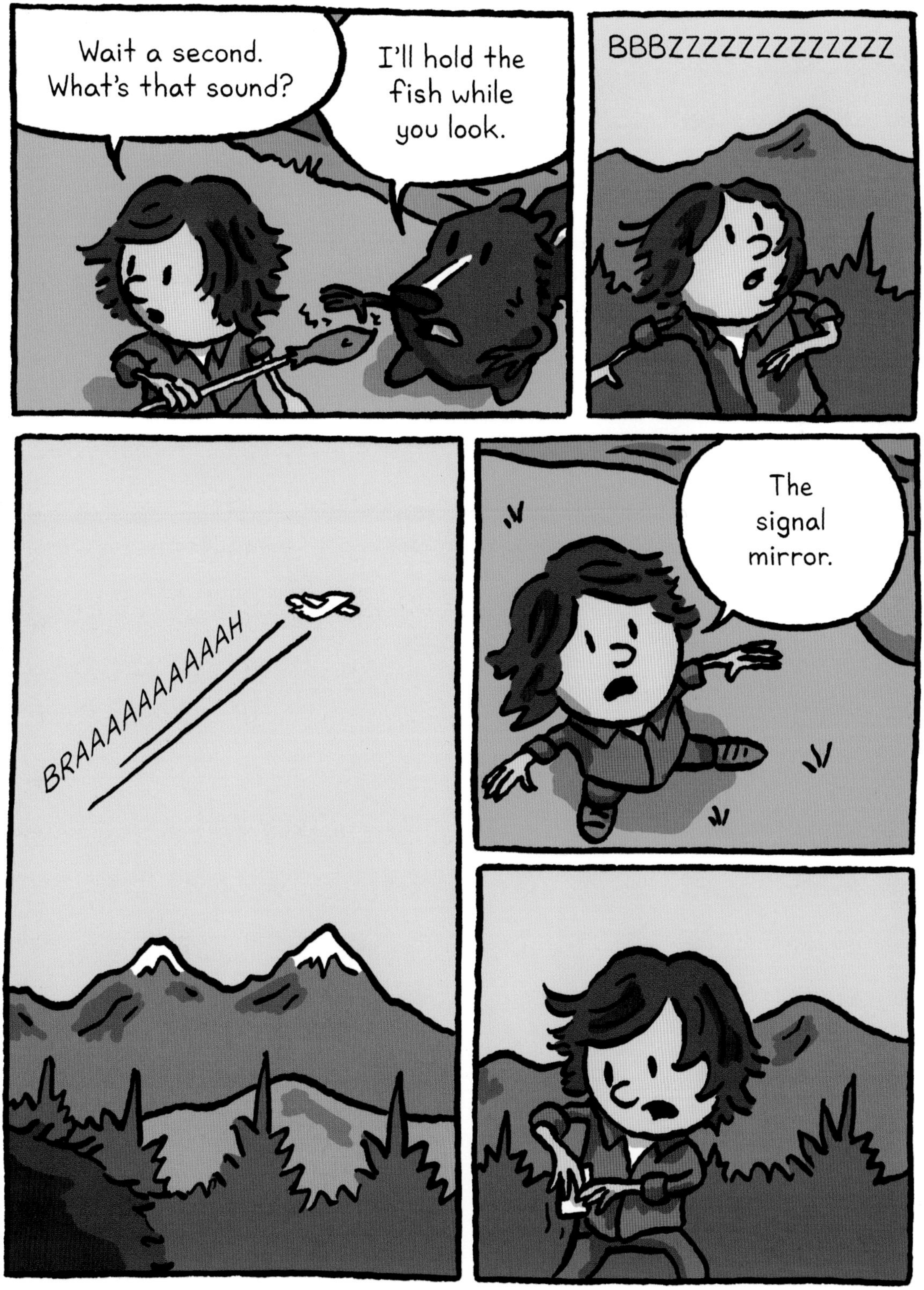
Wait a second. What's that sound?
I'll hold the fish while you look.
BBBZZZZZZZZZZZZZ
BRAAAAAAAAAAH
The signal mirror.

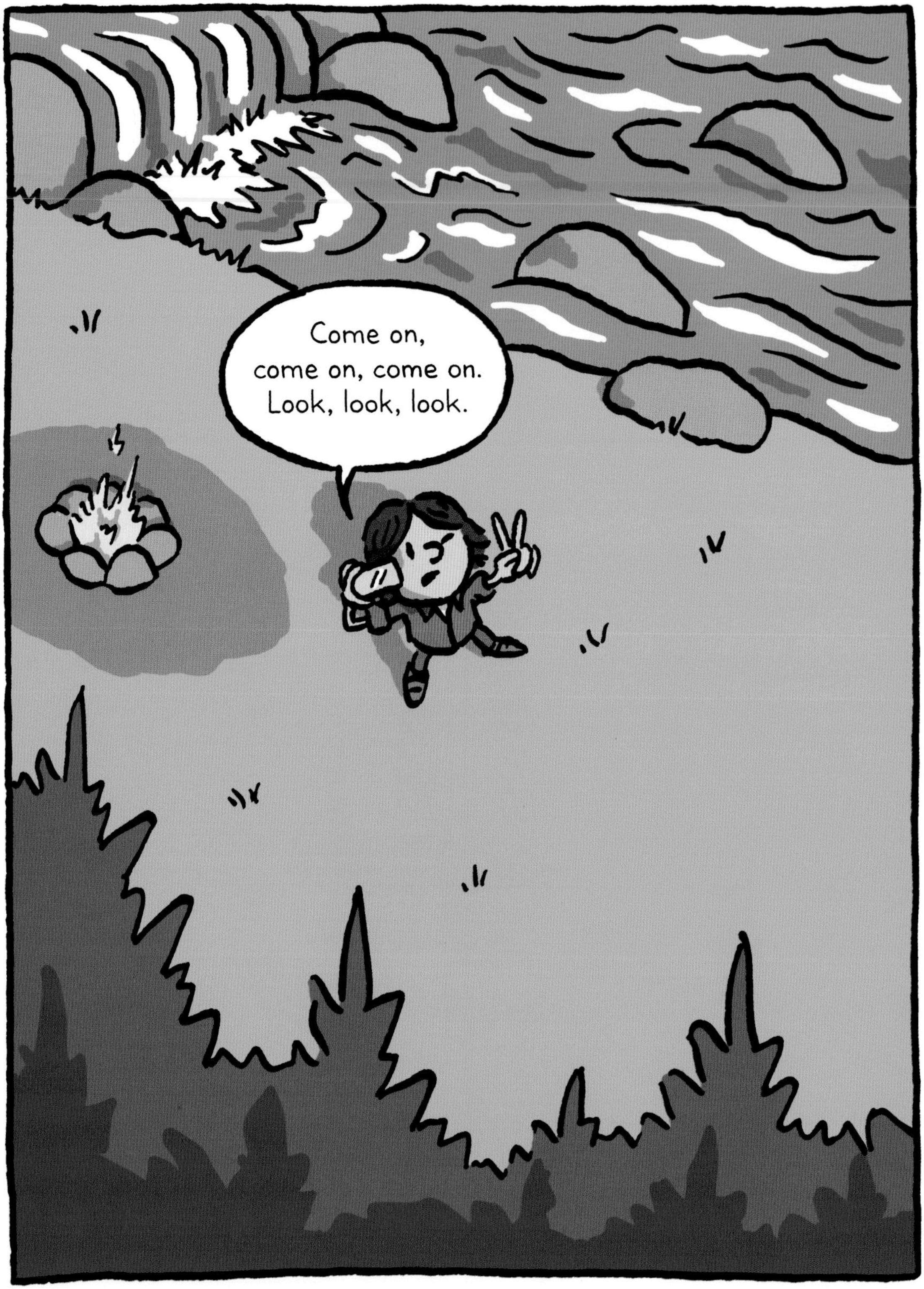
Come on,
come on, come on.
Look, look, look.

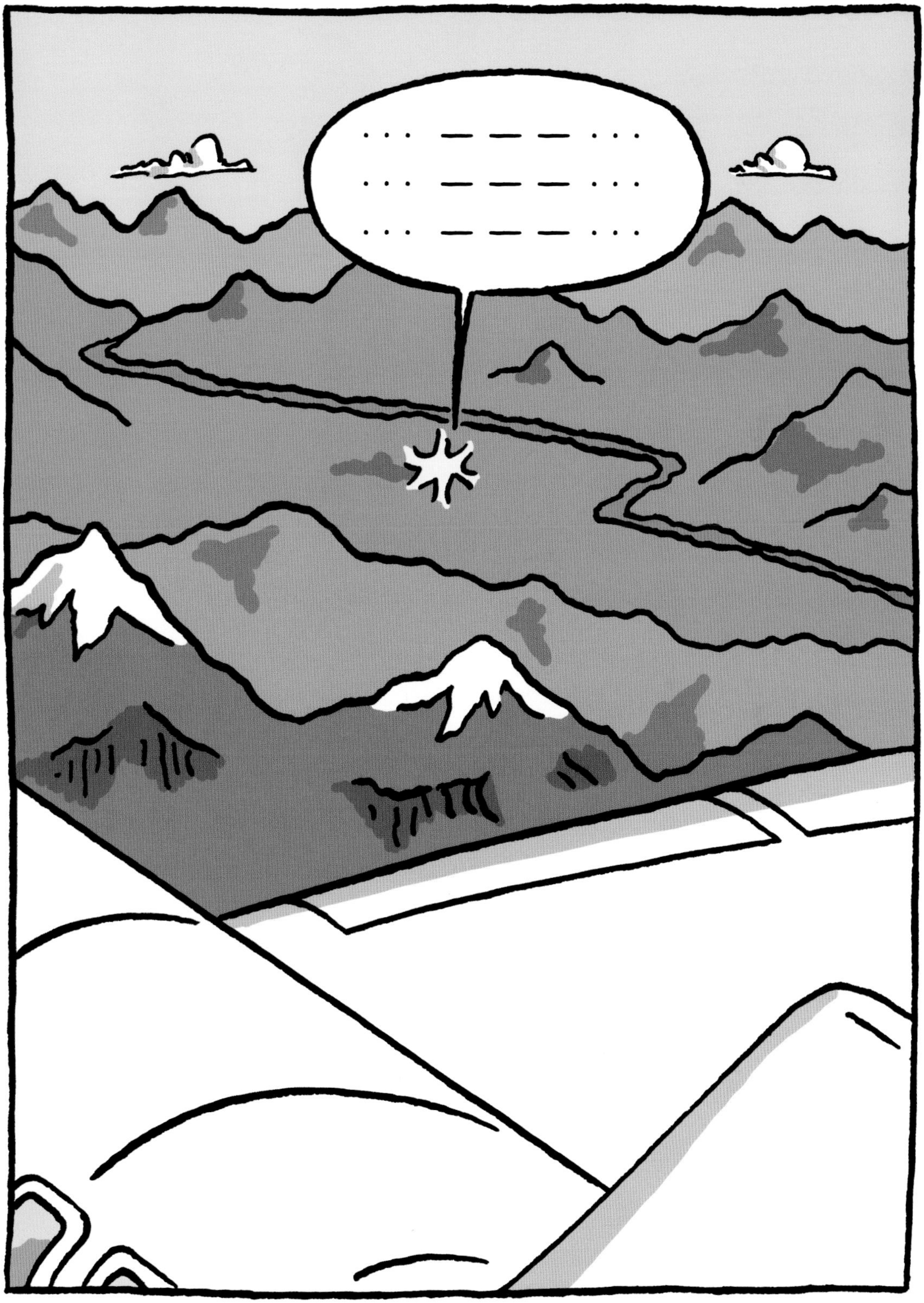

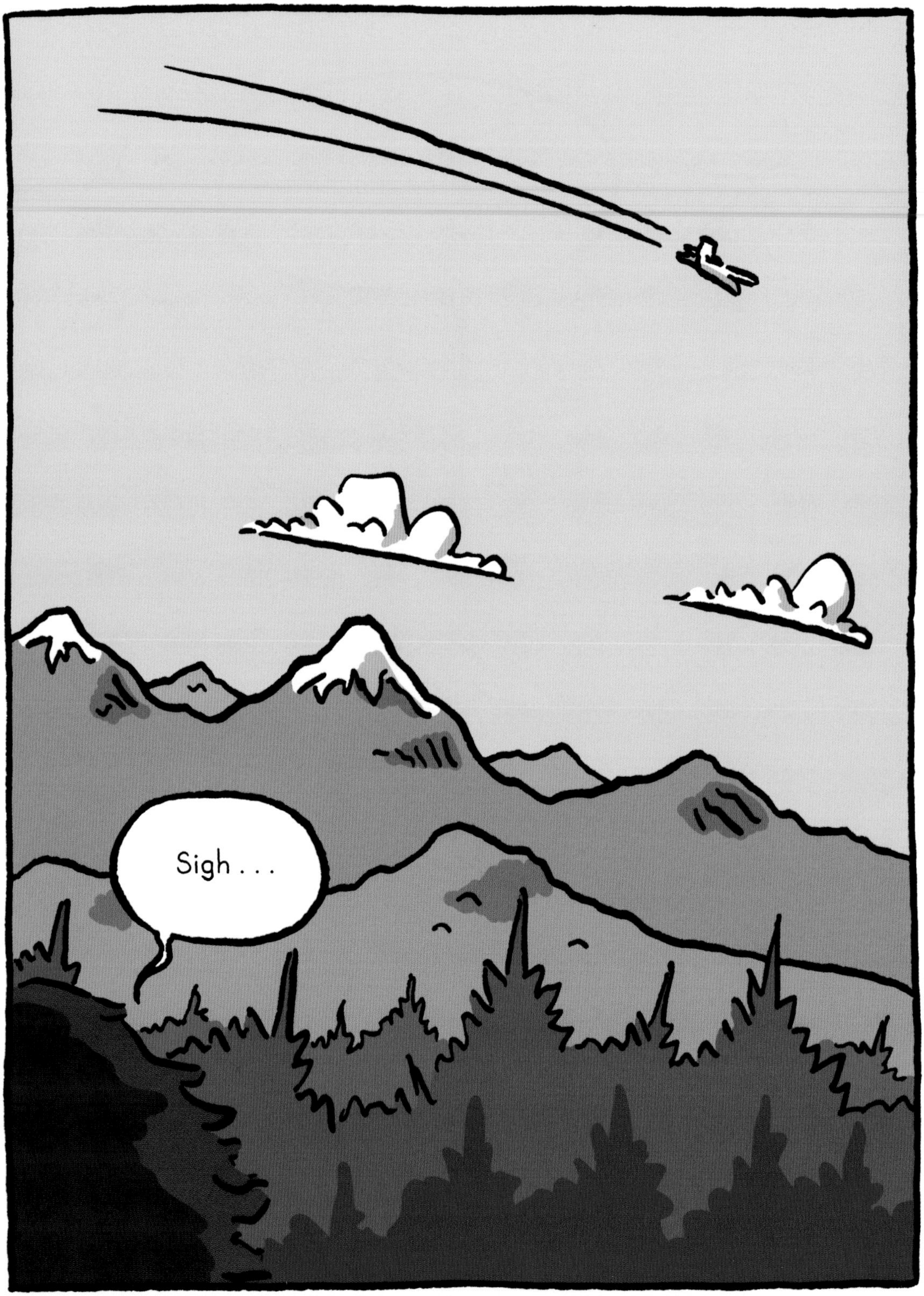
Sigh . . .

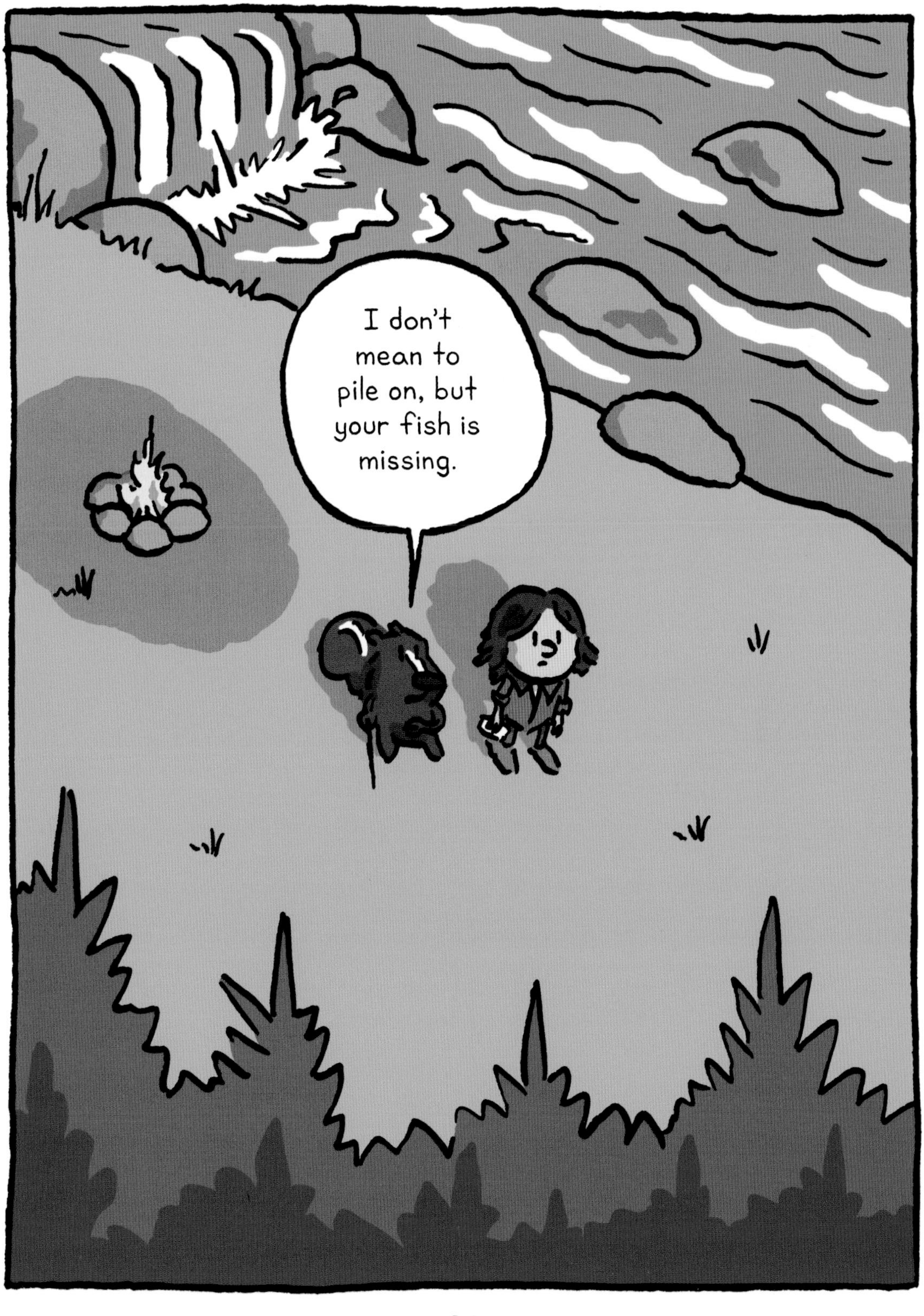
I don't mean to pile on, but your fish is missing.

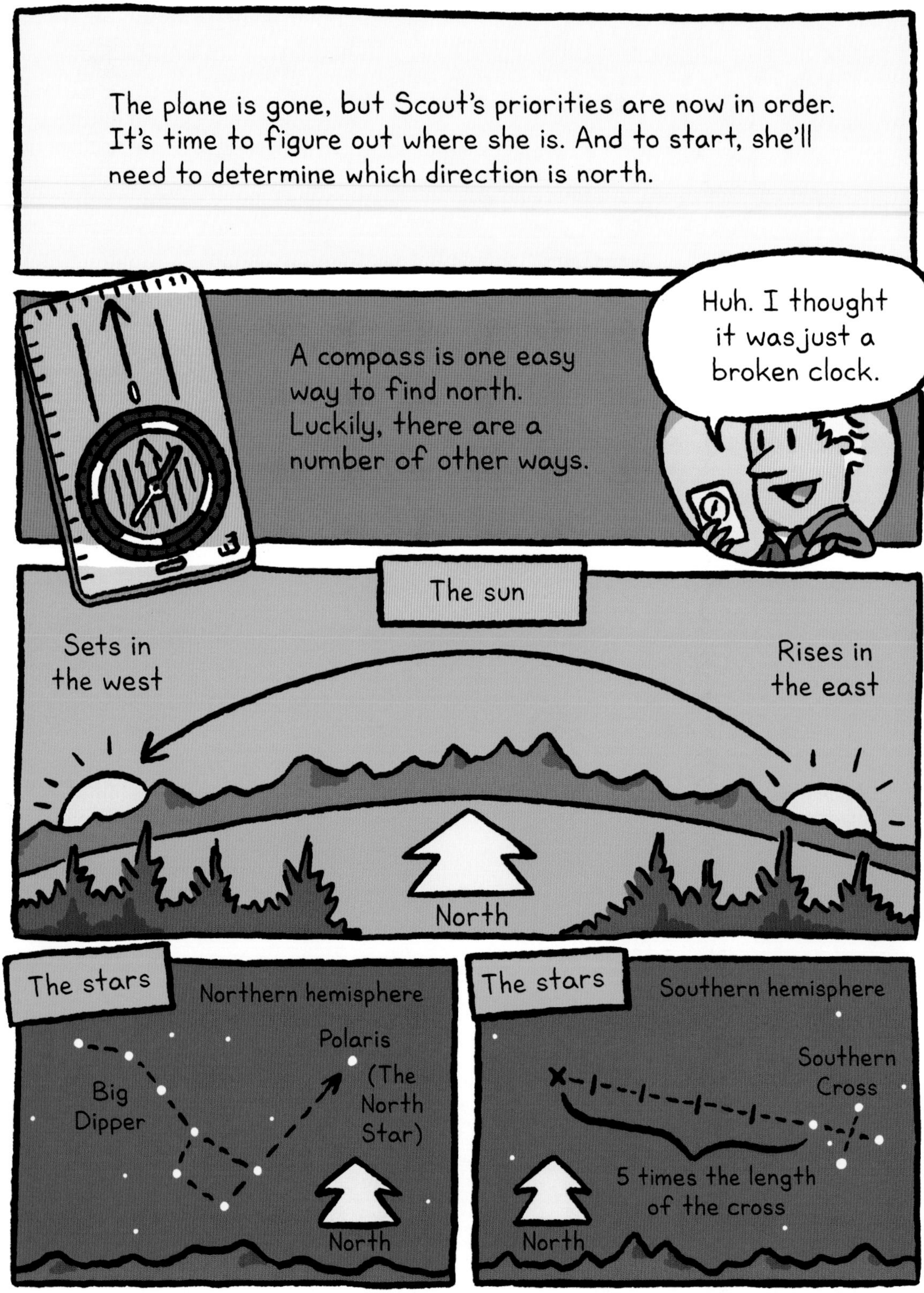
The plane is gone, but Scout's priorities are now in order. It's time to figure out where she is. And to start, she'll need to determine which direction is north.
A compass is one easy way to find north. Luckily, there are a number of other ways.
Huh. I thought it was just a broken clock.
The sun
Sets in the west
Rises in the east
North
The stars
Northern hemisphere
Big Dipper
Polaris (The North Star)
North
The stars
Southern hemisphere
Southern Cross
5 times the length of the cross
North

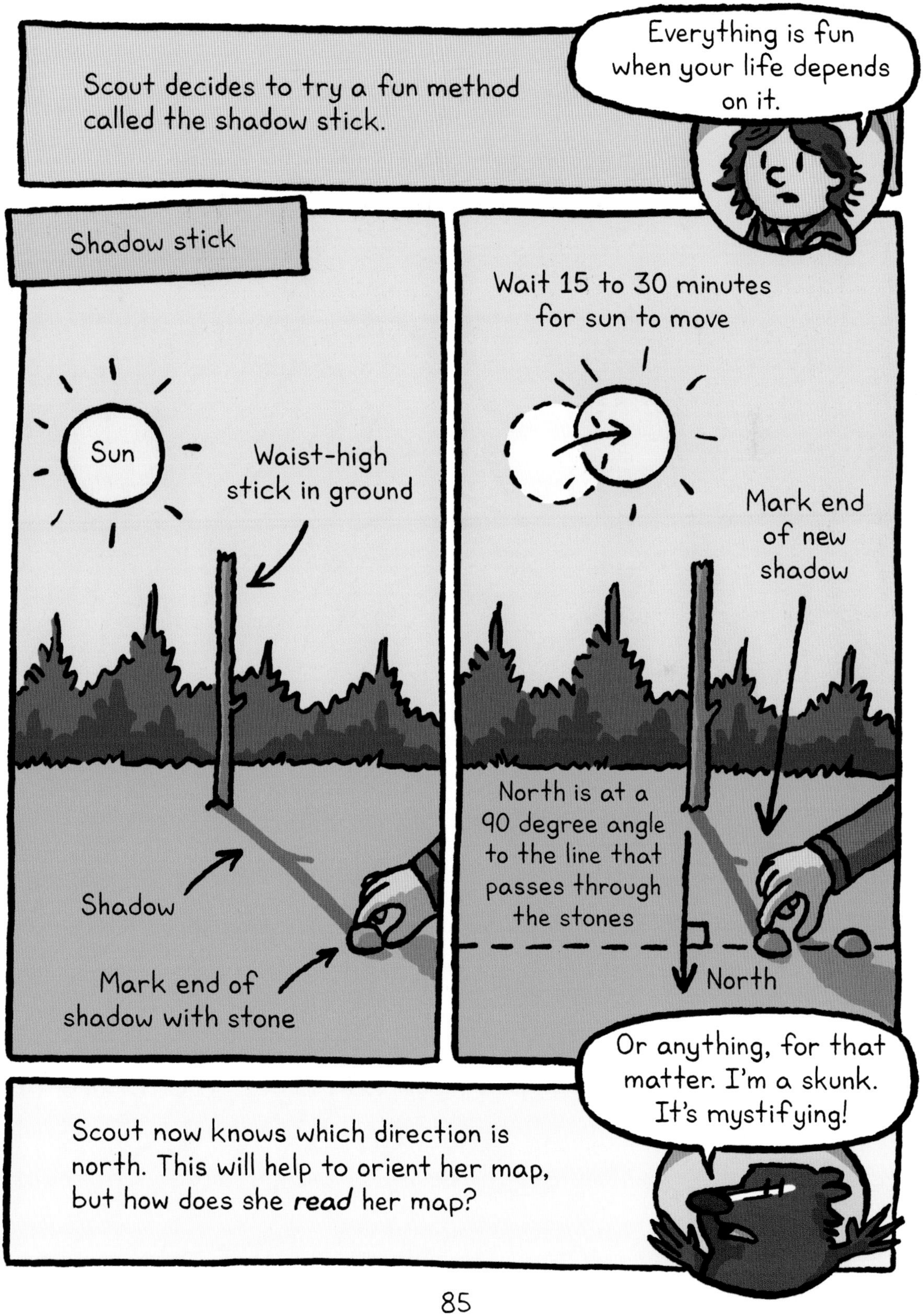
Scout decides to try a fun method called the shadow stick.
Everything is fun when your life depends on it.
Shadow stick
Sun
Waist-high stick in ground
Shadow
Mark end of shadow with stone
Wait 15 to 30 minutes for sun to move
Mark end of new shadow
North is at a 90 degree angle to the line that passes through the stones
North
Scout now knows which direction is north. This will help to orient her map, but how does she *read* her map?
Or anything, for that matter. I'm a skunk. It's mystifying!

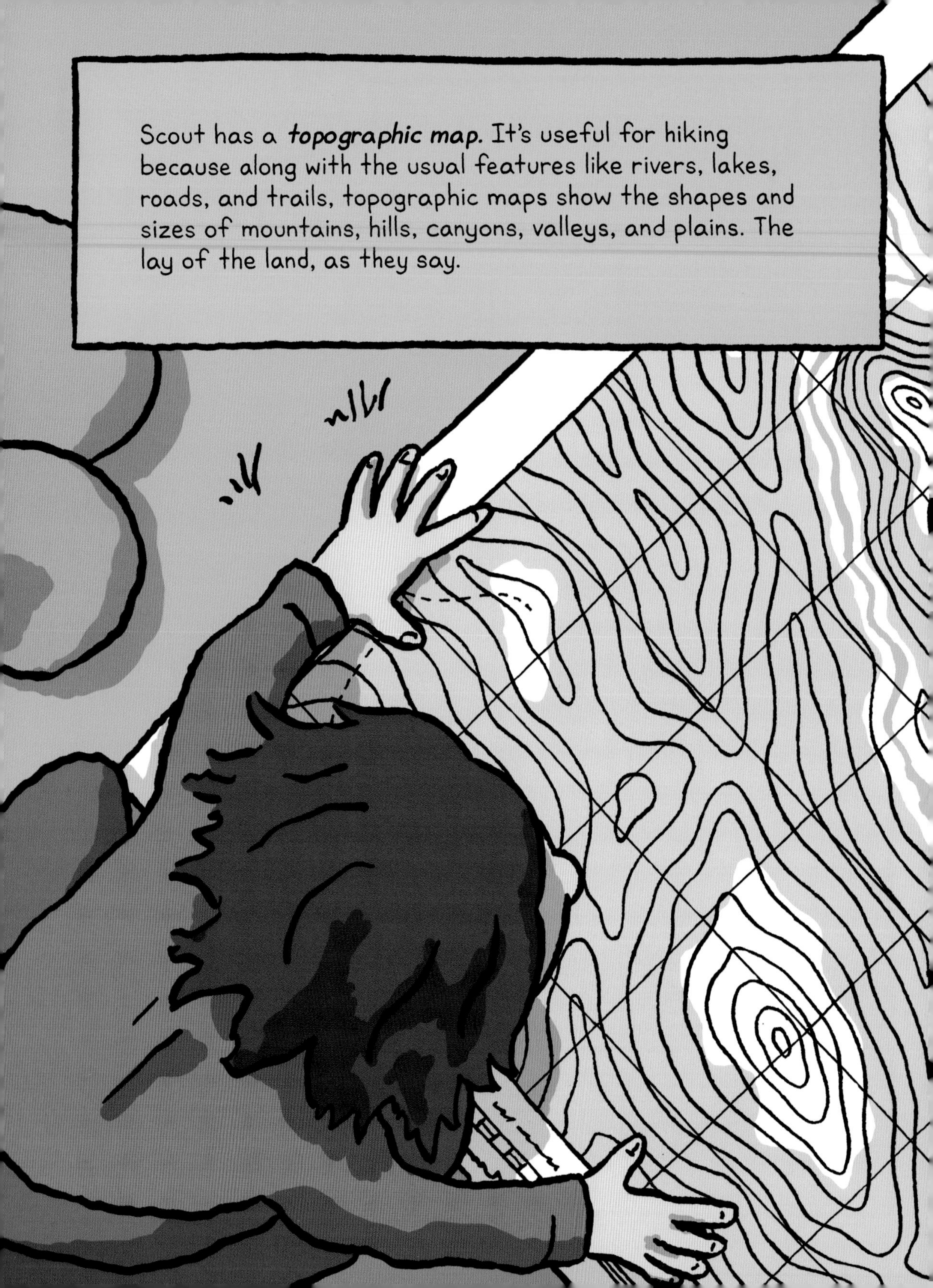
Scout has a ***topographic map.*** It's useful for hiking because along with the usual features like rivers, lakes, roads, and trails, topographic maps show the shapes and sizes of mountains, hills, canyons, valleys, and plains. The lay of the land, as they say.

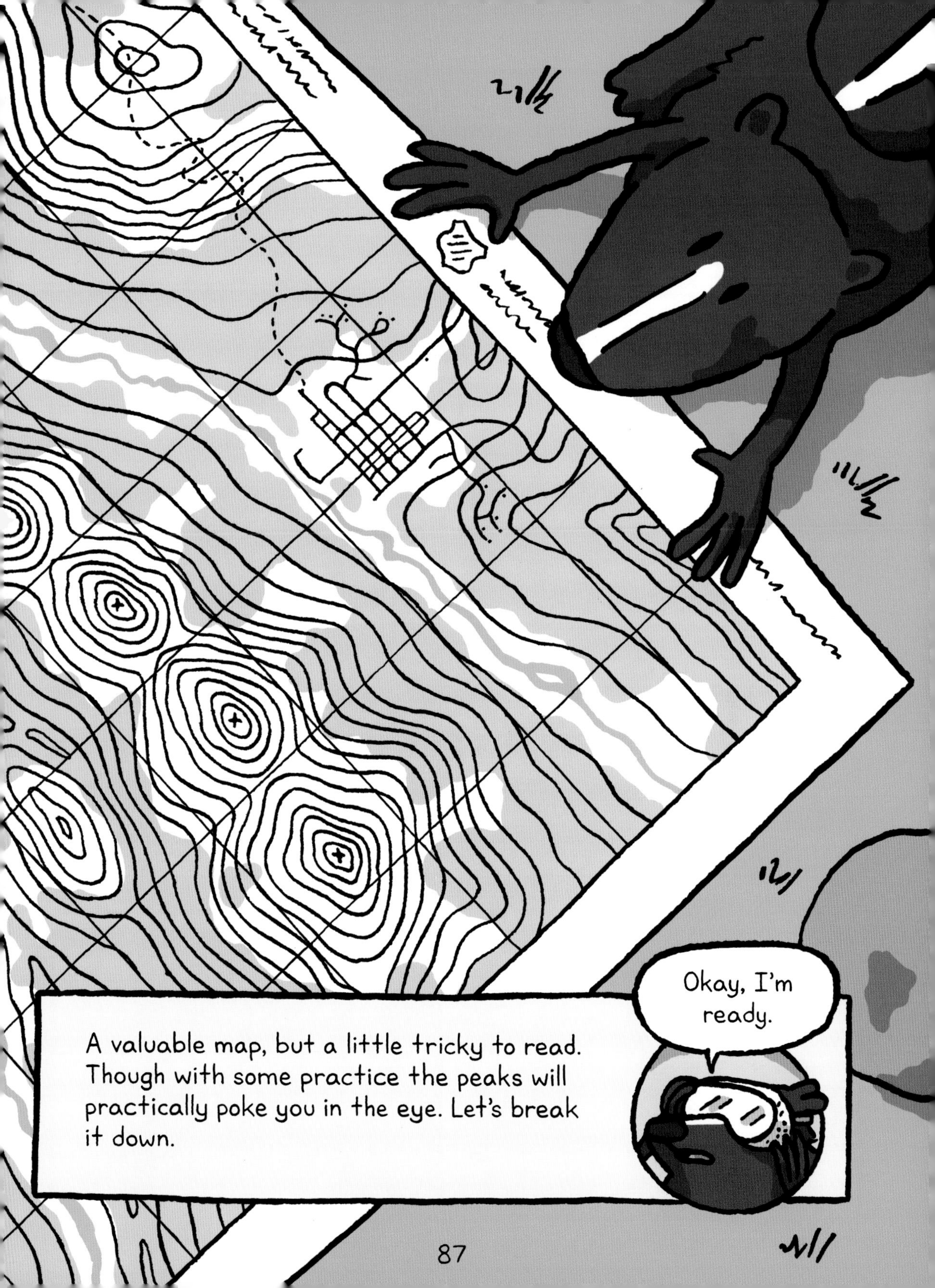
A valuable map, but a little tricky to read. Though with some practice the peaks will practically poke you in the eye. Let's break it down.
Okay, I'm ready.

Topographic Maps

Think of an island in the ocean. Trace a line around the island where the land meets the water. This is at zero feet above sea level.

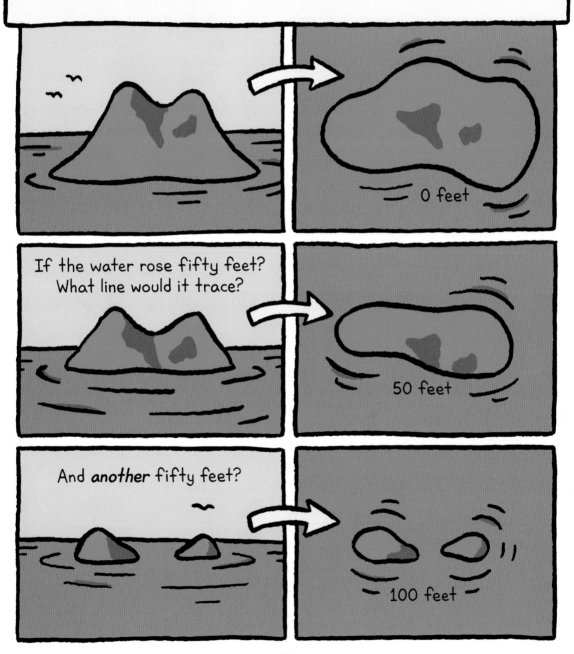

If the water rose fifty feet? What line would it trace?

And **another** fifty feet?

0 feet

50 feet

100 feet

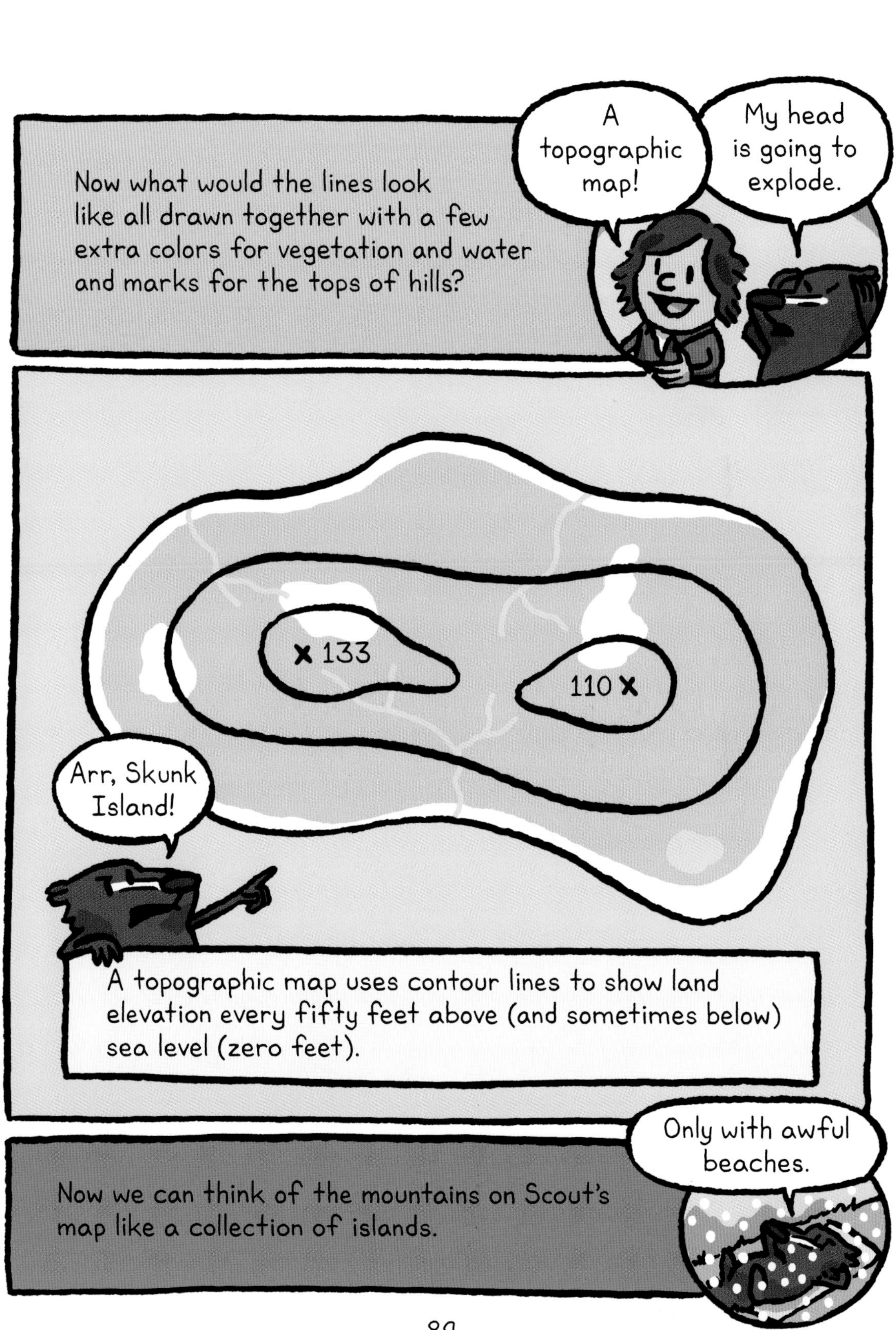

Now what would the lines look like all drawn together with a few extra colors for vegetation and water and marks for the tops of hills?

A topographic map!

My head is going to explode.

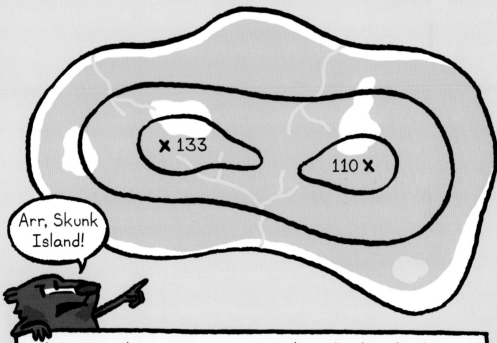

x 133

110 **x**

Arr, Skunk Island!

A topographic map uses contour lines to show land elevation every fifty feet above (and sometimes below) sea level (zero feet).

Now we can think of the mountains on Scout's map like a collection of islands.

Only with awful beaches.

Reading Scout's Map

Scout points her body and her map north in order to visualize where she is.

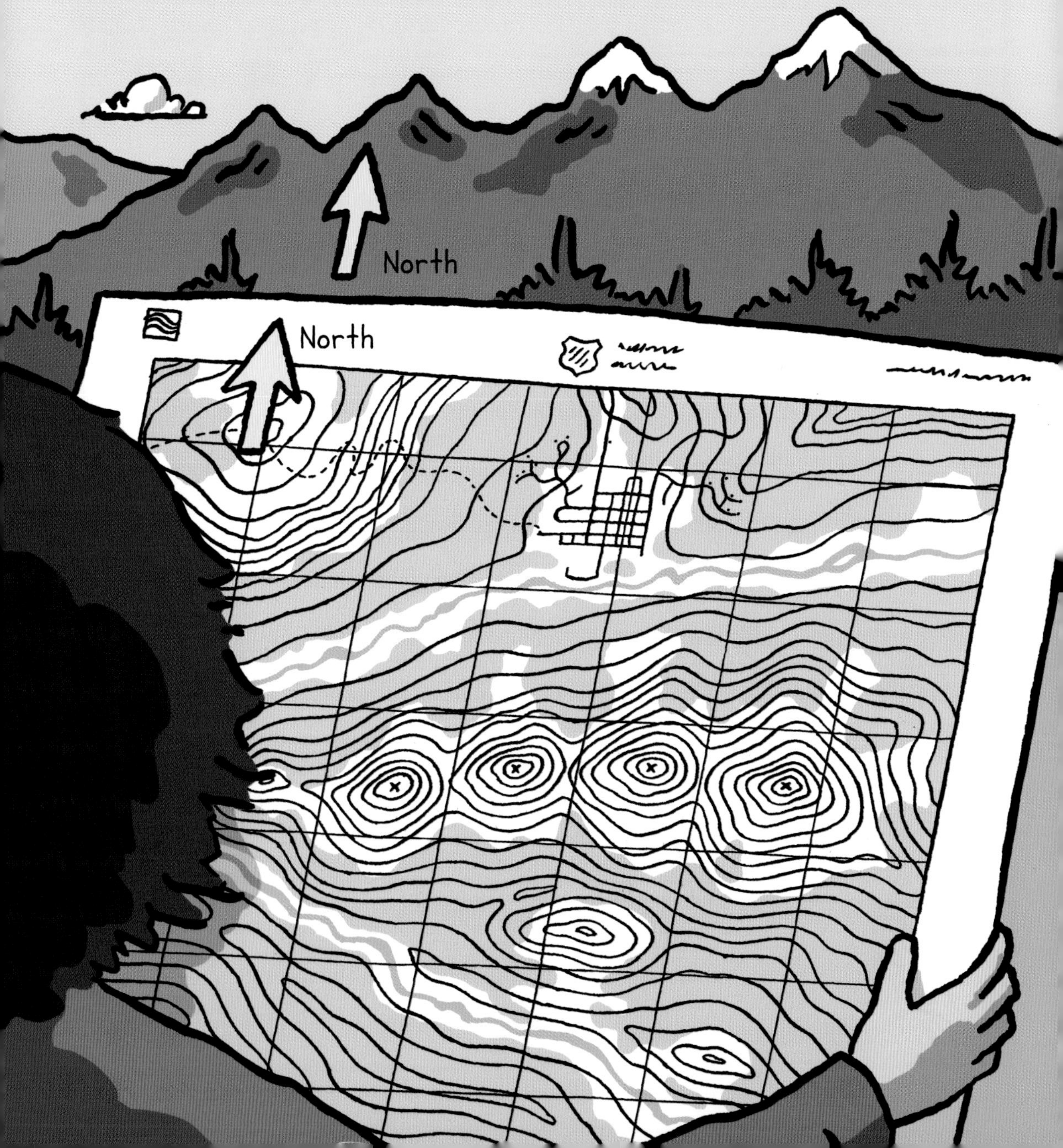
North
North

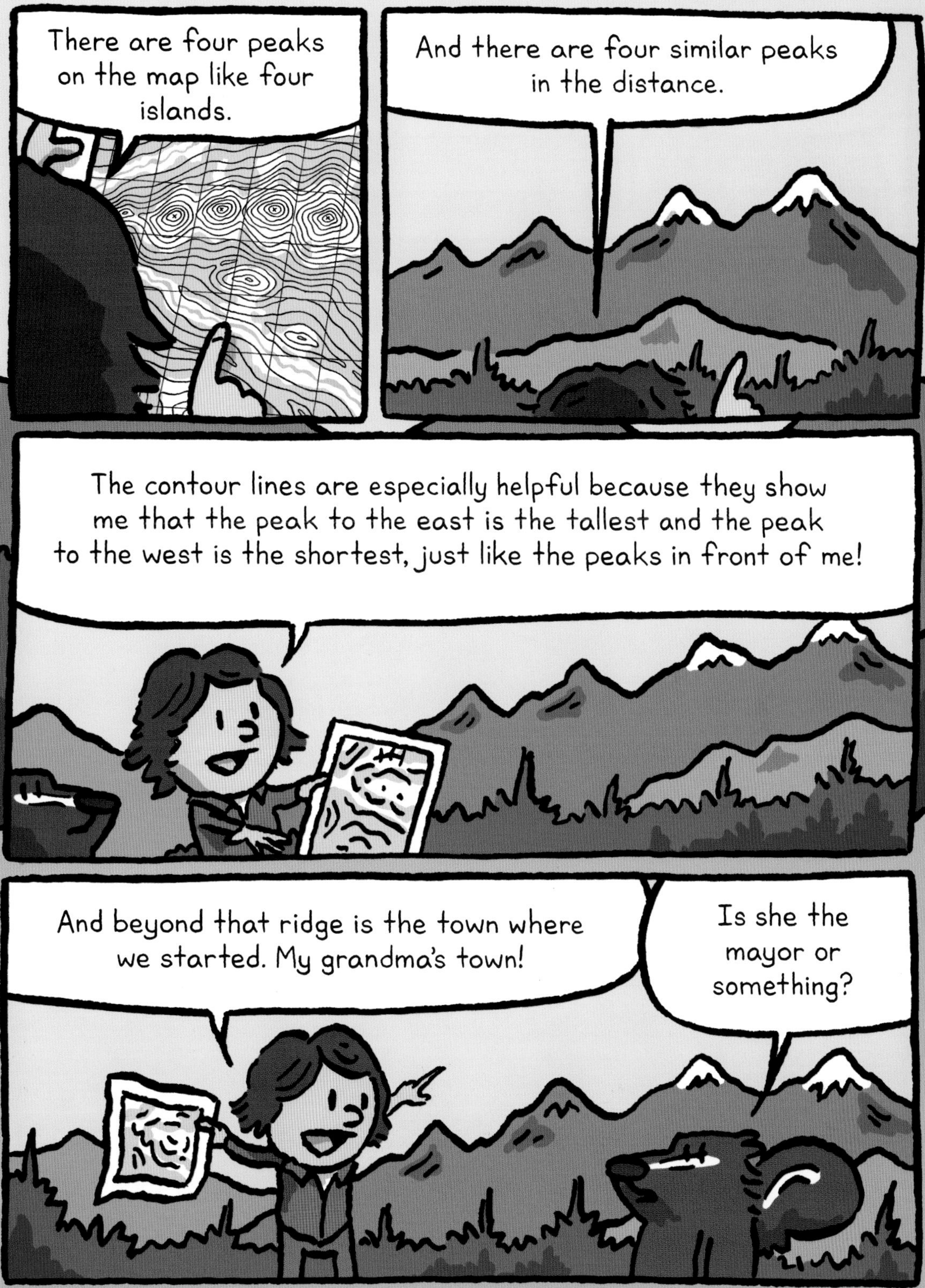
There are four peaks on the map like four islands.
And there are four similar peaks in the distance.
The contour lines are especially helpful because they show me that the peak to the east is the tallest and the peak to the west is the shortest, just like the peaks in front of me!
And beyond that ridge is the town where we started. My grandma's town!
Is she the mayor or something?

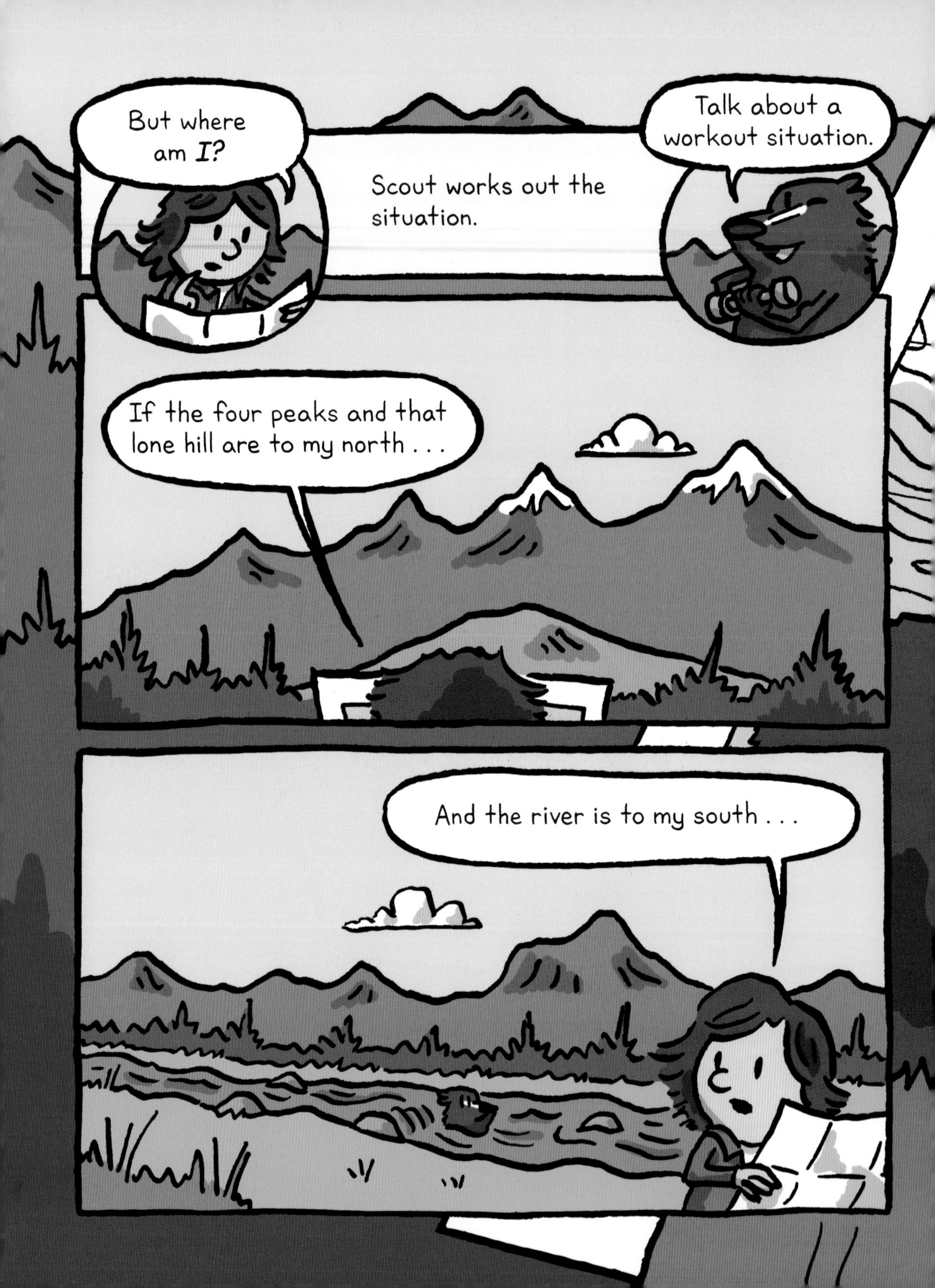
But where am I?
Scout works out the situation.
Talk about a workout situation.
If the four peaks and that lone hill are to my north . . .
And the river is to my south . . .

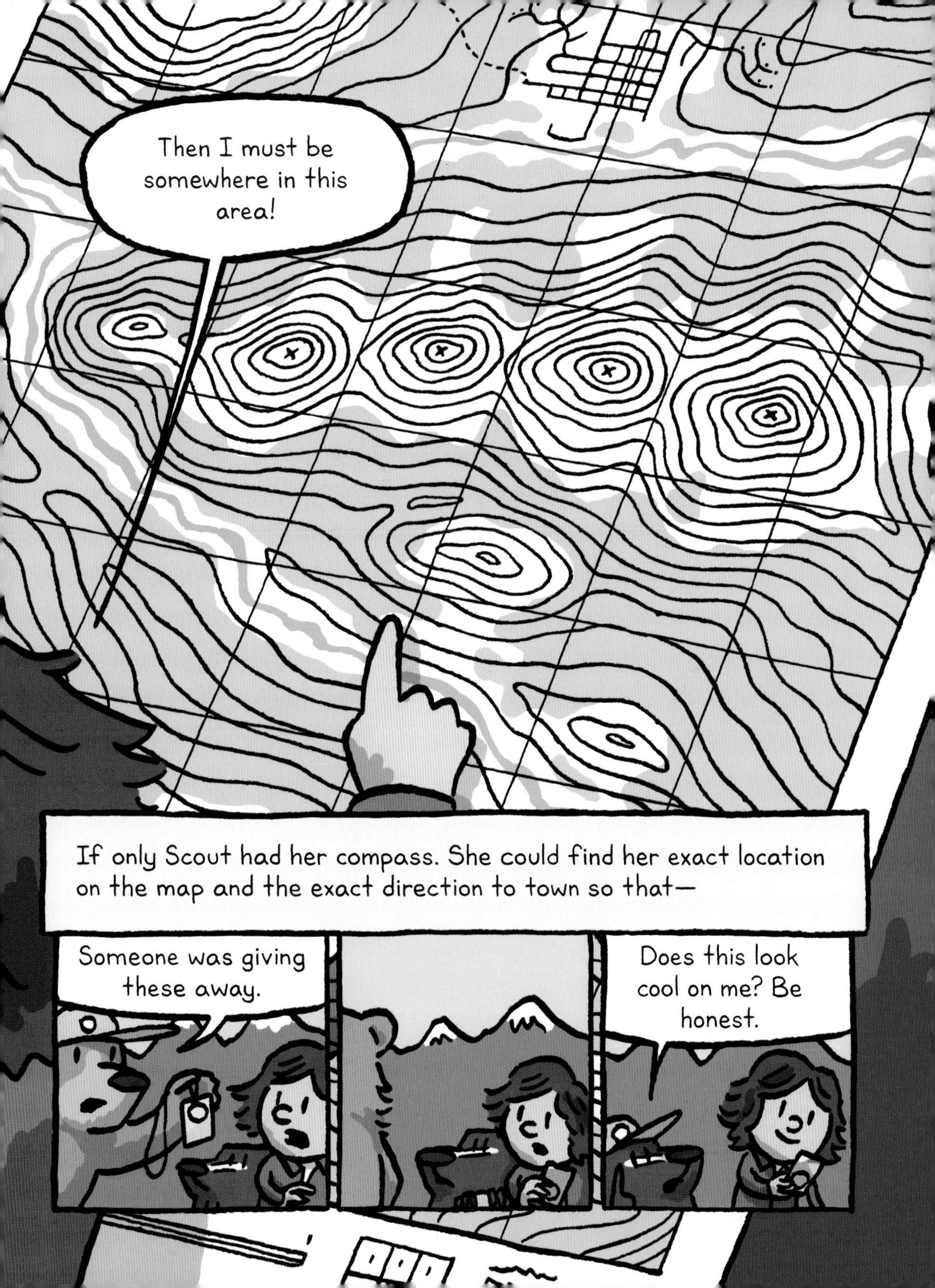
Then I must be somewhere in this area!
If only Scout had her compass. She could find her exact location on the map and the exact direction to town so that—
Someone was giving these away.
Does this look cool on me? Be honest.

Using a Compass

It will be helpful, if not lifesaving, for Scout to figure out her exact location. To do so, she'll use her map, compass, pencil, and two prominent features. The tall peaks to the east and west should do nicely.

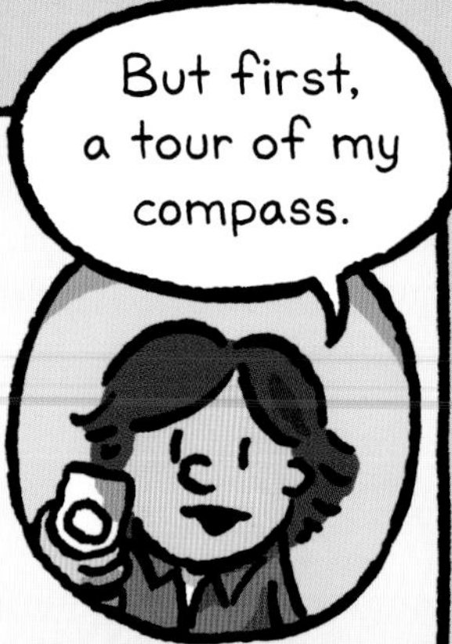
But first, a tour of my compass.

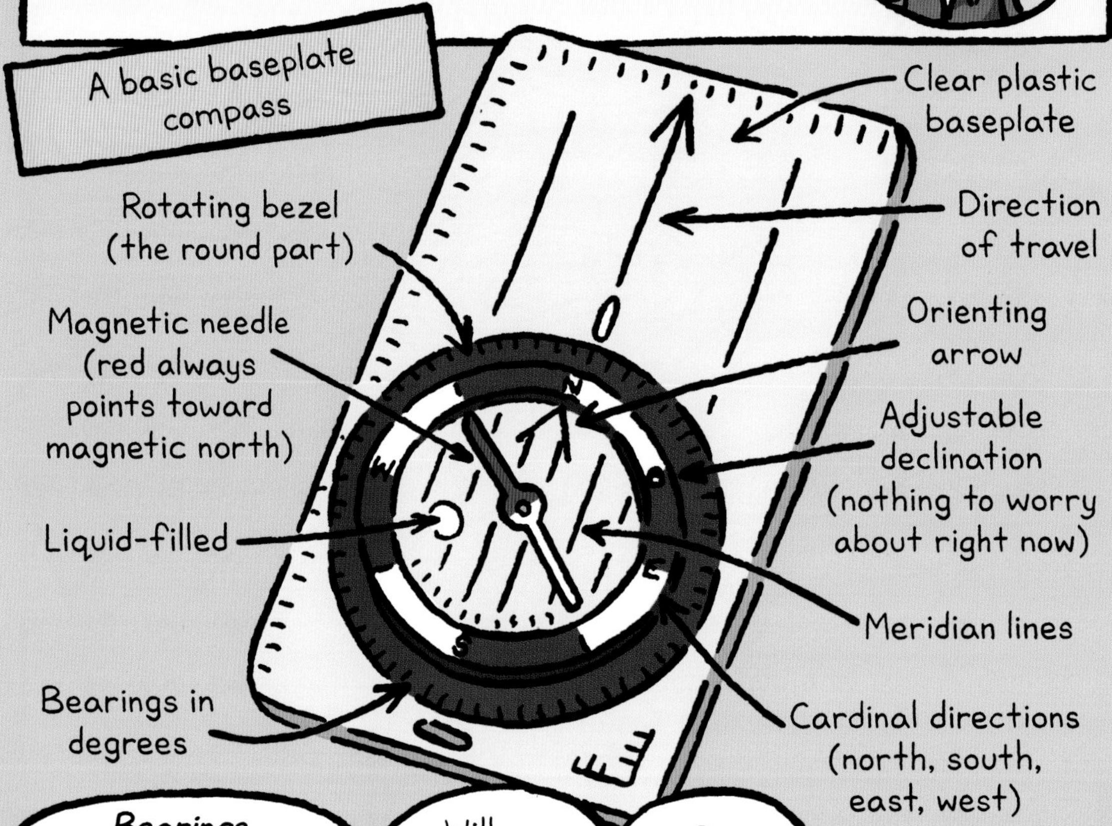
A basic baseplate compass
Clear plastic baseplate
Direction of travel
Rotating bezel (the round part)
Magnetic needle (red always points toward magnetic north)
Orienting arrow
Adjustable declination (nothing to worry about right now)
Liquid-filled
Meridian lines
Bearings in degrees
Cardinal directions (north, south, east, west)
N
S
E

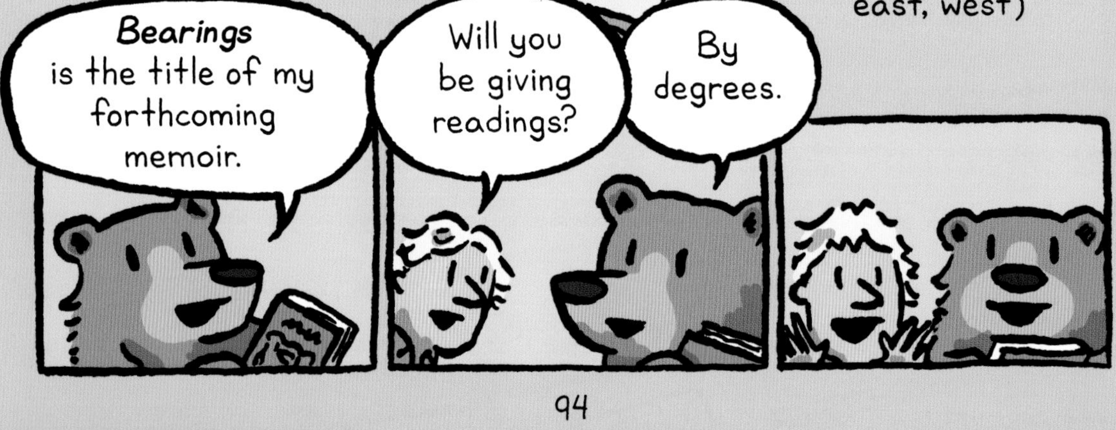
Bearings is the title of my forthcoming memoir.
Will you be giving readings?
By degrees.

Now then, to find her location, Scout first points her compass at the peak to the west. She rotates the bezel until the orienting arrow is lined up with the red end of the needle.

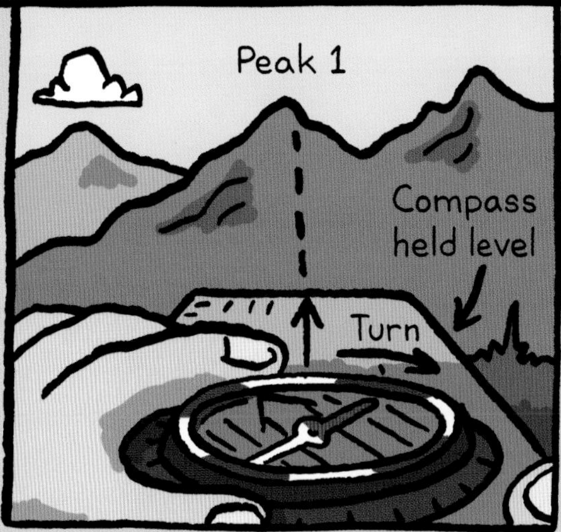
Peak 1
Compass held level
Turn

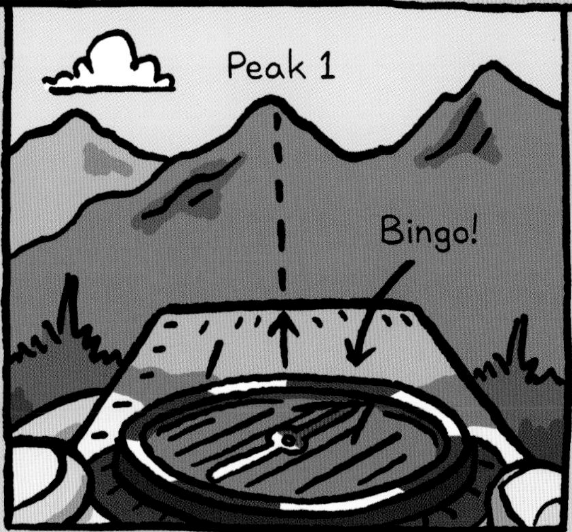
Peak 1
Bingo!

She then places the compass on the map, lines up the orienting arrow with the north-south meridian lines of the map (without rotating the bezel), slides the compass edge up to the correct peak, and draws a line.

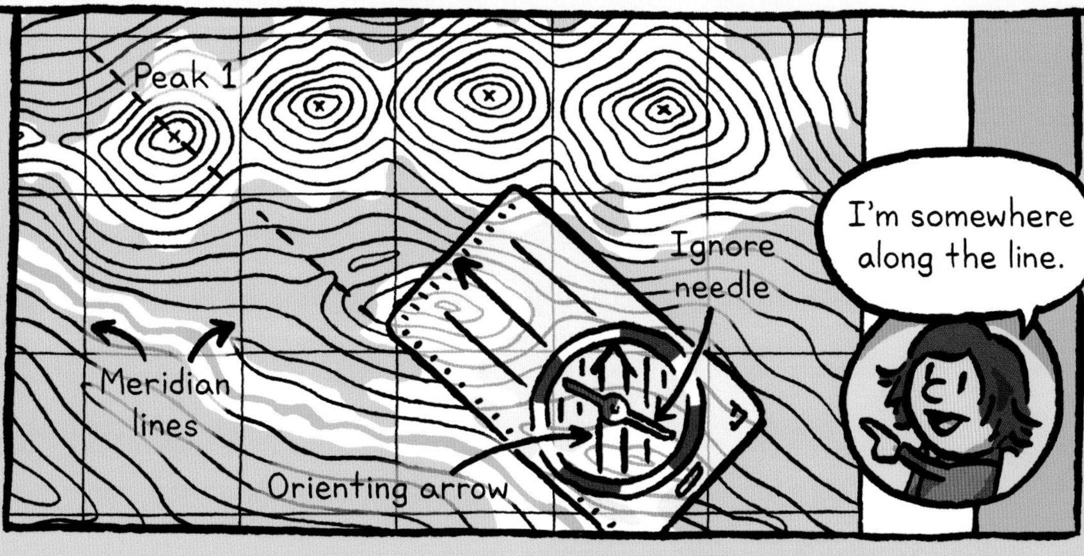
Peak 1
I'm somewhere along the line.
Ignore needle
Meridian lines
Orienting arrow

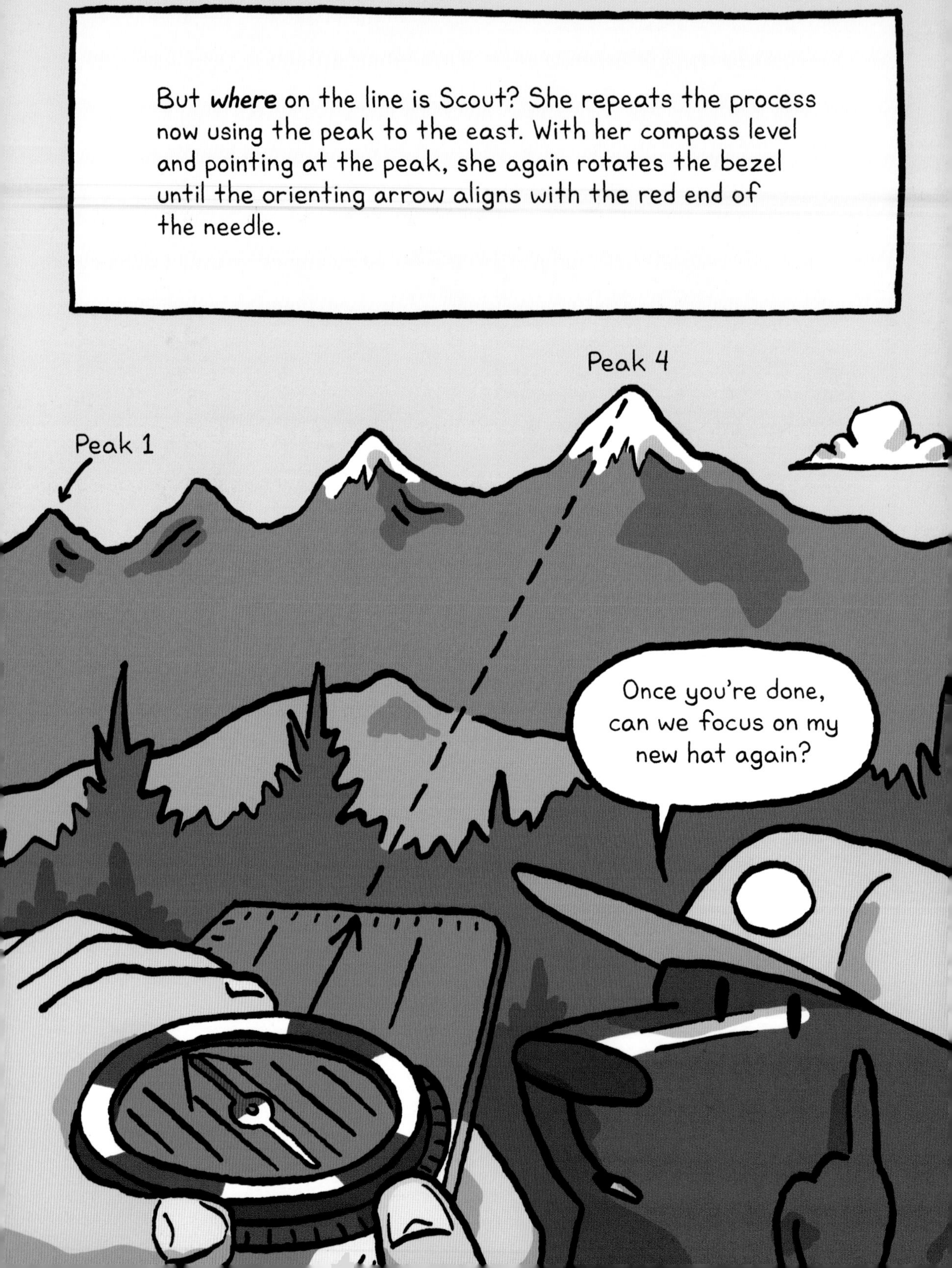
But *where* on the line is Scout? She repeats the process now using the peak to the east. With her compass level and pointing at the peak, she again rotates the bezel until the orienting arrow aligns with the red end of the needle.
Peak 4
Peak 1
Once you're done, can we focus on my new hat again?

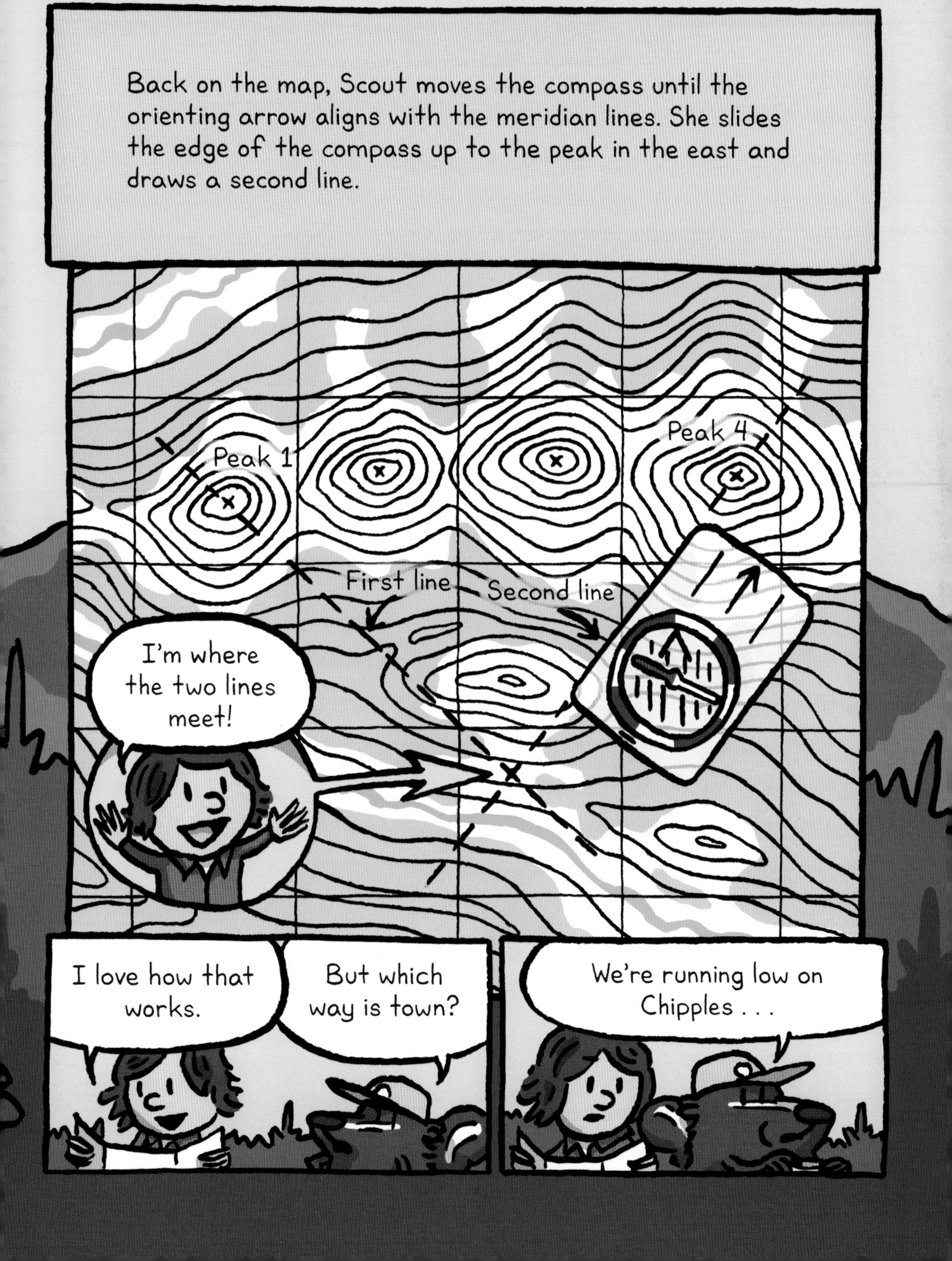

Back on the map, Scout moves the compass until the orienting arrow aligns with the meridian lines. She slides the edge of the compass up to the peak in the east and draws a second line.
Peak 1
Peak 4
First line
Second line
I'm where the two lines meet!
I love how that works.
But which way is town?
We're running low on Chipples . . .

Finding Town

To find town, Scout does the same thing but backward.

1. She draws a line from her location to town.
2. She aligns her compass edge with the line.
3. She then rotates the bezel until the orienting arrow matches the meridian lines.

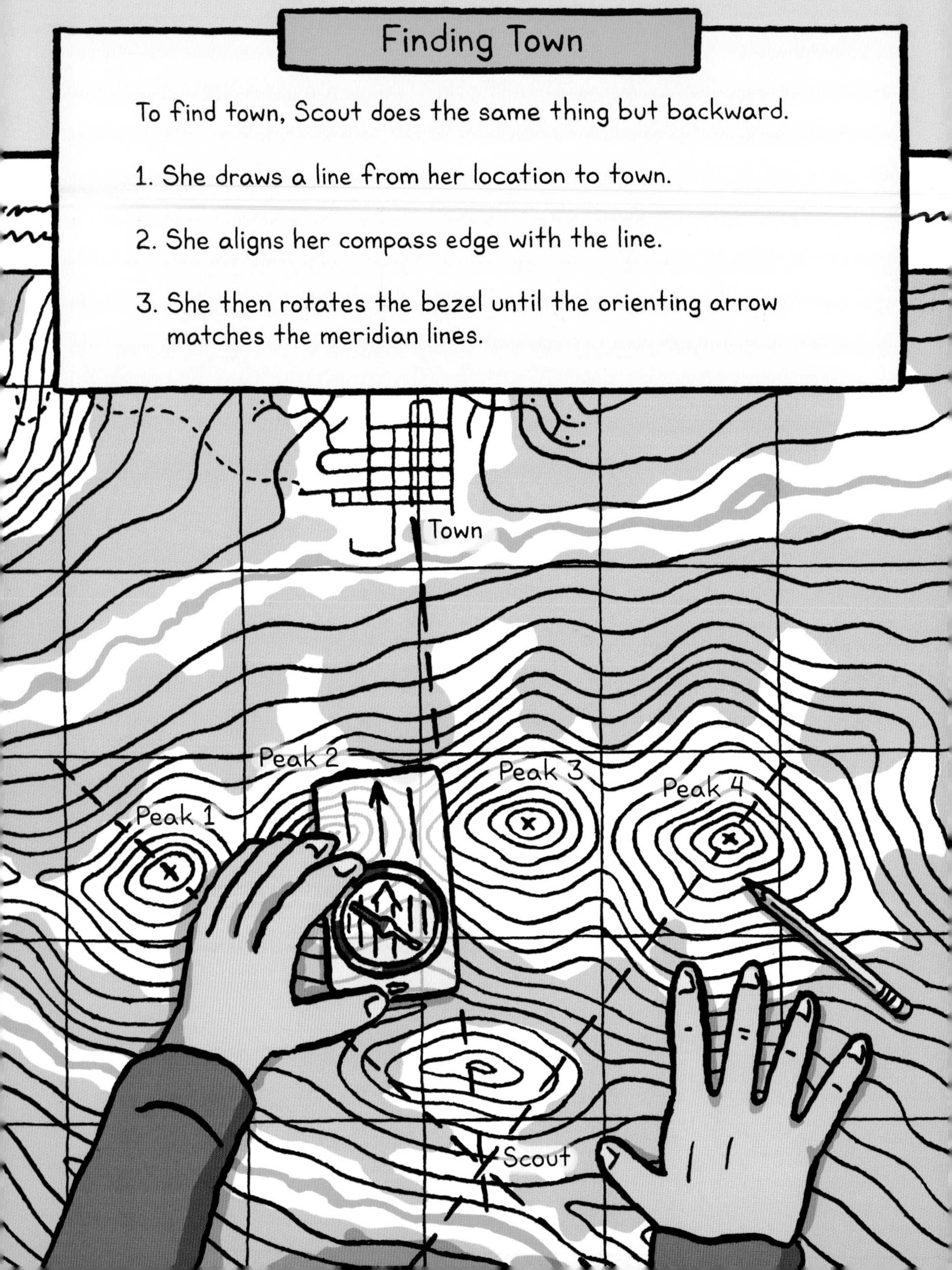
Town
Peak 2
Peak 3
Peak 4
Peak 1
Scout

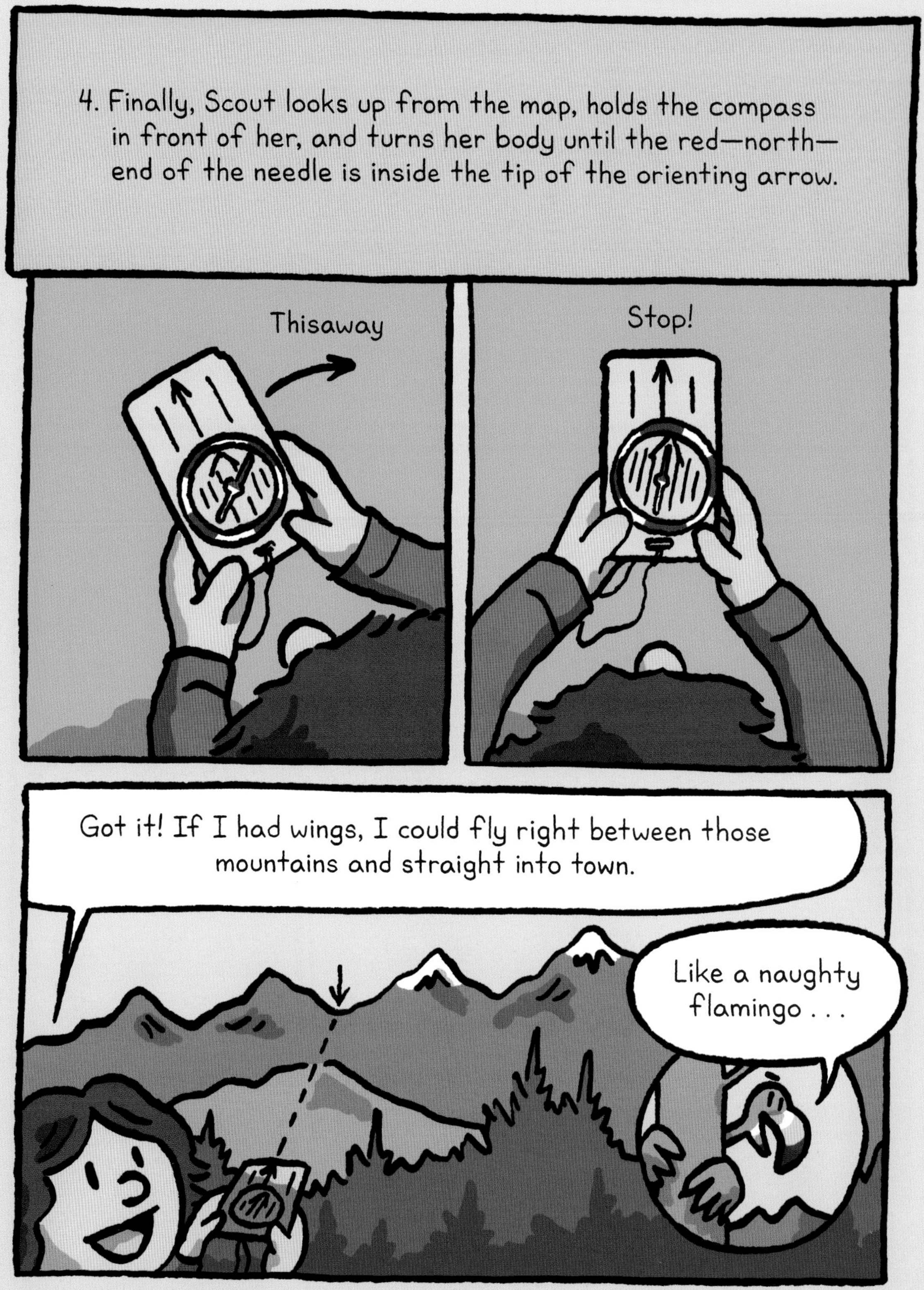
4. Finally, Scout looks up from the map, holds the compass in front of her, and turns her body until the red—north—end of the needle is inside the tip of the orienting arrow.
Thisaway
Stop!
Got it! If I had wings, I could fly right between those mountains and straight into town.
Like a naughty flamingo . . .

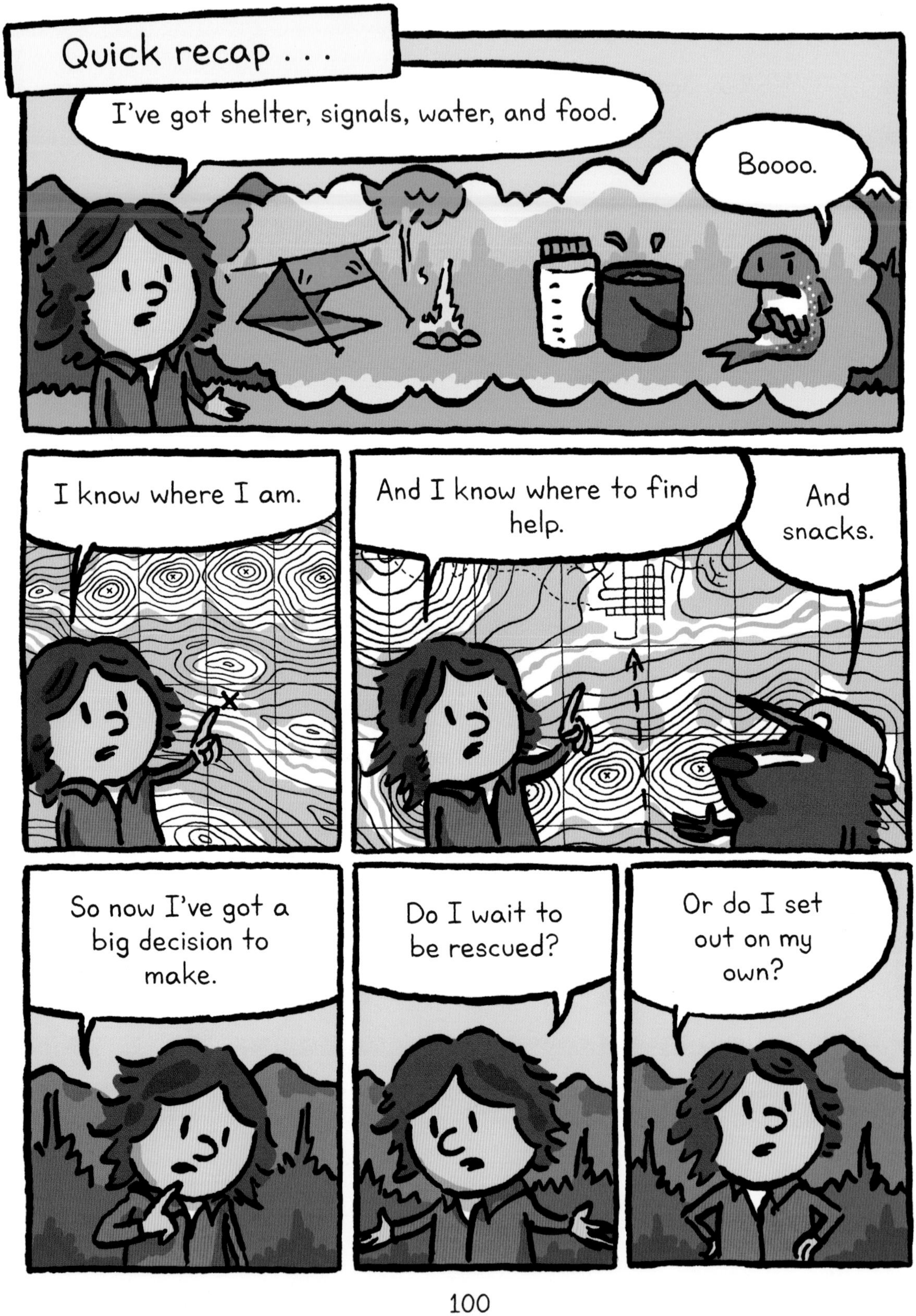
Quick recap . . .
I've got shelter, signals, water, and food.
Boooo.
I know where I am.
And I know where to find help.
And snacks.
So now I've got a big decision to make.
Do I wait to be rescued?
Or do I set out on my own?

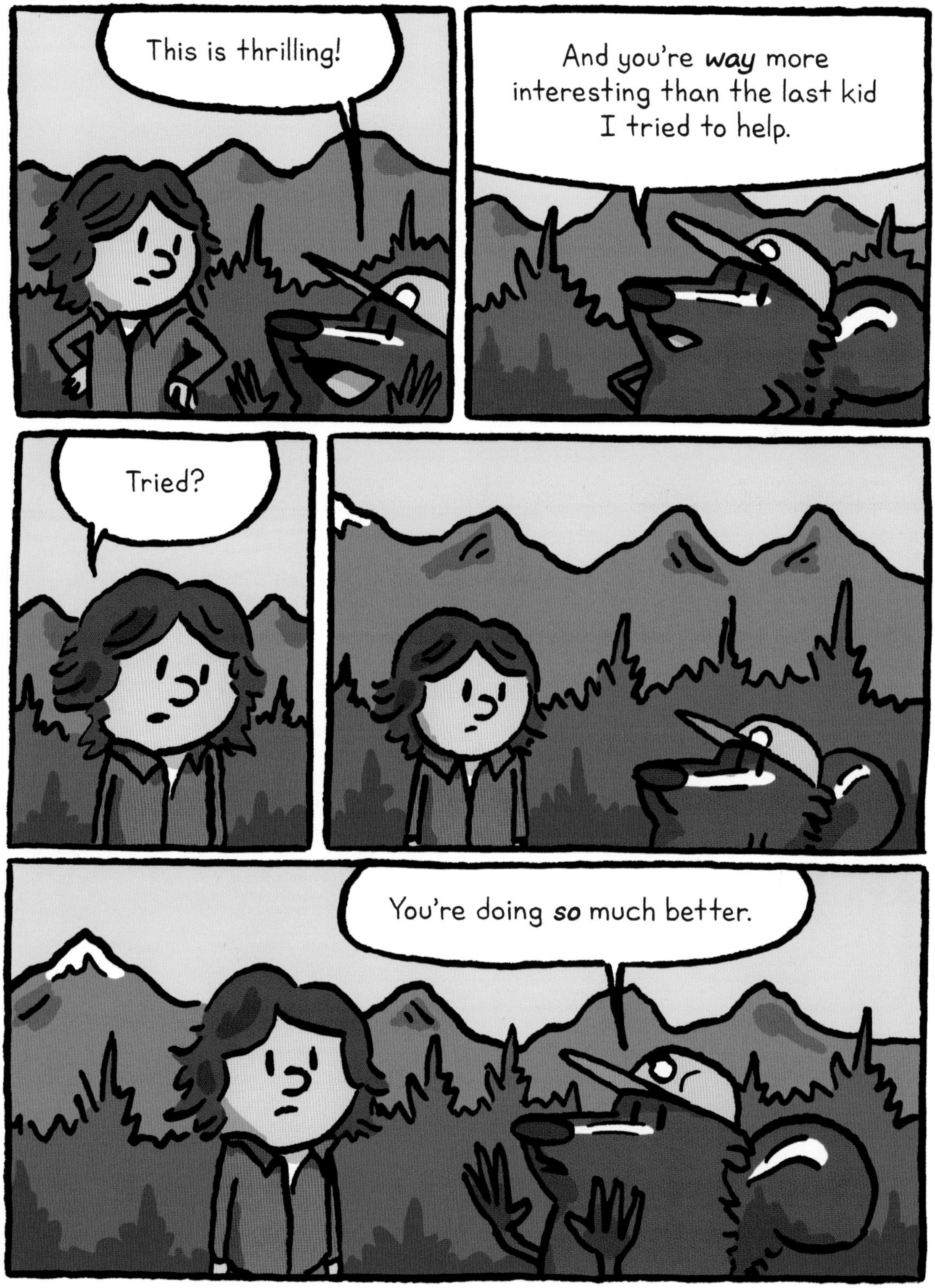
This is thrilling!
And you're *way* more interesting than the last kid I tried to help.
Tried?
You're doing *so* much better.

Route Finding

Before weighing whether to head off on foot, Scout will use her map to figure out exactly what routes she might take. She'll then need to estimate the length of each route, her own hiking speed, **and** the kind of terrain she may encounter.

Distance

To figure distance, Scout lays a piece of string along each route on the map and then measures it using the scale bar at the bottom of the map.

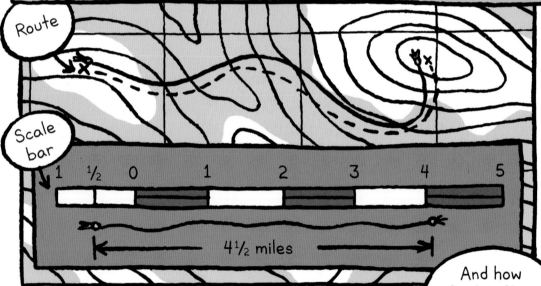

Route

Scale bar

1   ½   0   1   2   3   4   5

4½ miles

Speed

Average hiking speed carrying gear

- 1½ miles per hour
- Add a half hour of time for every 1,000 feet of elevation gain

And how fast with a large skunk in her pack?

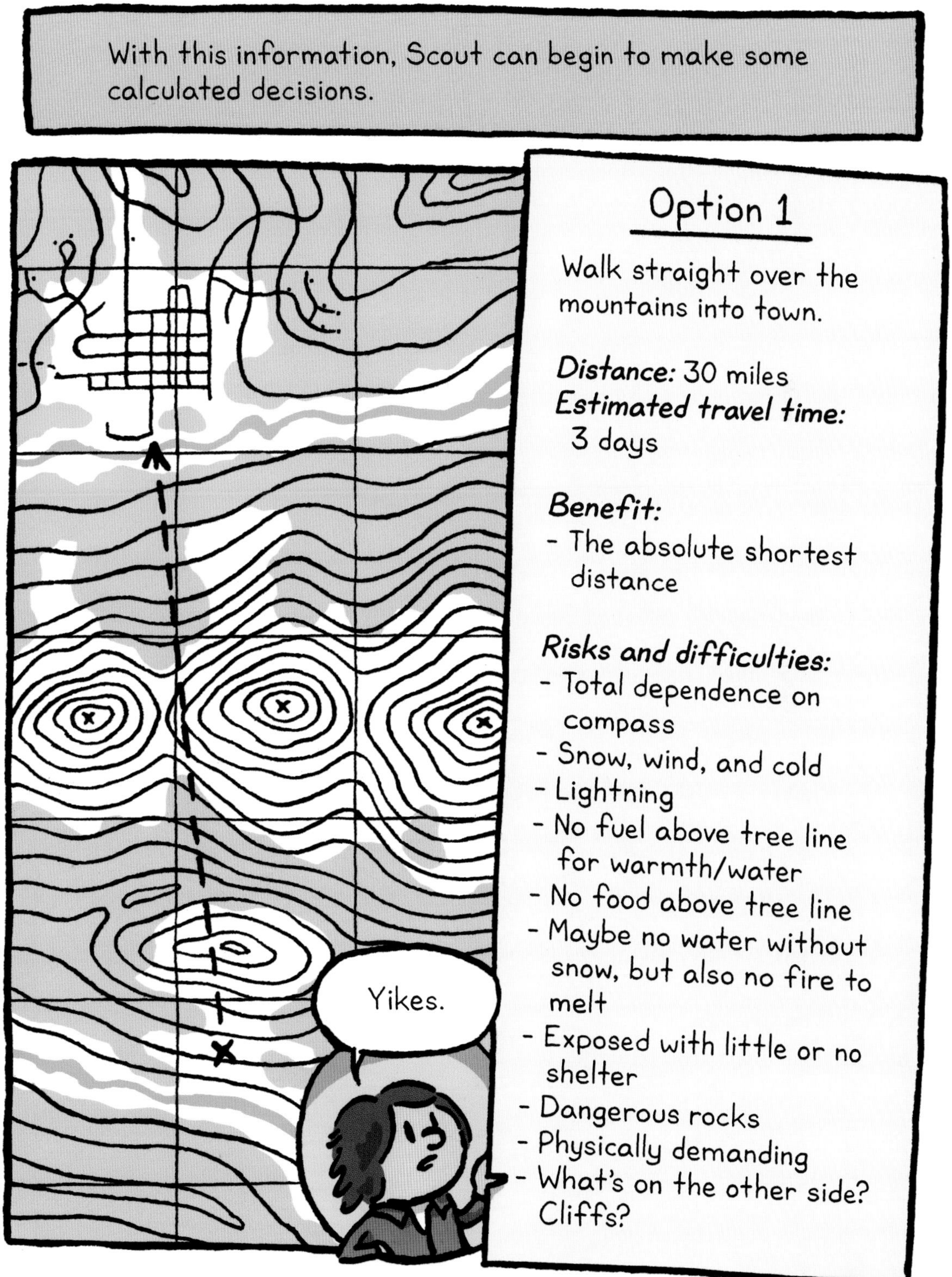
With this information, Scout can begin to make some calculated decisions.
Option 1
Walk straight over the mountains into town.
Distance: 30 miles
Estimated travel time: 3 days
Benefit:
- The absolute shortest distance
Risks and difficulties:
- Total dependence on compass
- Snow, wind, and cold
- Lightning
- No fuel above tree line for warmth/water
- No food above tree line
- Maybe no water without snow, but also no fire to melt
- Exposed with little or no shelter
- Dangerous rocks
- Physically demanding
- What's on the other side? Cliffs?
Yikes.

Option 2

Walk along the side of the river to town.

Distance: 50 miles
Estimated travel time: 5 days

Benefits:
- Easy route finding
- Water, food, and fuel the entire way
- Slowly walking downhill
- Might find original trail
- Scout is more likely to be found or stumble across people

Risks and difficulties:
- Longest distance option
- Possible steep canyon walls
- Flash flooding
- More likely to run into bears

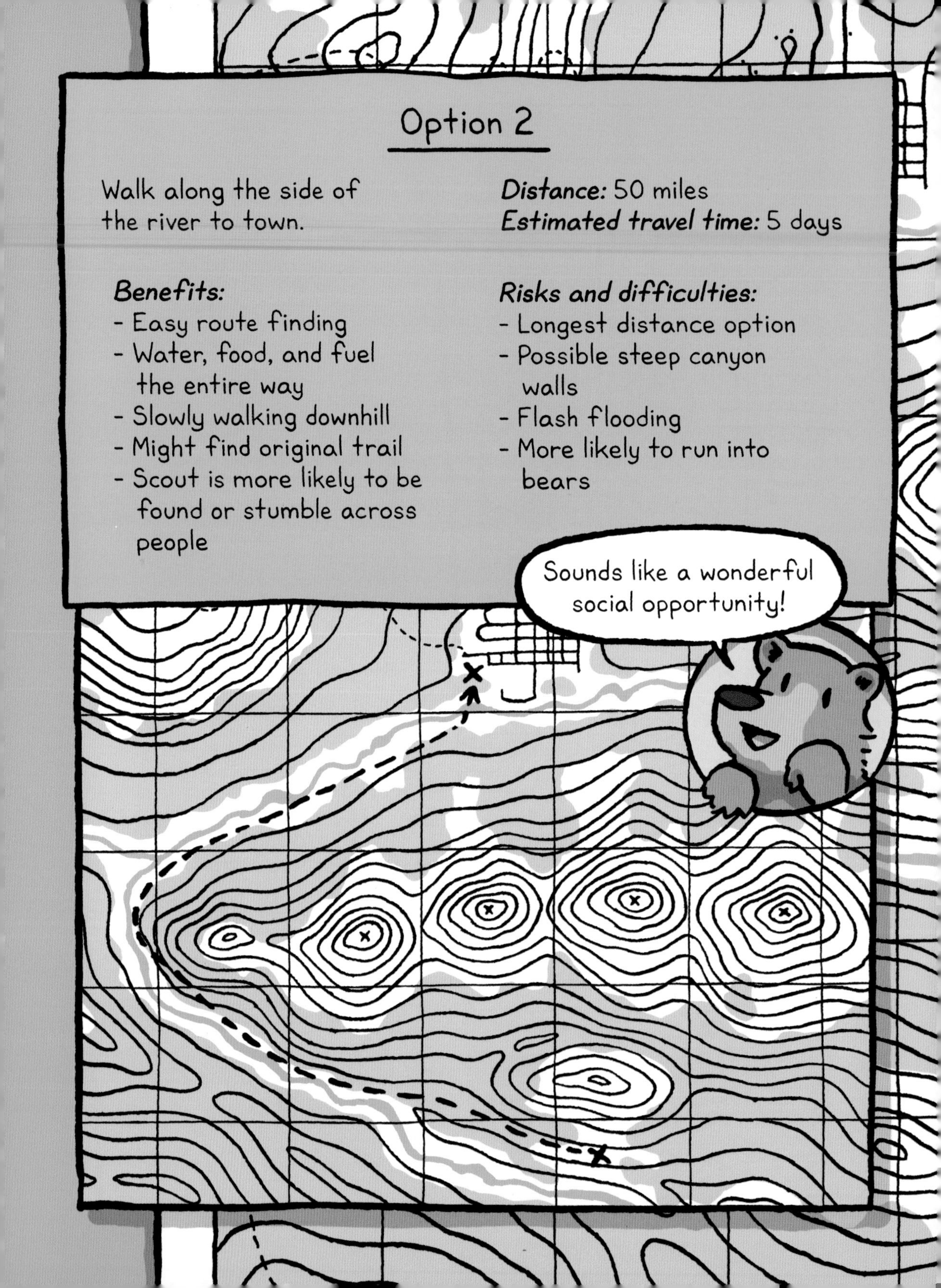
Sounds like a wonderful social opportunity!

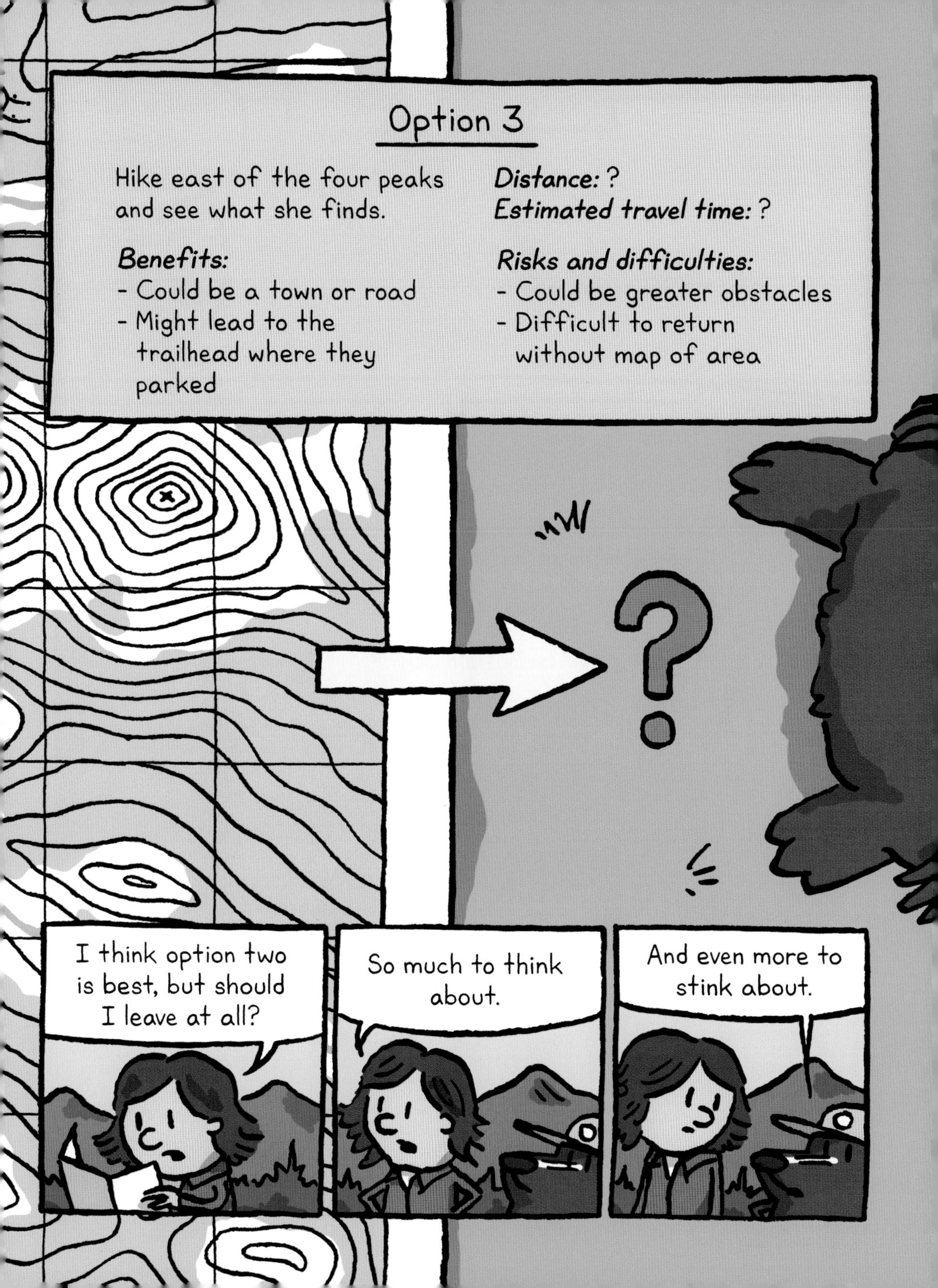
Option 3
Hike east of the four peaks and see what she finds.
Distance: ?
Estimated travel time: ?
Benefits:
- Could be a town or road
- Might lead to the trailhead where they parked
Risks and difficulties:
- Could be greater obstacles
- Difficult to return without map of area
I think option two is best, but should I leave at all?
So much to think about.
And even more to stink about.

Decision Time

The best plan, almost always, is to stay in one place and wait for help. Being on the move makes Scout more difficult to find. No signals. No fires. No campsite.

And so much walking. Ugh.

On the move

She could be under trees when an aircraft passes by.

Scout may wander into an area that has already been searched.

She would also have to set up a shelter and possibly make a fire every night of the trip, rain or shine.

How well does a wet fire bow work?

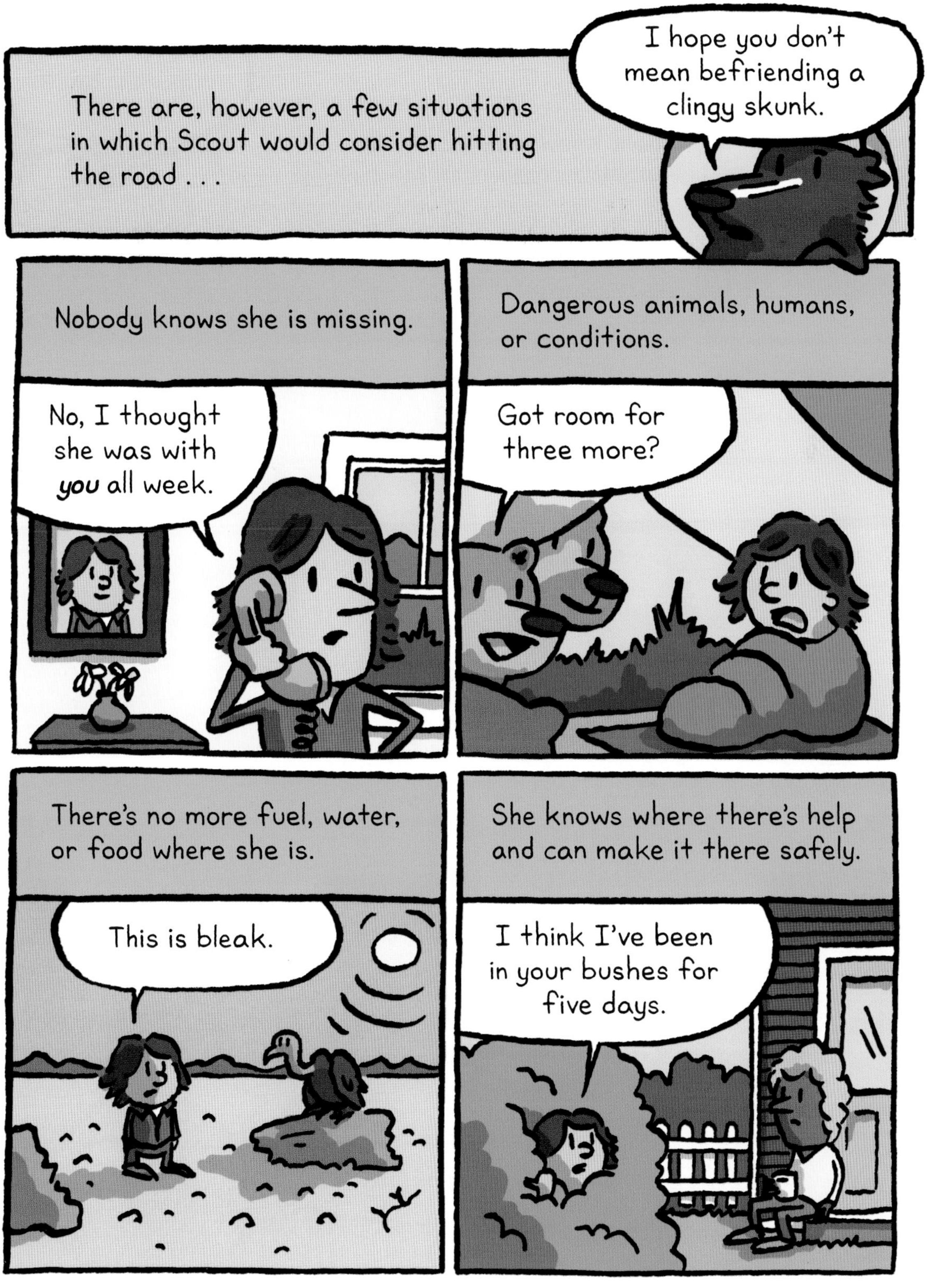
There are, however, a few situations in which Scout would consider hitting the road . . .
I hope you don't mean befriending a clingy skunk.
Nobody knows she is missing.
No, I thought she was with *you* all week.
Dangerous animals, humans, or conditions.
Got room for three more?
There's no more fuel, water, or food where she is.
This is bleak.
She knows where there's help and can make it there safely.
I think I've been in your bushes for five days.

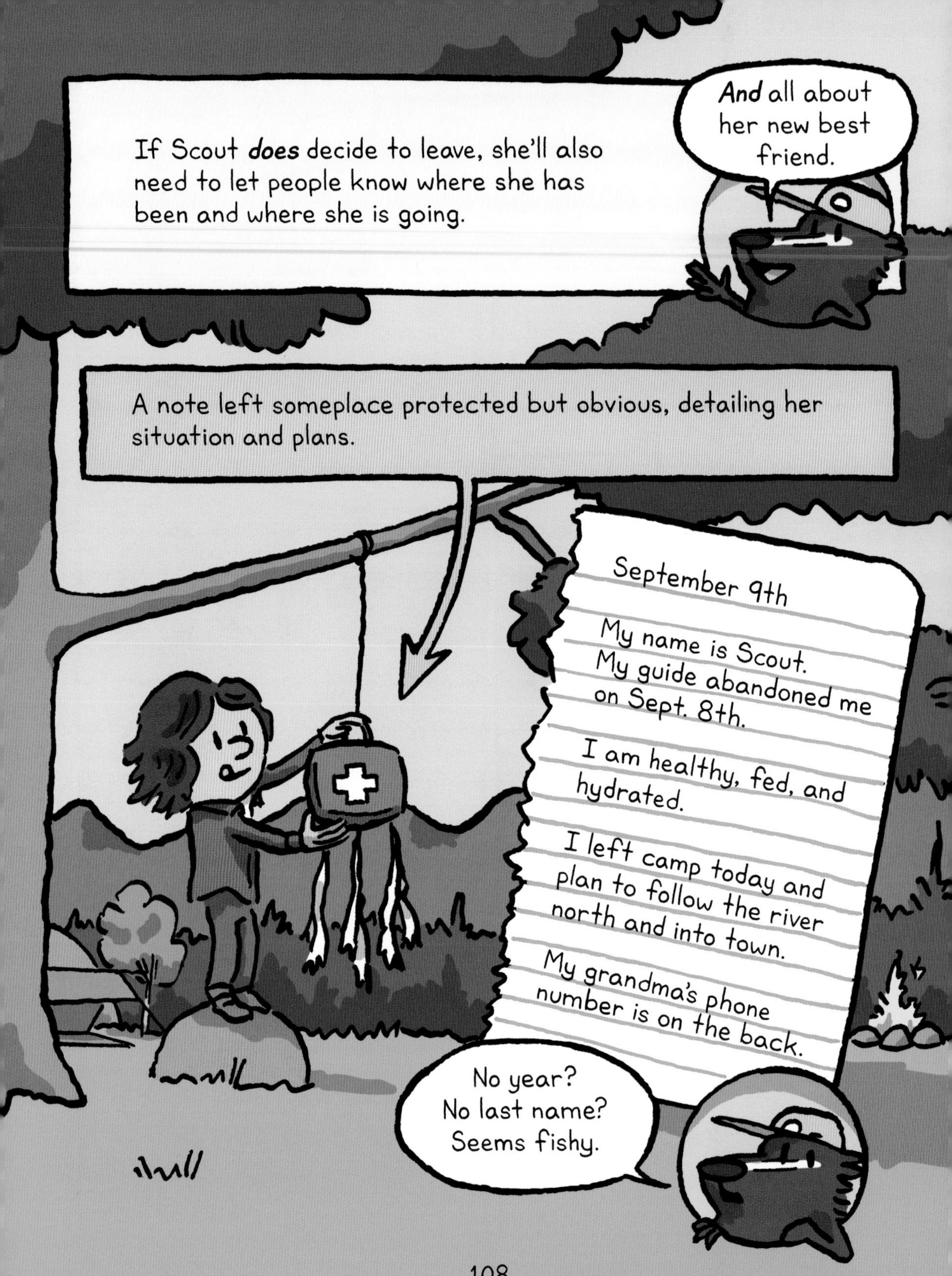
If Scout *does* decide to leave, she'll also need to let people know where she has been and where she is going.
And all about her new best friend.
A note left someplace protected but obvious, detailing her situation and plans.
September 9th
My name is Scout. My guide abandoned me on Sept. 8th.
I am healthy, fed, and hydrated.
I left camp today and plan to follow the river north and into town.
My grandma's phone number is on the back.
No year? No last name? Seems fishy.

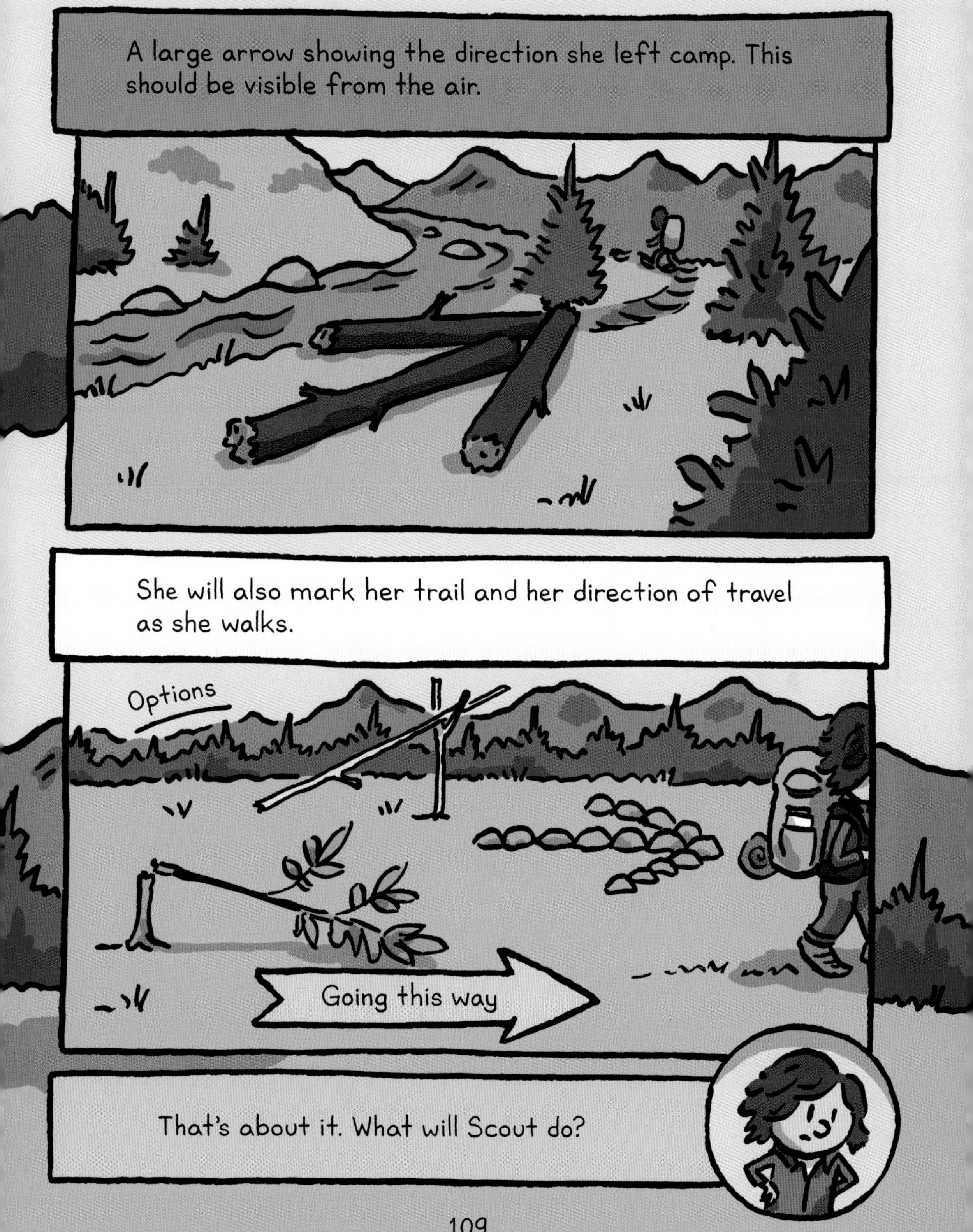

A large arrow showing the direction she left camp. This should be visible from the air.
She will also mark her trail and her direction of travel as she walks.
Options
Going this way
That's about it. What will Scout do?

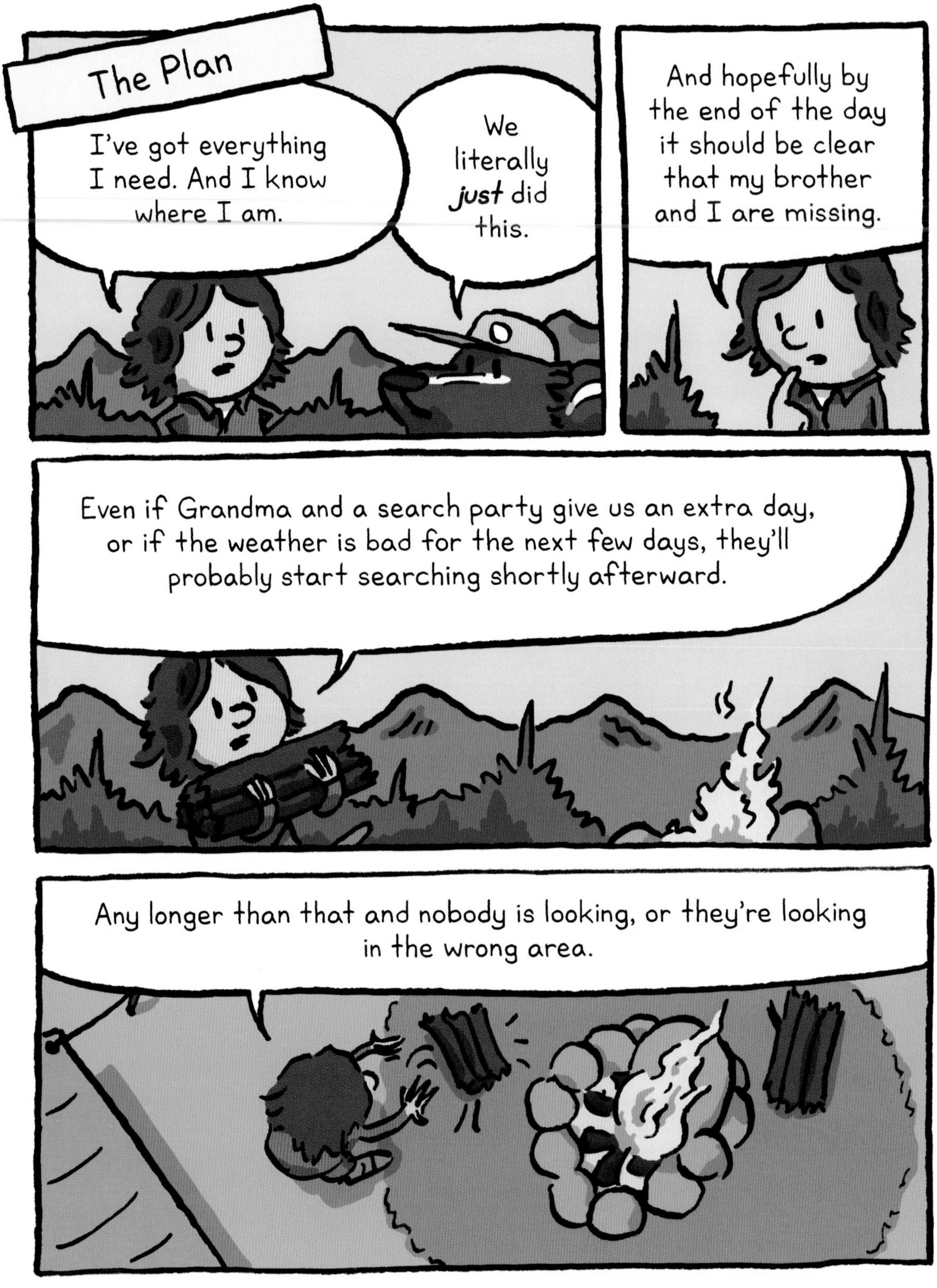
The Plan
I've got everything I need. And I know where I am.
We literally *just* did this.
And hopefully by the end of the day it should be clear that my brother and I are missing.
Even if Grandma and a search party give us an extra day, or if the weather is bad for the next few days, they'll probably start searching shortly afterward.
Any longer than that and nobody is looking, or they're looking in the wrong area.

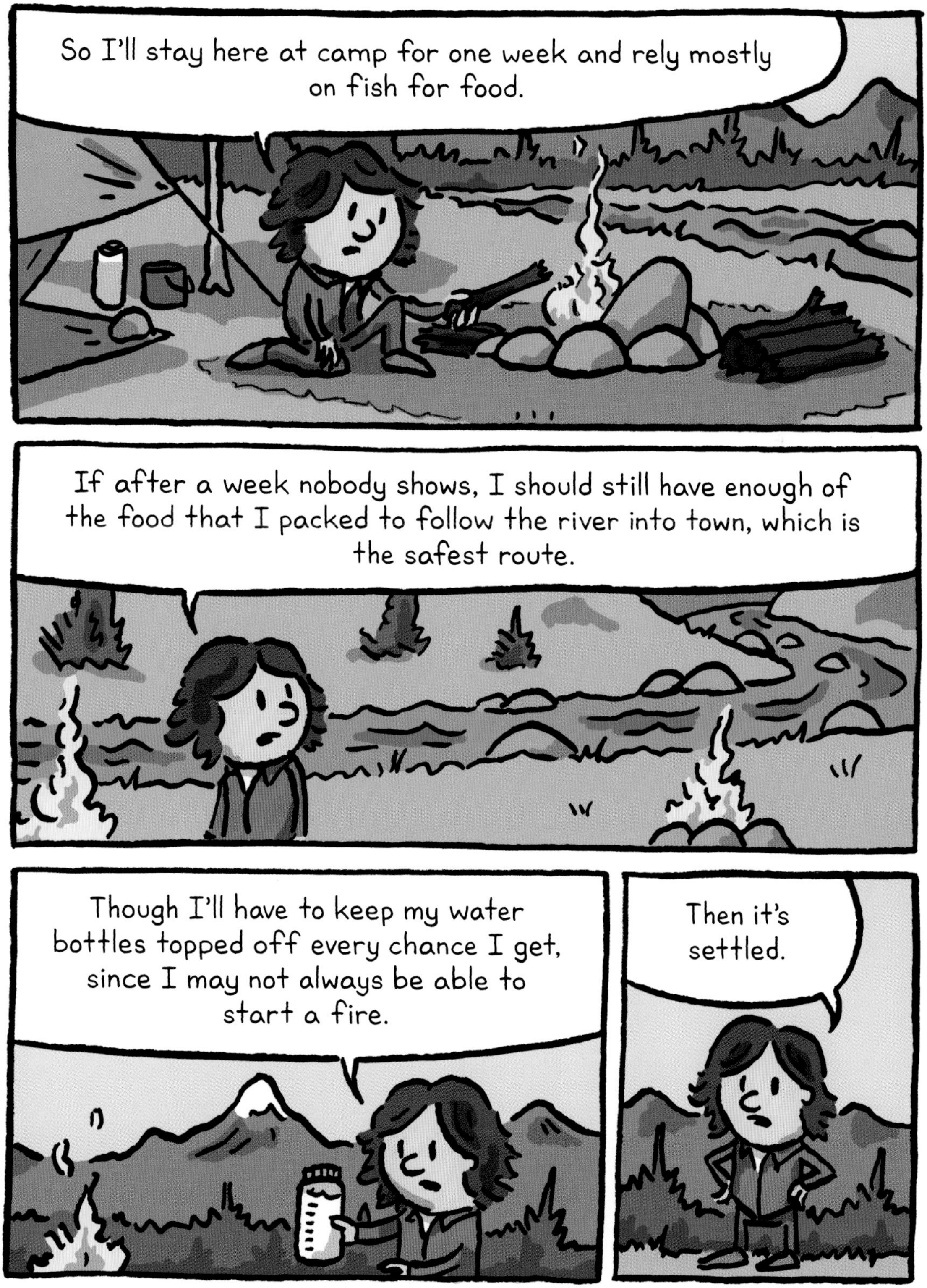
So I'll stay here at camp for one week and rely mostly on fish for food.
If after a week nobody shows, I should still have enough of the food that I packed to follow the river into town, which is the safest route.
Though I'll have to keep my water bottles topped off every chance I get, since I may not always be able to start a fire.
Then it's settled.

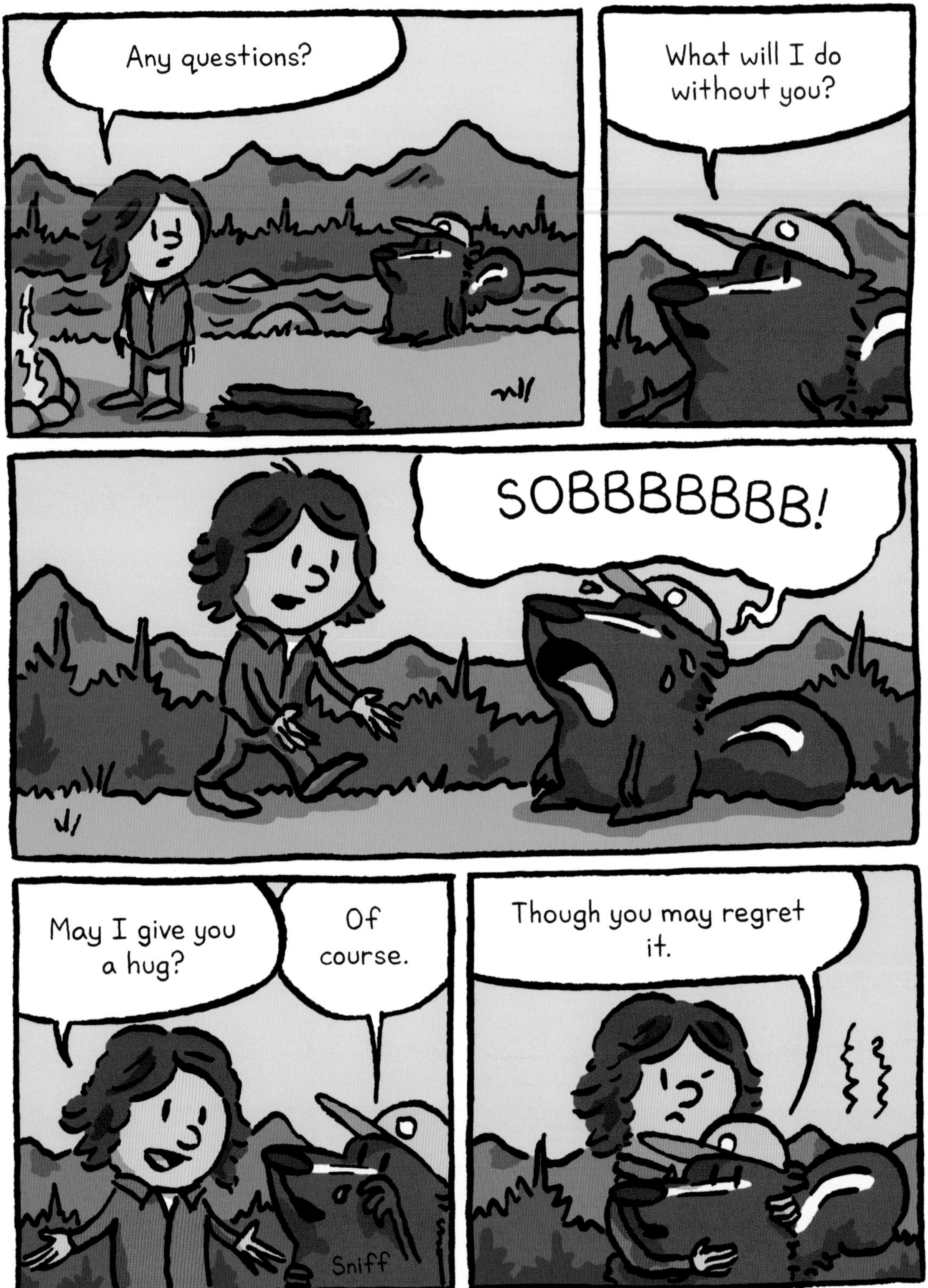
Any questions?
What will I do without you?
SOBBBBBBB!
May I give you a hug?
Of course.
Sniff
Though you may regret it.

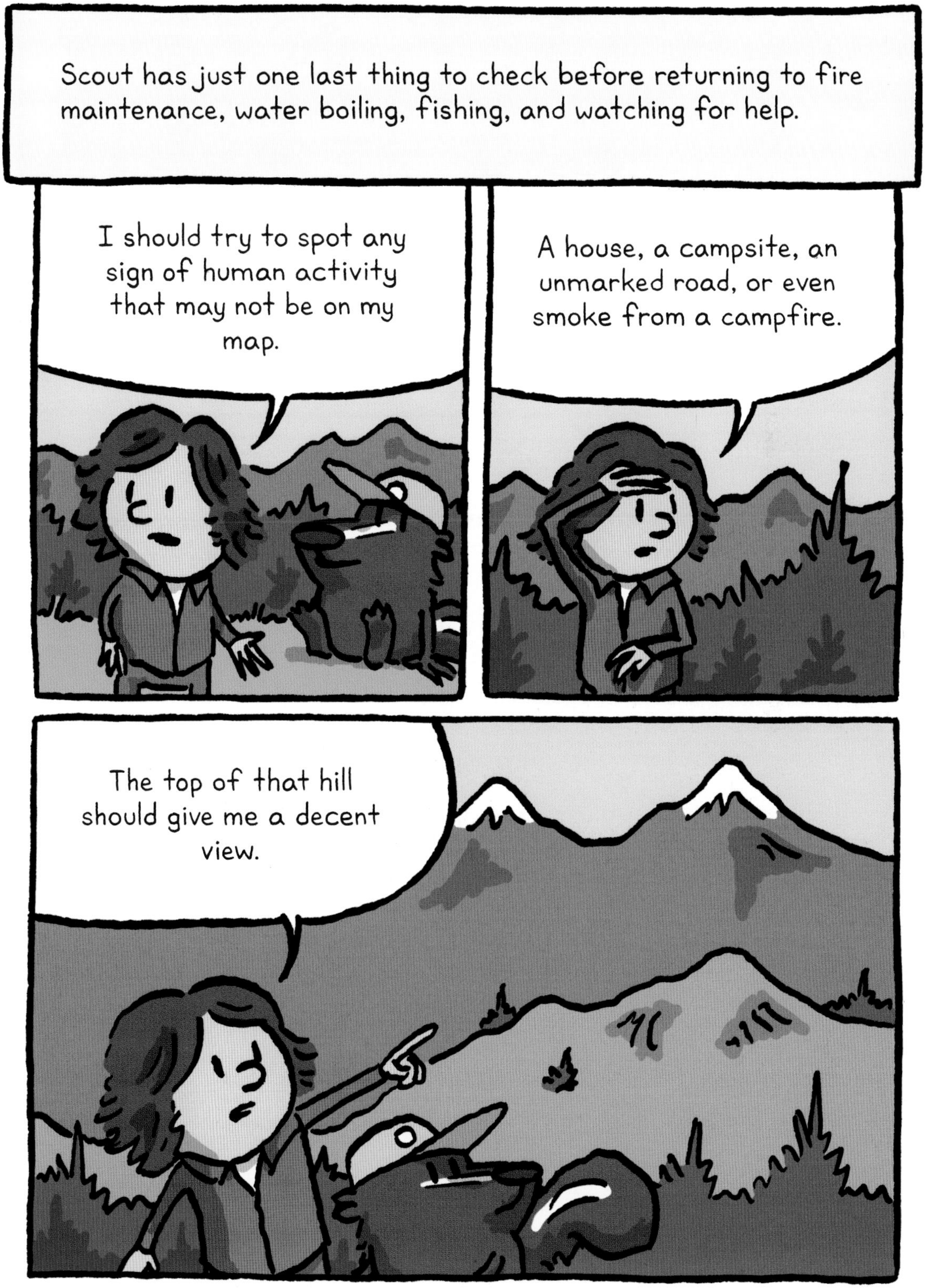
Scout has just one last thing to check before returning to fire maintenance, water boiling, fishing, and watching for help.
I should try to spot any sign of human activity that may not be on my map.
A house, a campsite, an unmarked road, or even smoke from a campfire.
The top of that hill should give me a decent view.

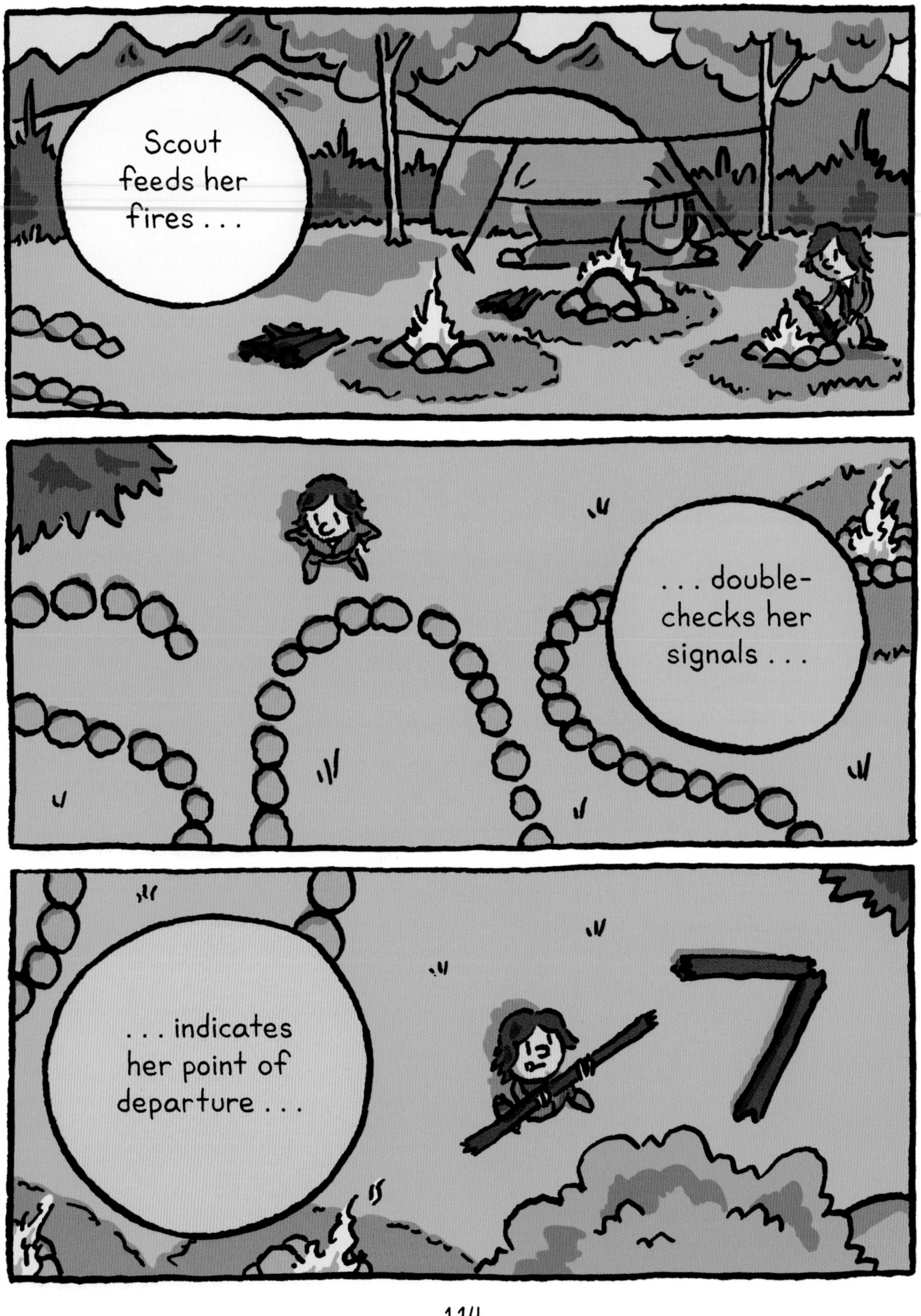
Scout feeds her fires . . .
. . . double-checks her signals . . .
. . . indicates her point of departure . . .

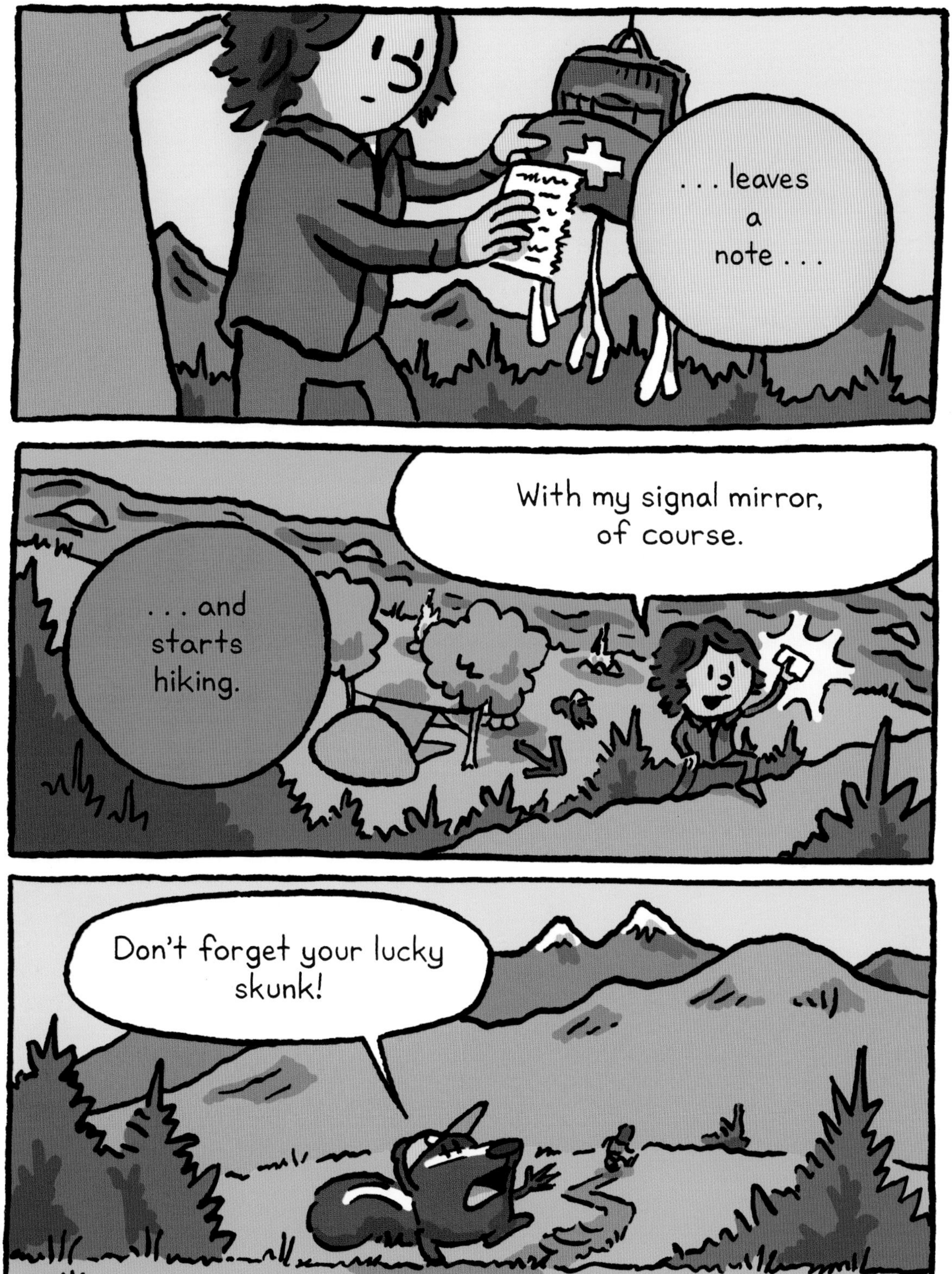
. . . leaves a note . . .
. . . and starts hiking.
With my signal mirror, of course.
Don't forget your lucky skunk!

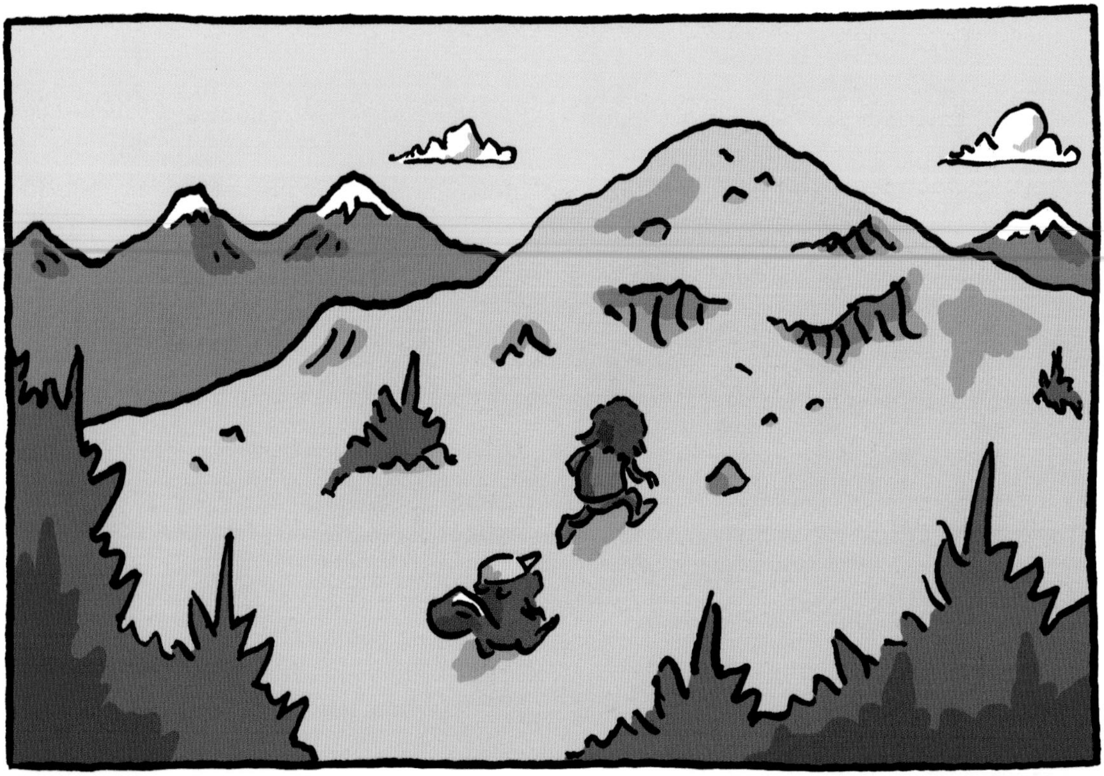

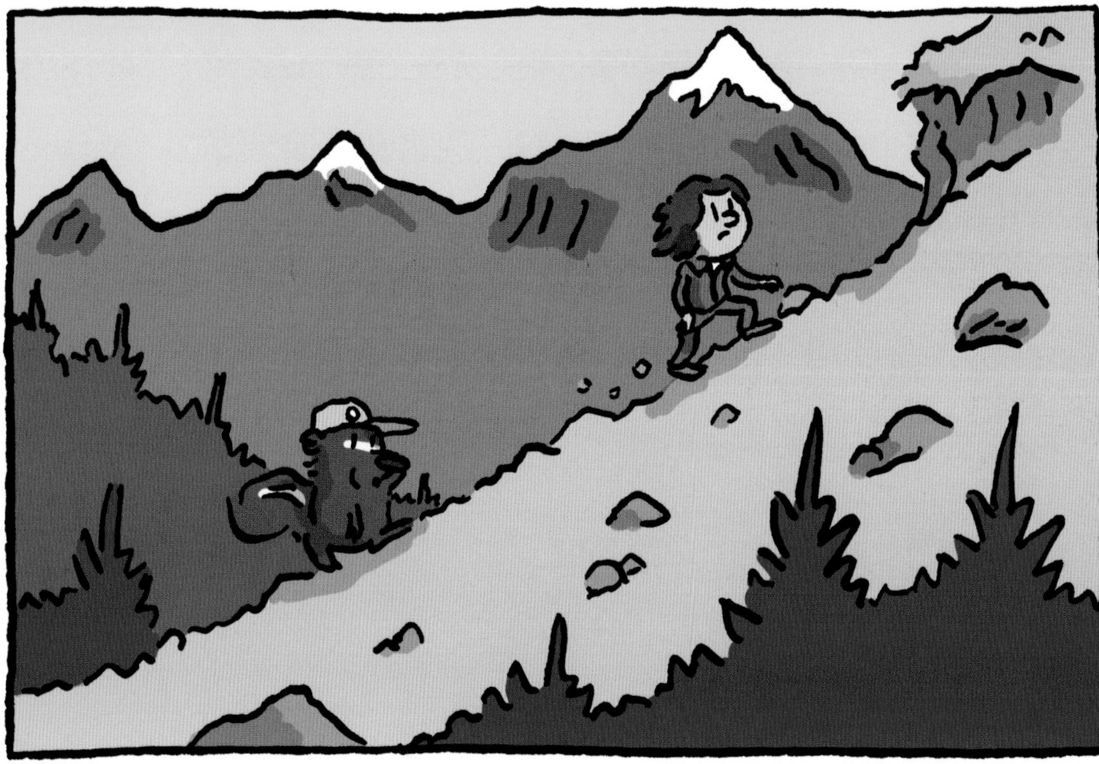

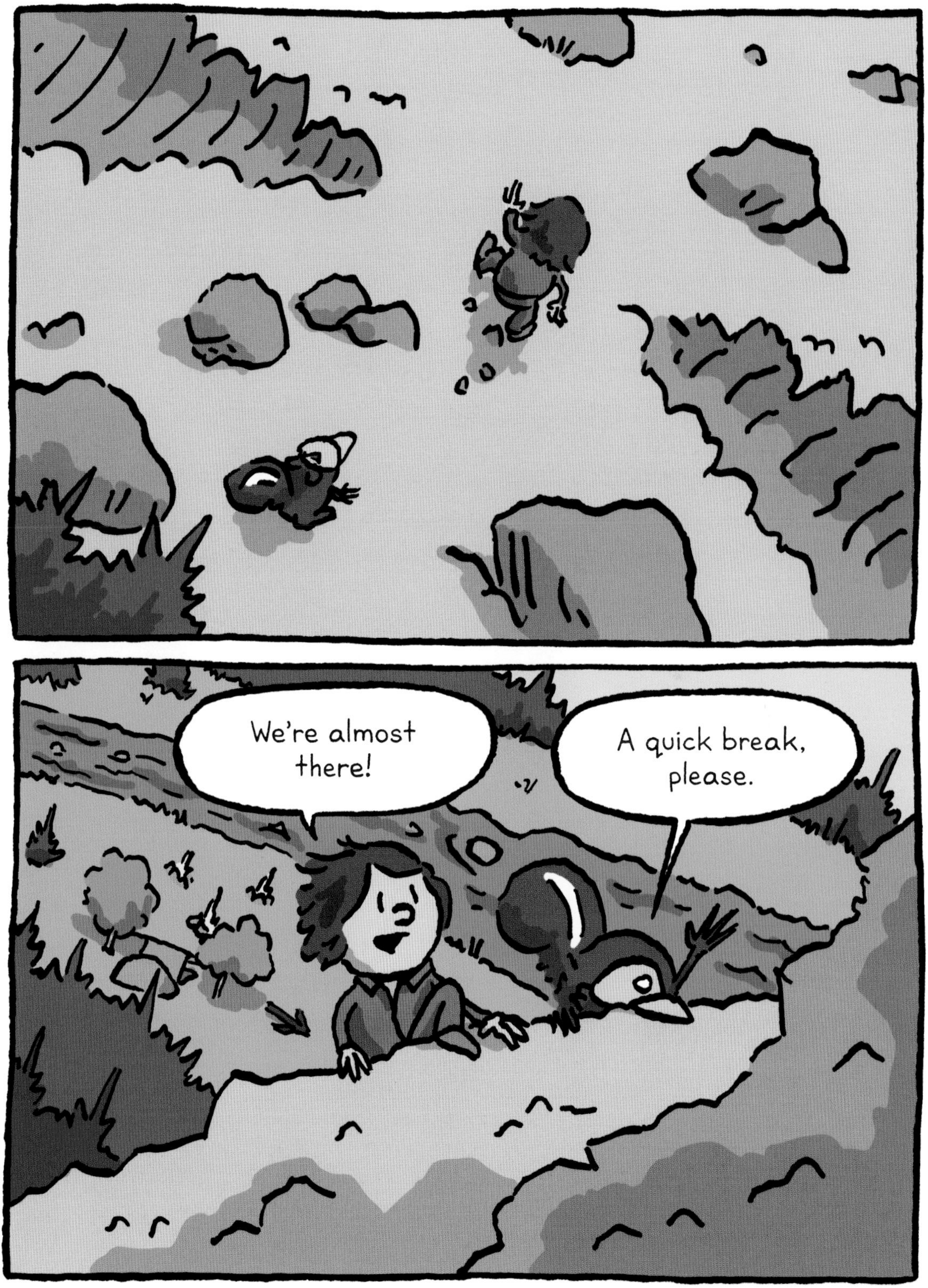
We're almost there!
A quick break, please.

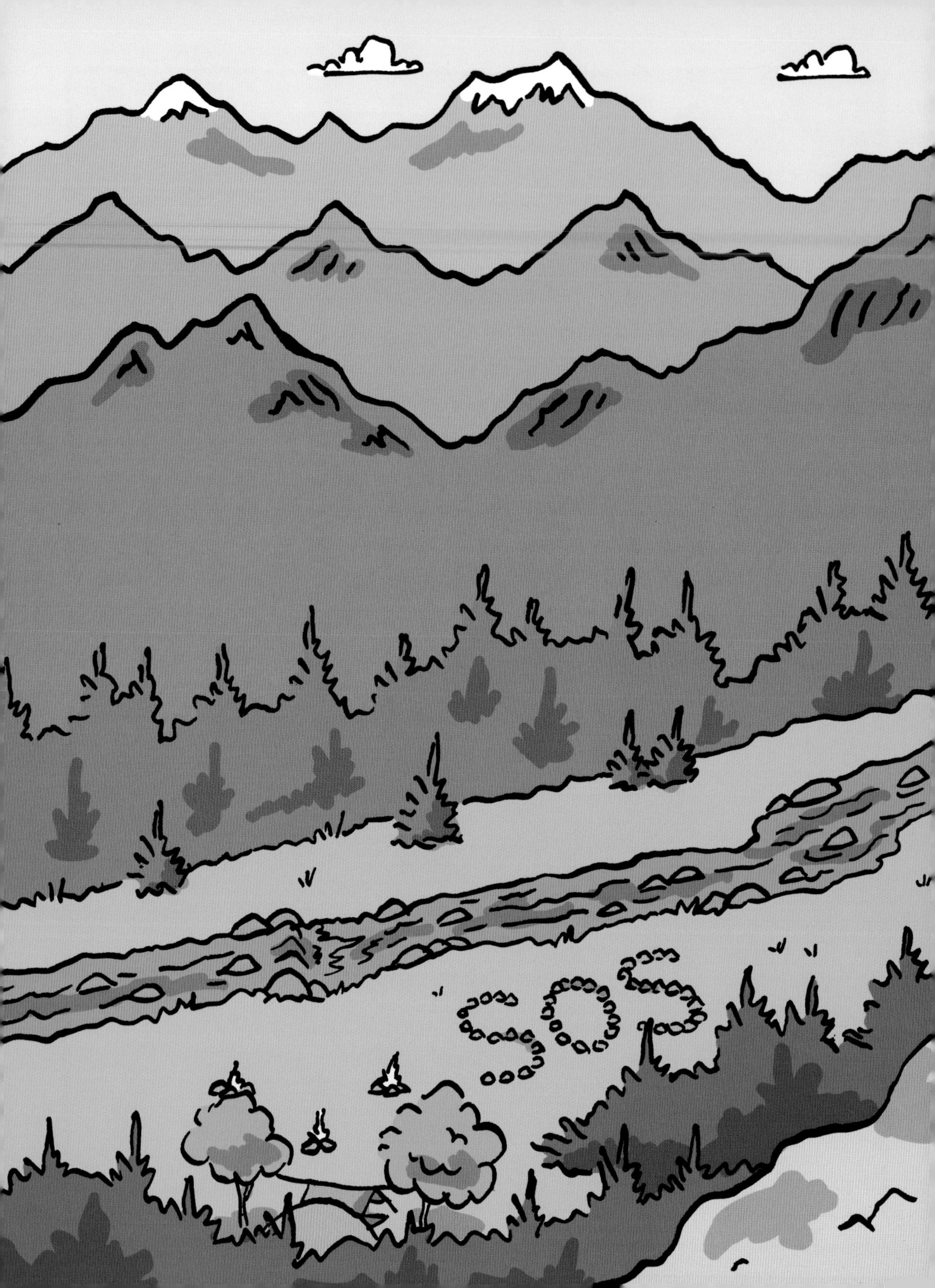
SOS

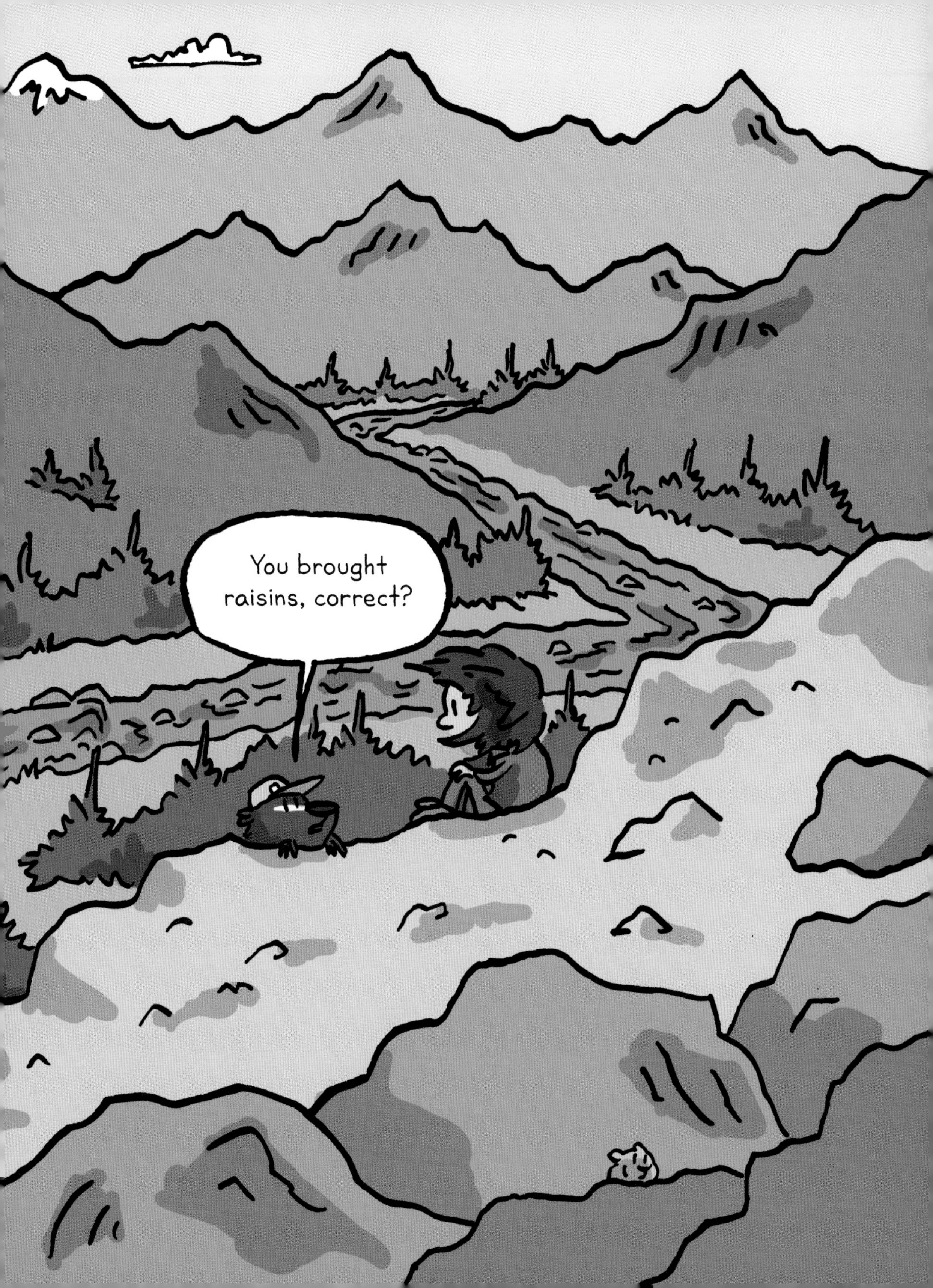
You brought raisins, correct?

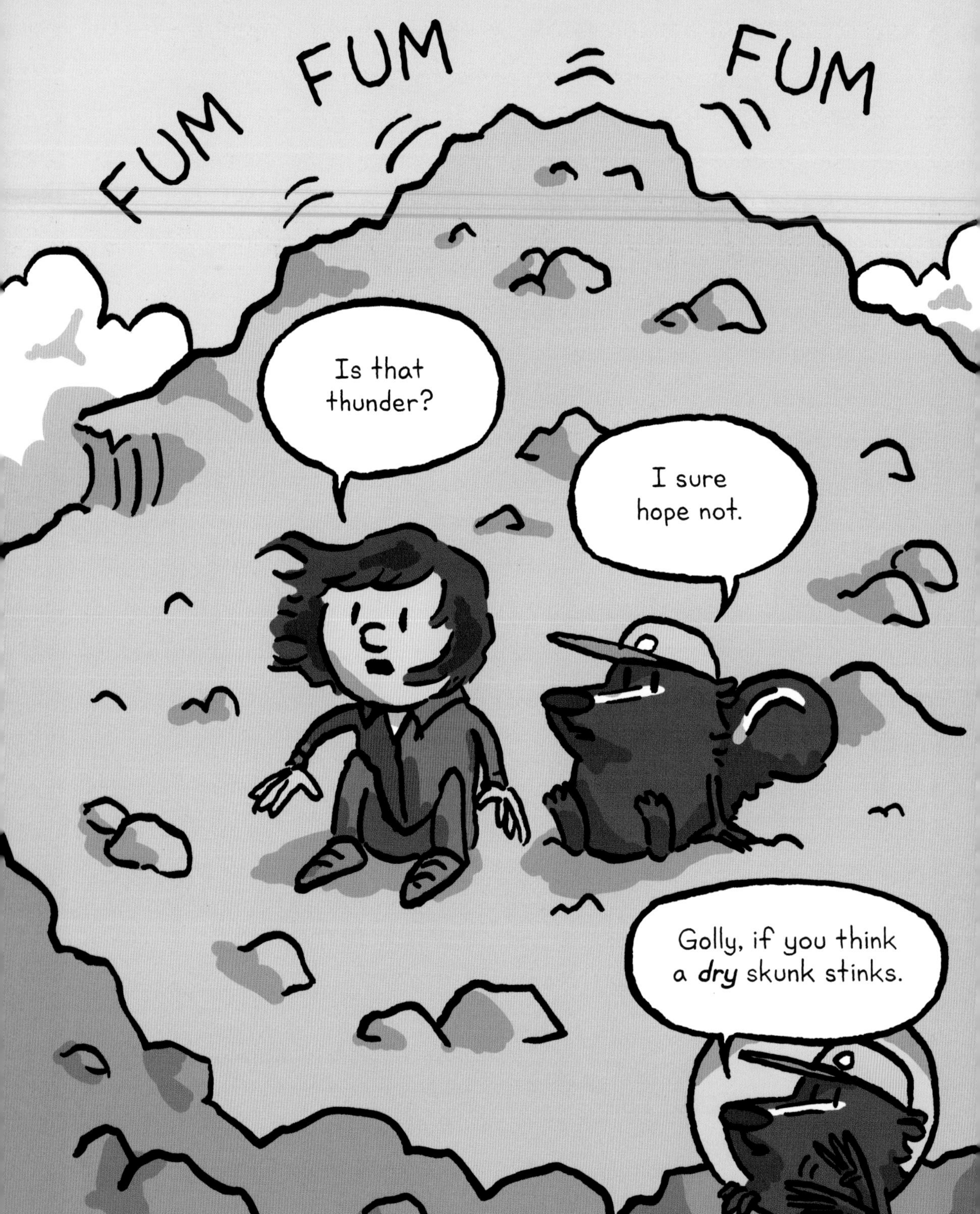
FUM FUM FUM
Is that thunder?
I sure hope not.
Golly, if you think a *dry* skunk stinks.

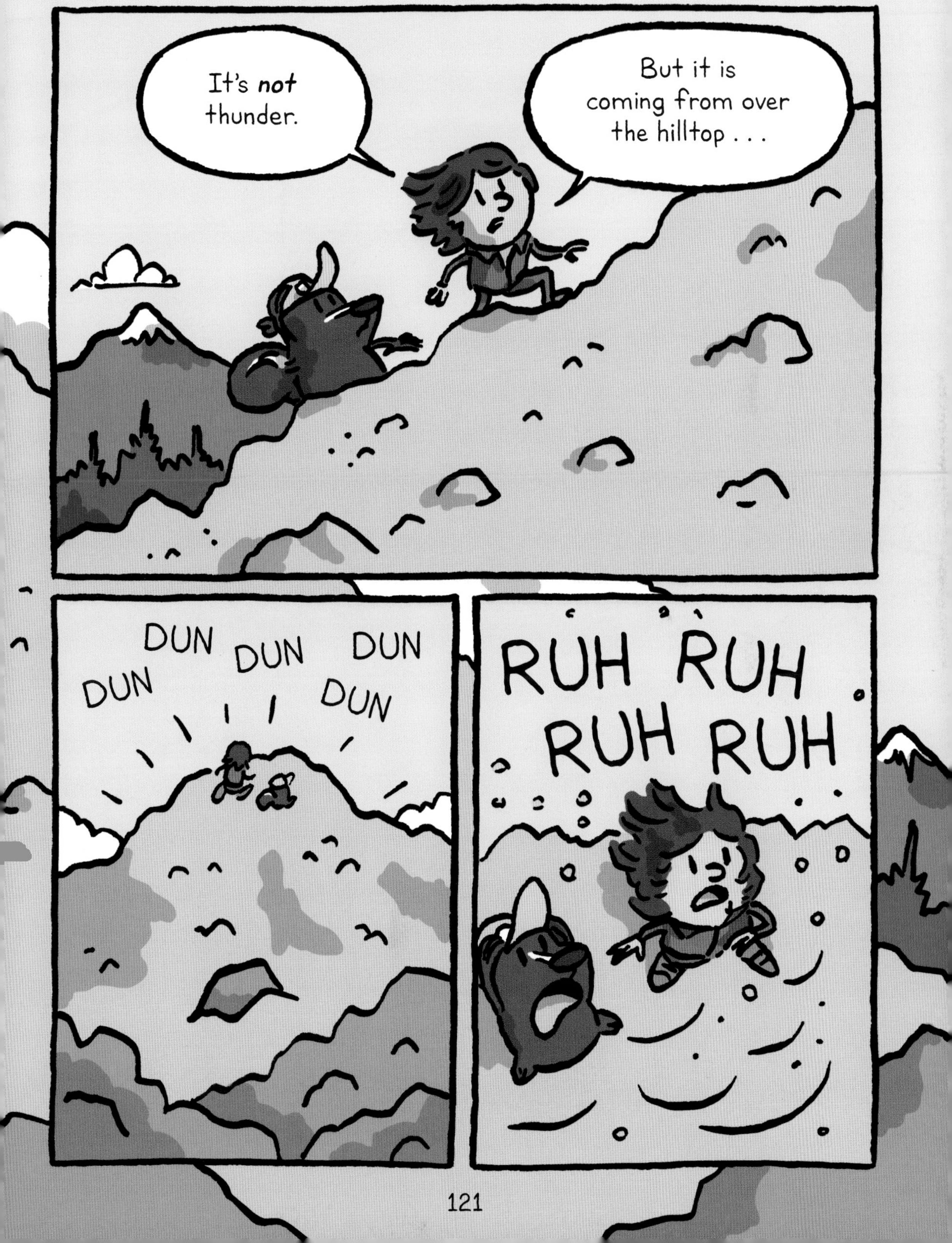

It's *not* thunder.
But it is coming from over the hilltop . . .
DUN
DUN
DUN
DUN
DUN
RUH RUH
RUH RUH

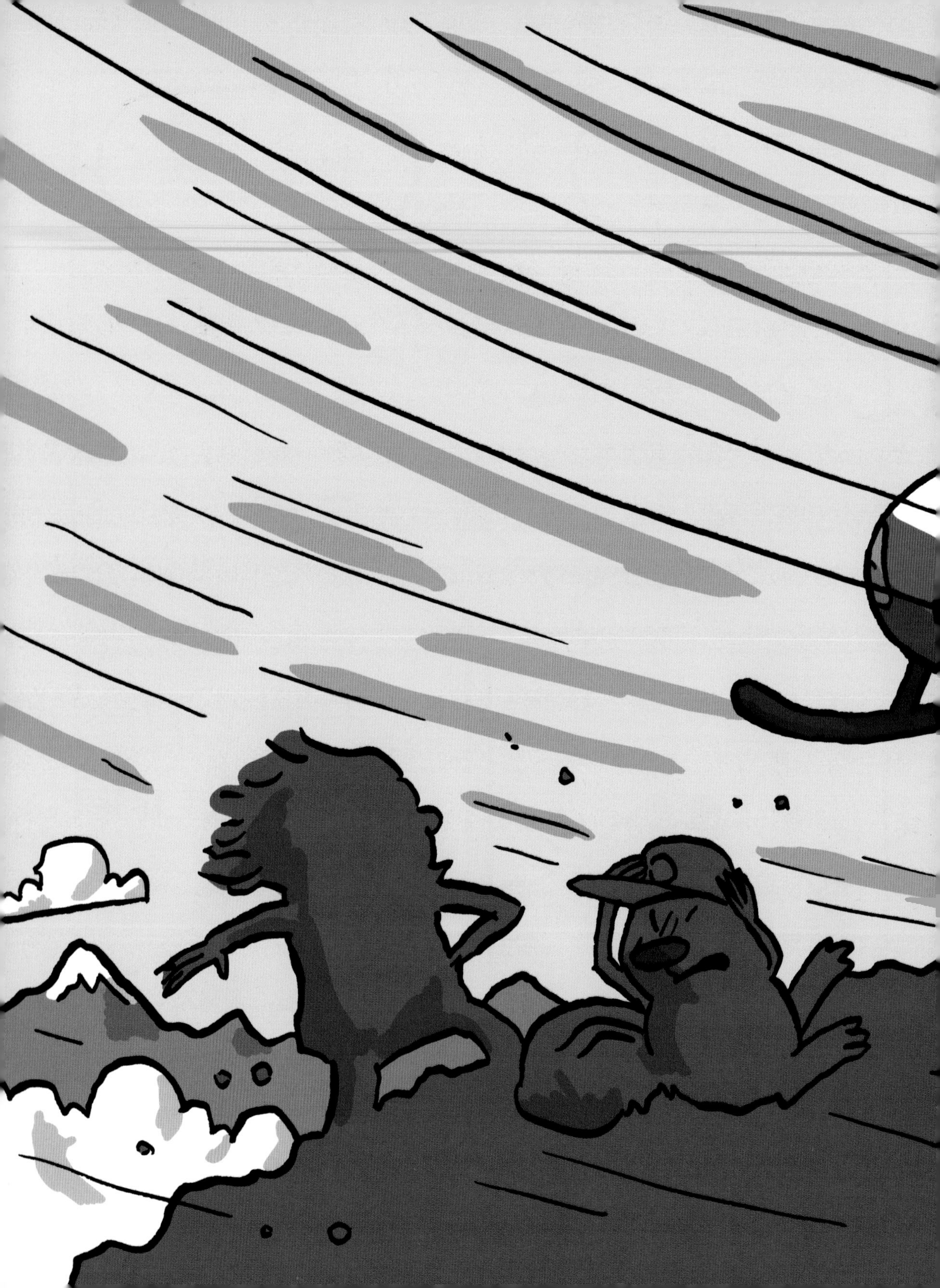

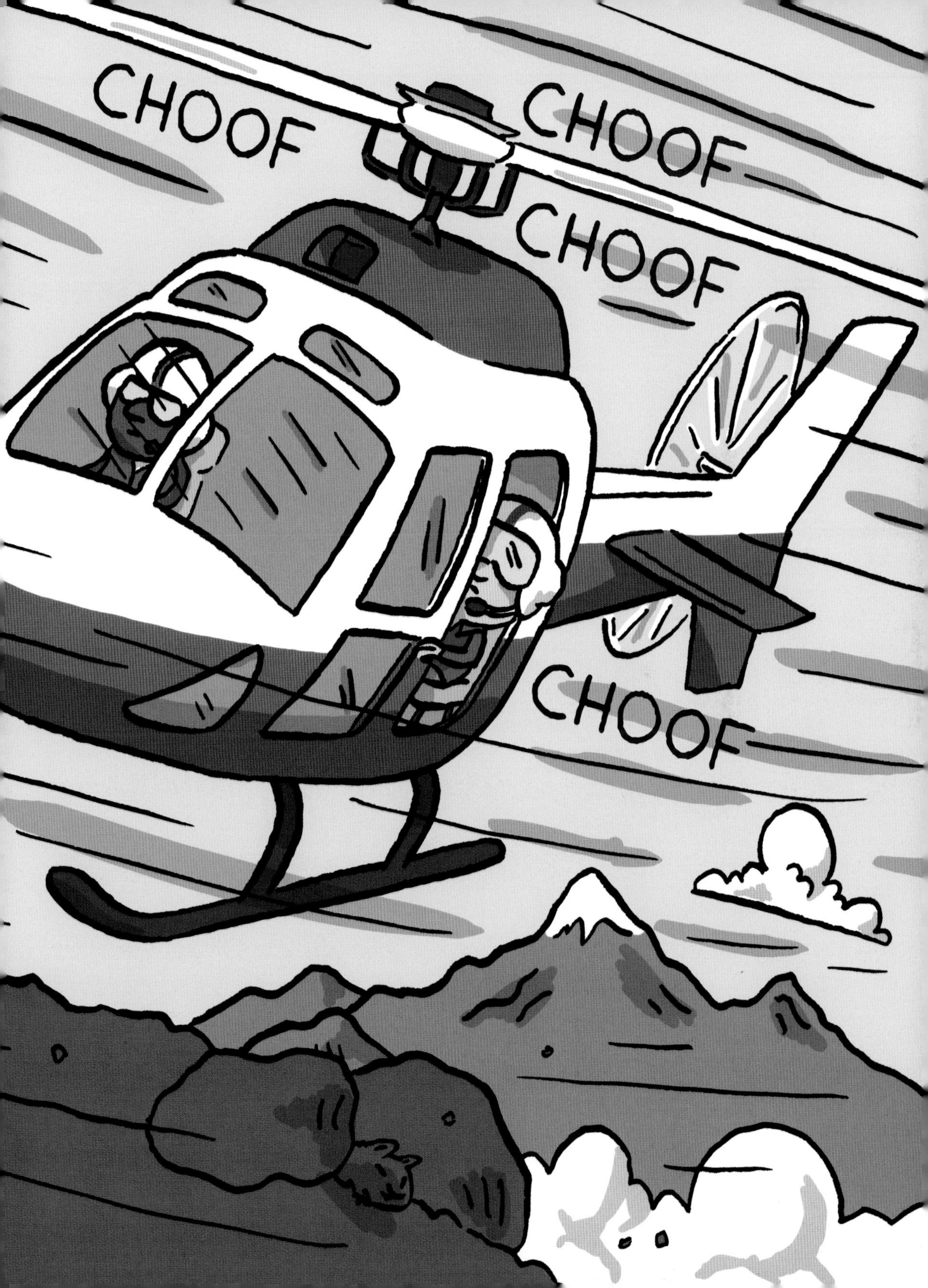
CHOOF
CHOOF
CHOOF
CHOOF

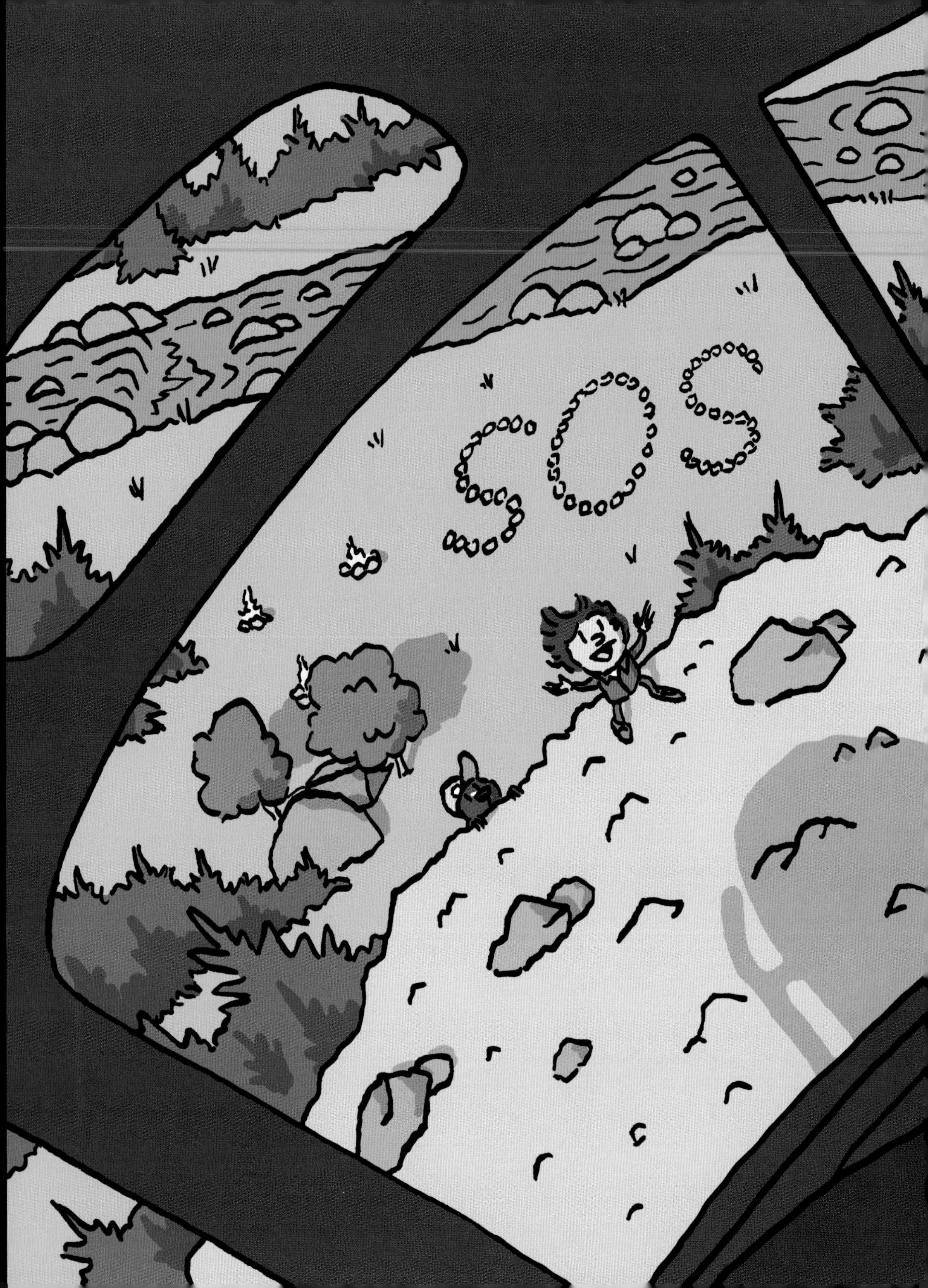
SOS

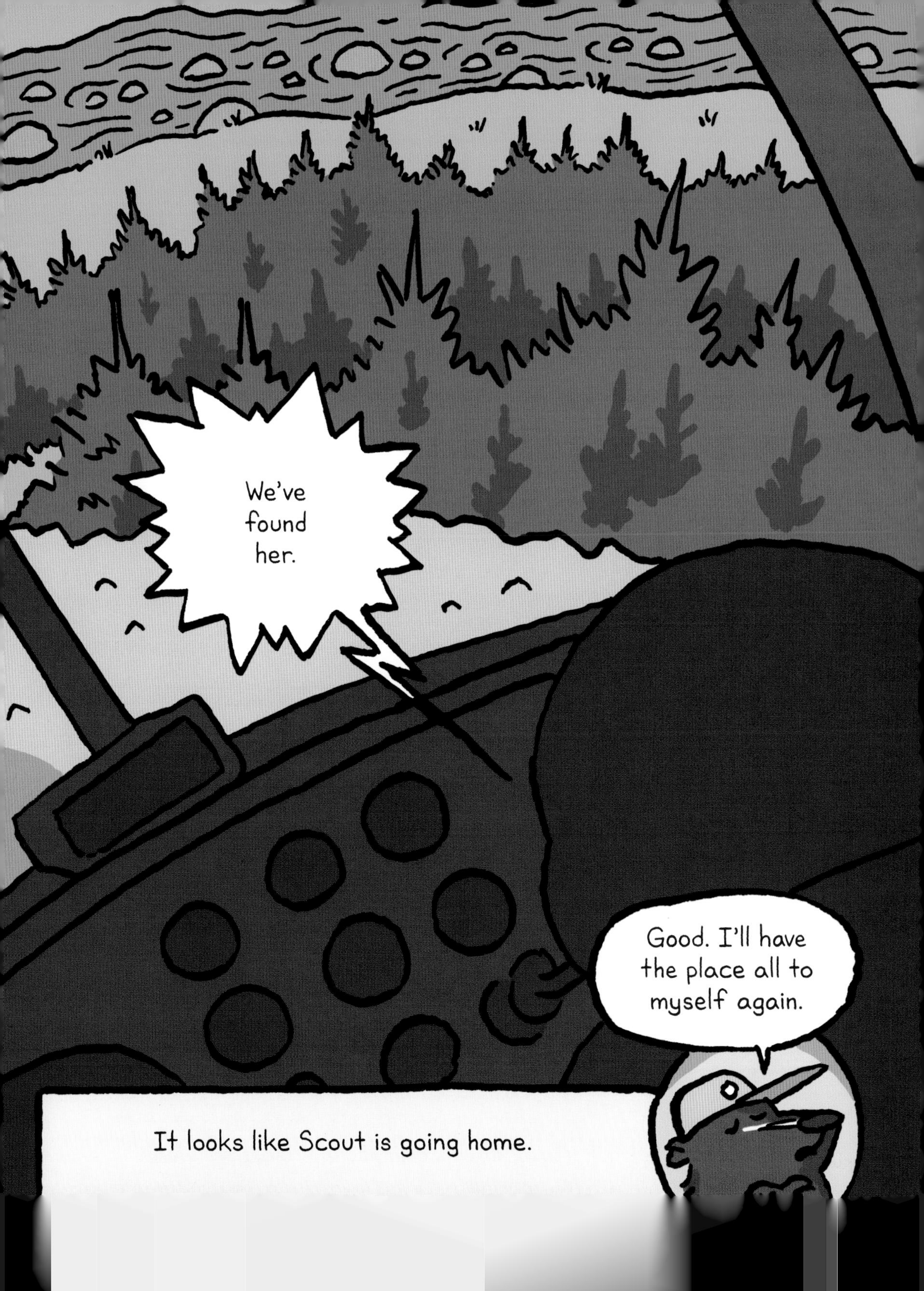
We've found her.
Good. I'll have the place all to myself again.
It looks like Scout is going home.

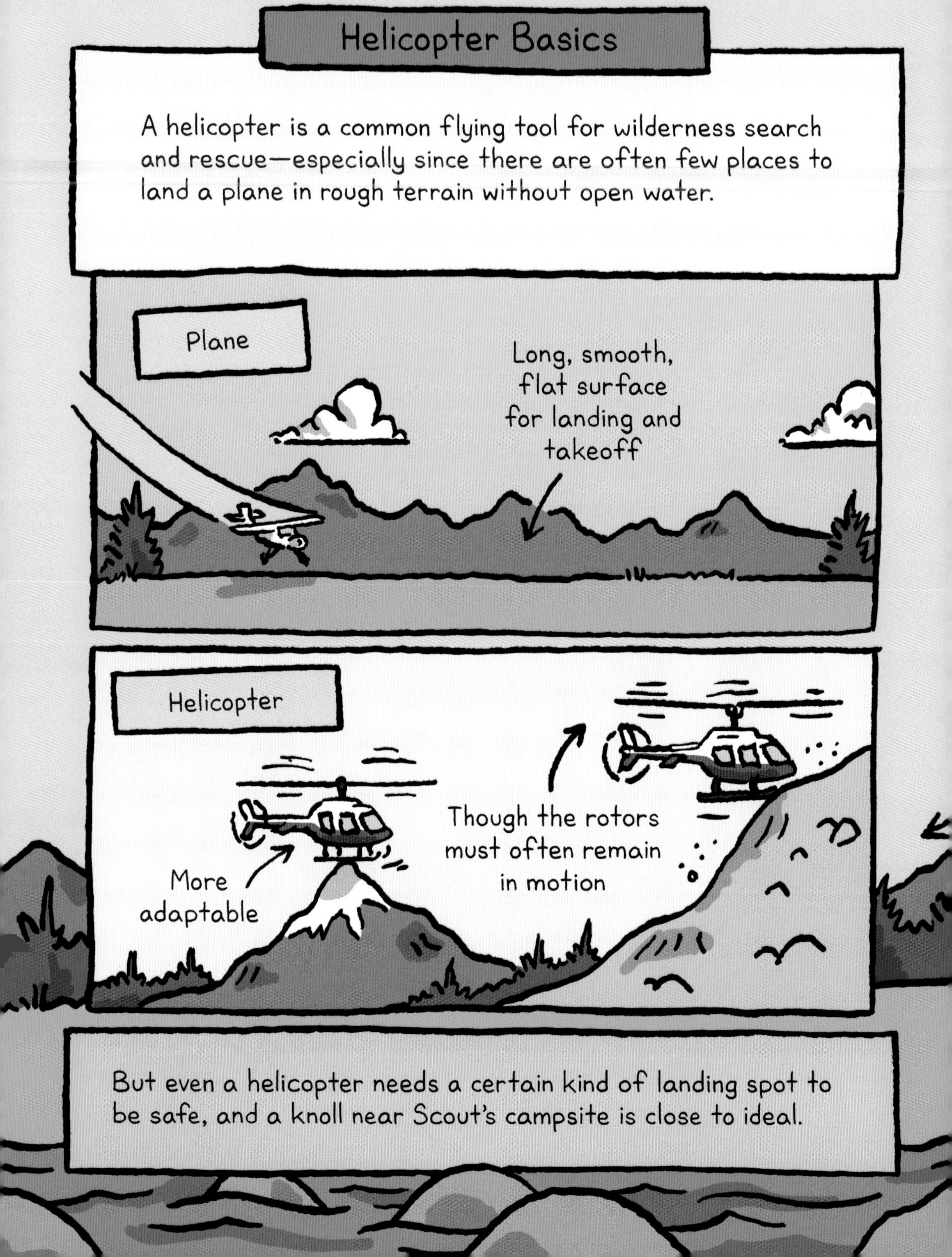
Helicopter Basics
A helicopter is a common flying tool for wilderness search and rescue—especially since there are often few places to land a plane in rough terrain without open water.
Plane
Long, smooth, flat surface for landing and takeoff
Helicopter
More adaptable
Though the rotors must often remain in motion
But even a helicopter needs a certain kind of landing spot to be safe, and a knoll near Scout's campsite is close to ideal.

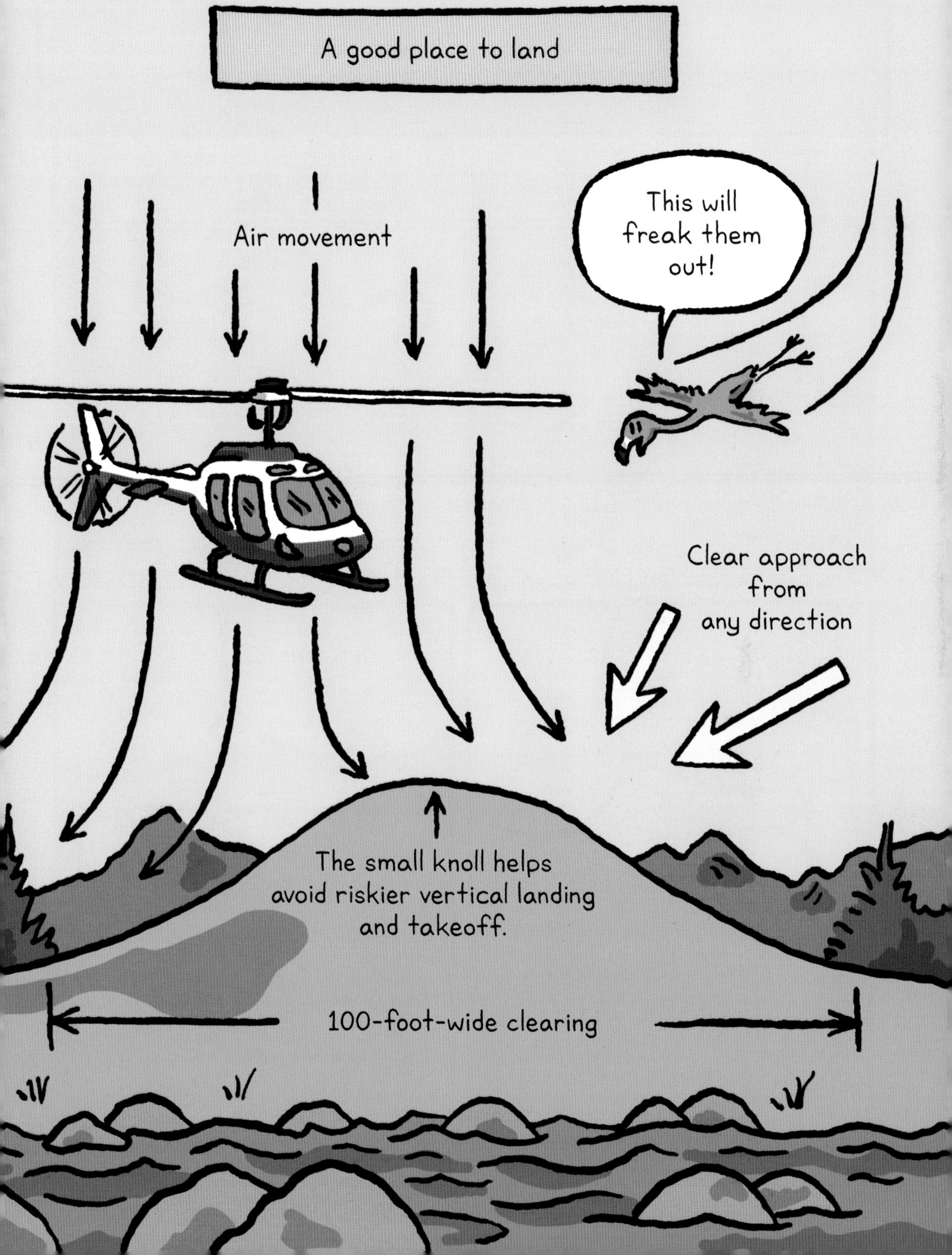
A good place to land
Air movement
This will freak them out!
Clear approach from any direction
The small knoll helps avoid riskier vertical landing and takeoff.
100-foot-wide clearing

Scout makes it back to camp and meets one of the members of the search party.

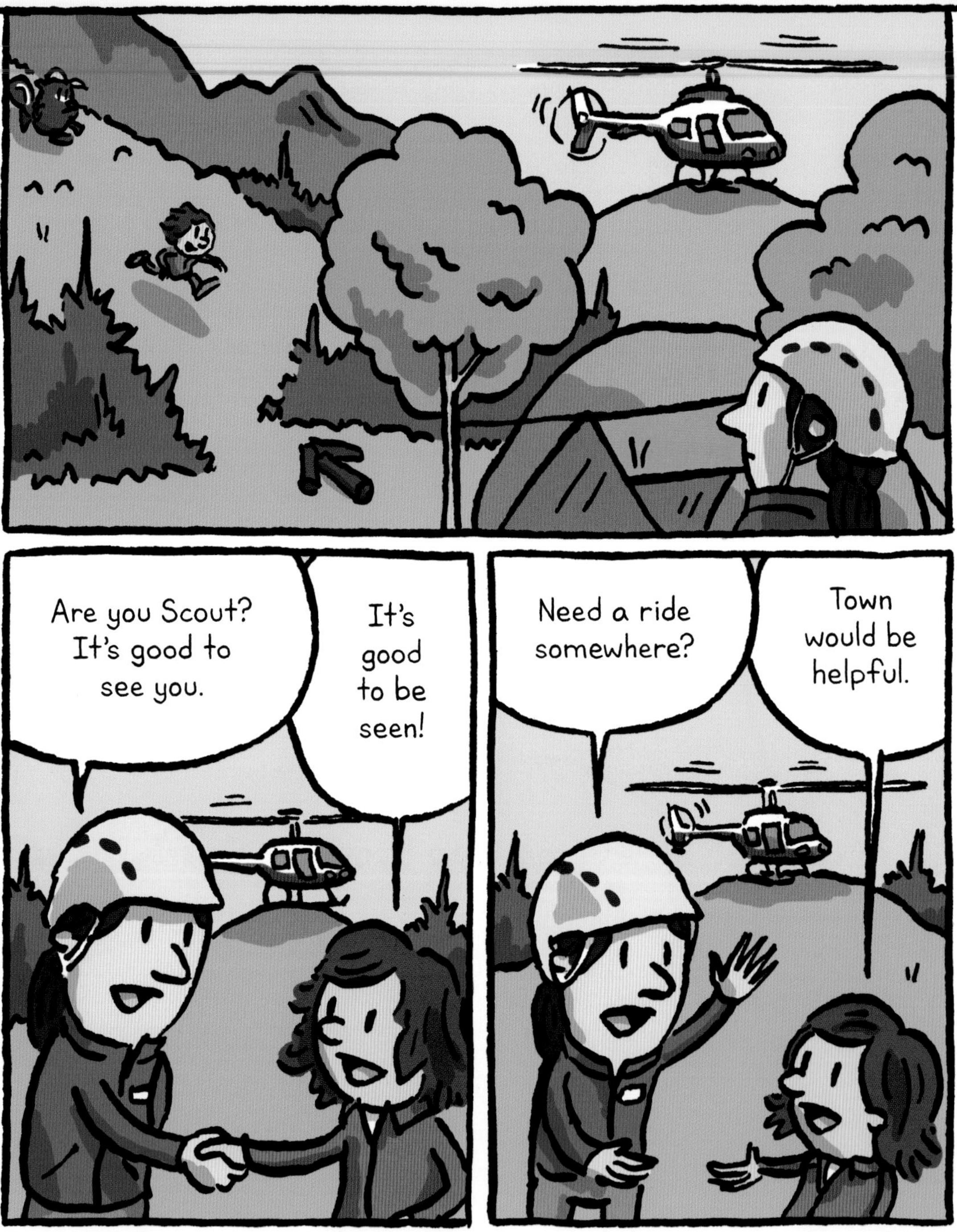

Are you Scout? It's good to see you.
It's good to be seen!
Need a ride somewhere?
Town would be helpful.

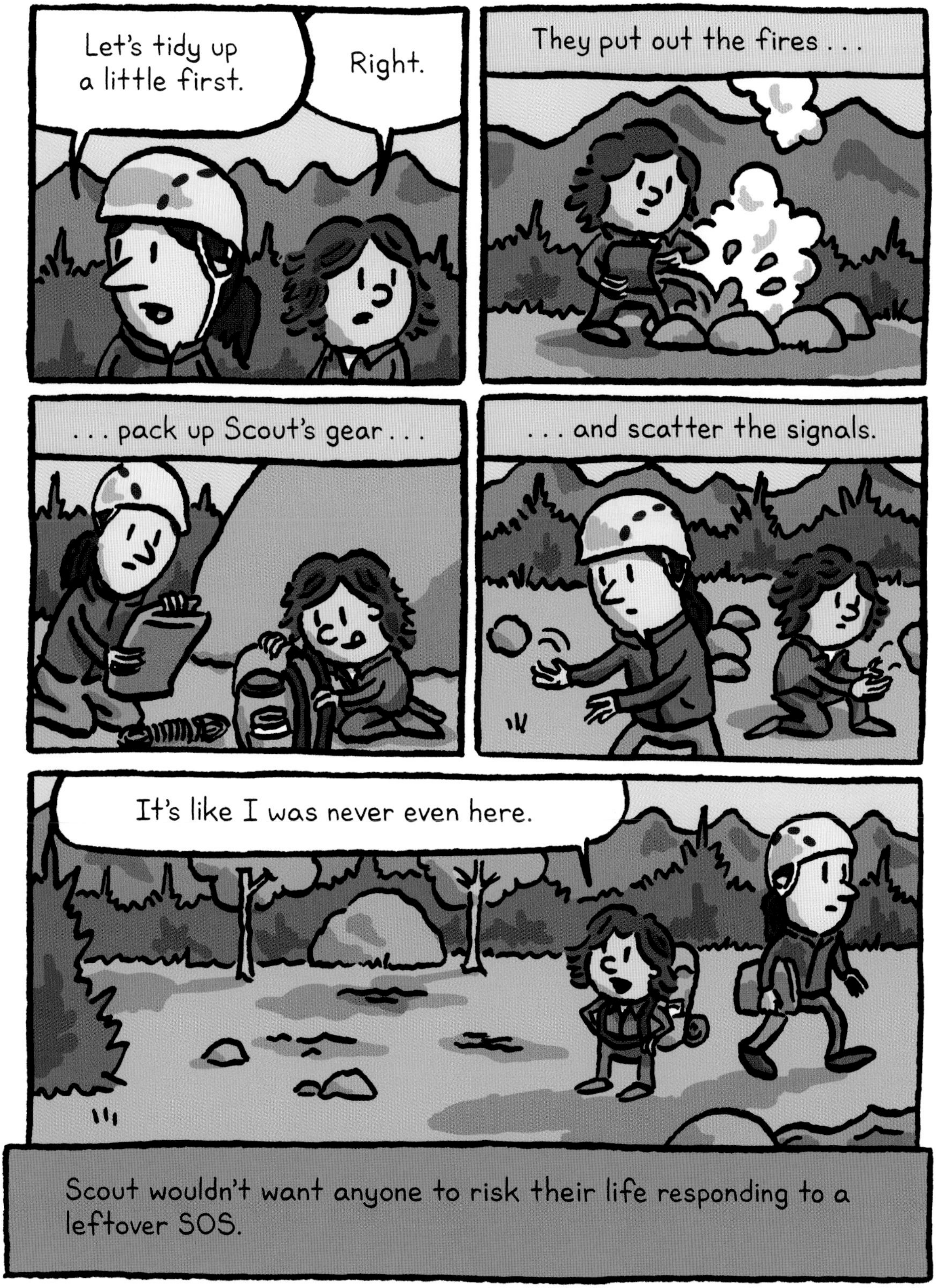
Let's tidy up a little first.
Right.
They put out the fires . . .
. . . pack up Scout's gear . . .
. . . and scatter the signals.
It's like I was never even here.
Scout wouldn't want anyone to risk their life responding to a leftover SOS.

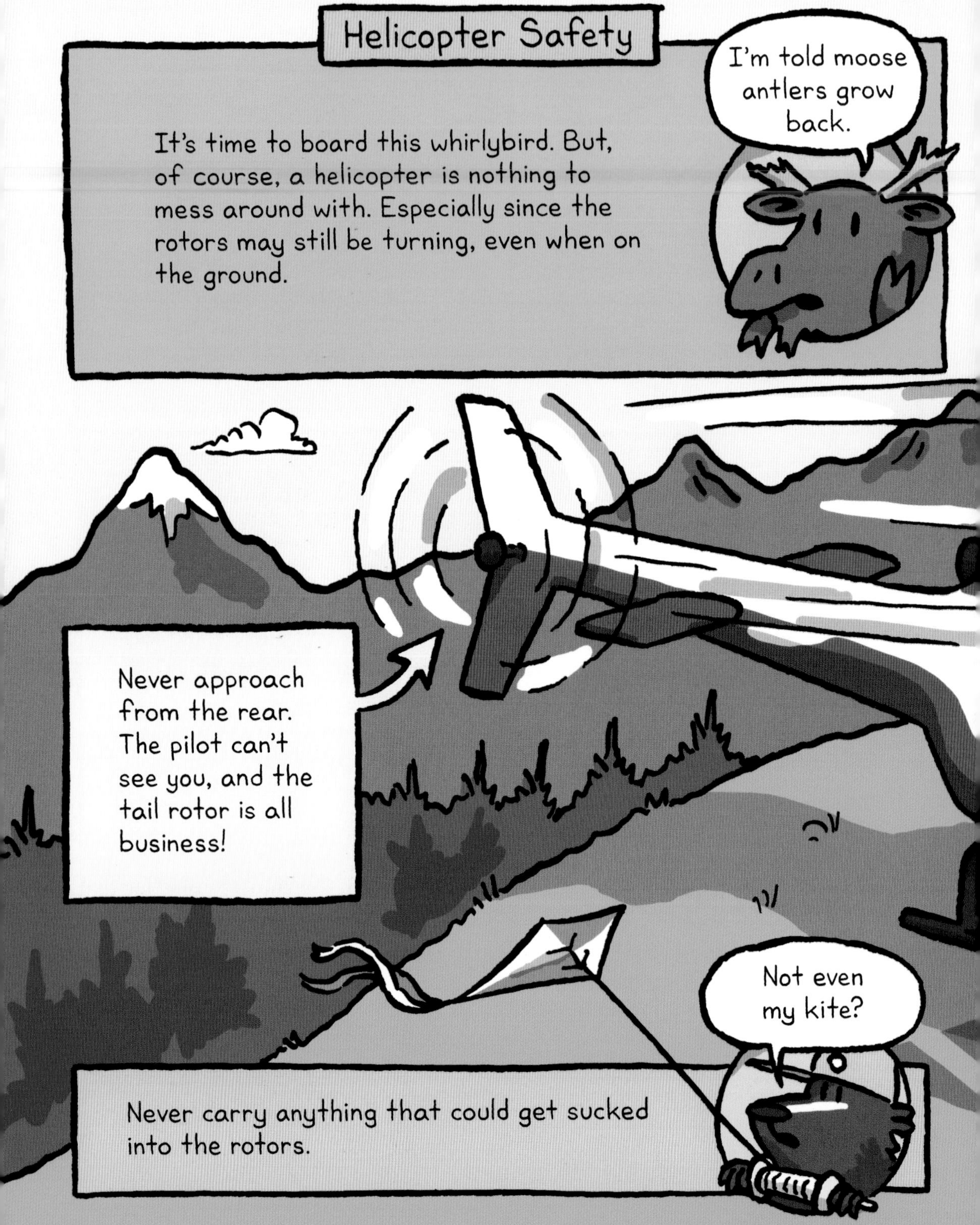

Helicopter Safety
It's time to board this whirlybird. But, of course, a helicopter is nothing to mess around with. Especially since the rotors may still be turning, even when on the ground.
I'm told moose antlers grow back.
Never approach from the rear. The pilot can't see you, and the tail rotor is all business!
Not even my kite?
Never carry anything that could get sucked into the rotors.

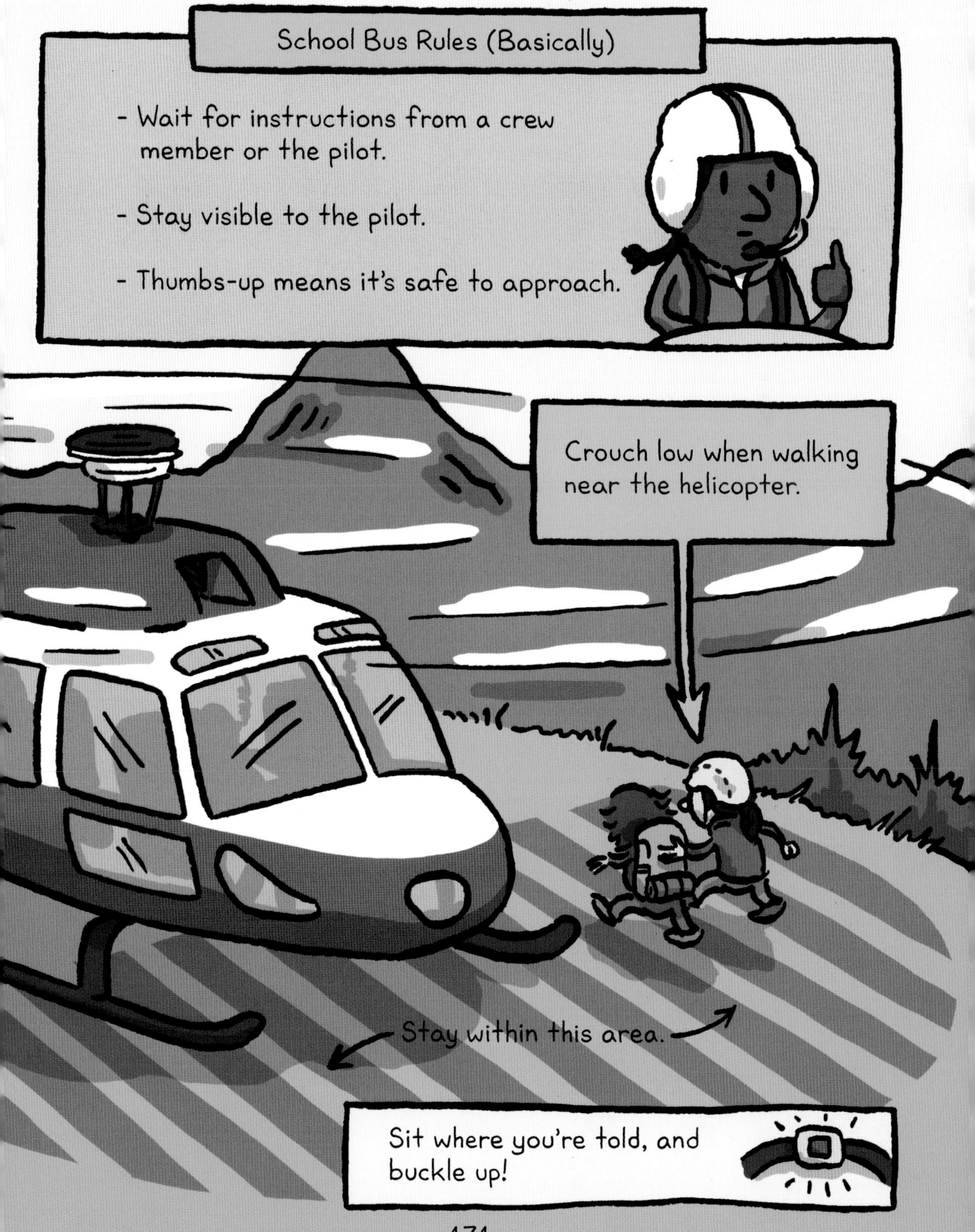
School Bus Rules (Basically)
- Wait for instructions from a crew member or the pilot.
- Stay visible to the pilot.
- Thumbs-up means it's safe to approach.
Crouch low when walking near the helicopter.
Stay within this area.
Sit where you're told, and buckle up!

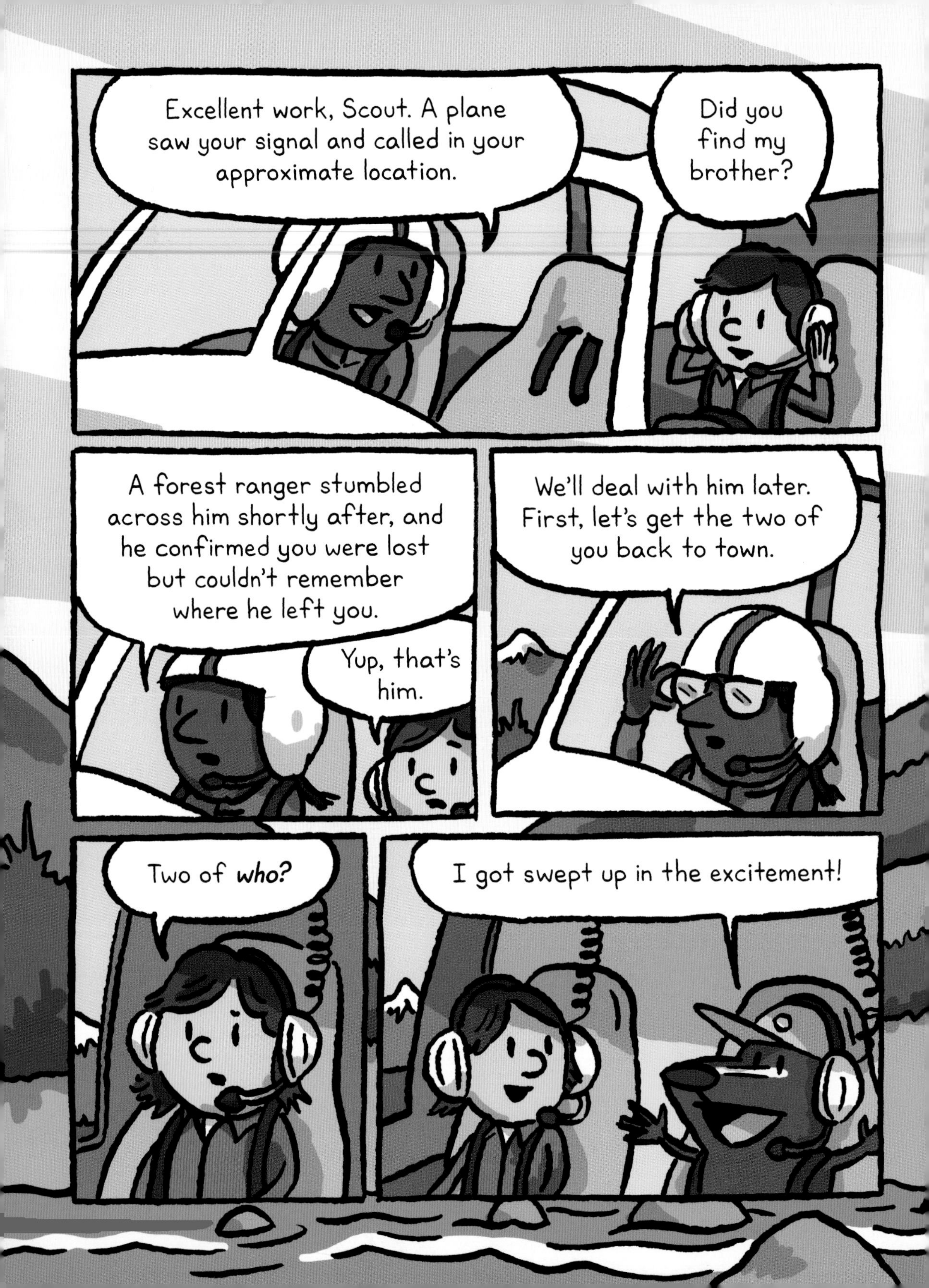
Excellent work, Scout. A plane saw your signal and called in your approximate location.
Did you find my brother?
A forest ranger stumbled across him shortly after, and he confirmed you were lost but couldn't remember where he left you.
Yup, that's him.
We'll deal with him later. First, let's get the two of you back to town.
Two of *who?*
I got swept up in the excitement!

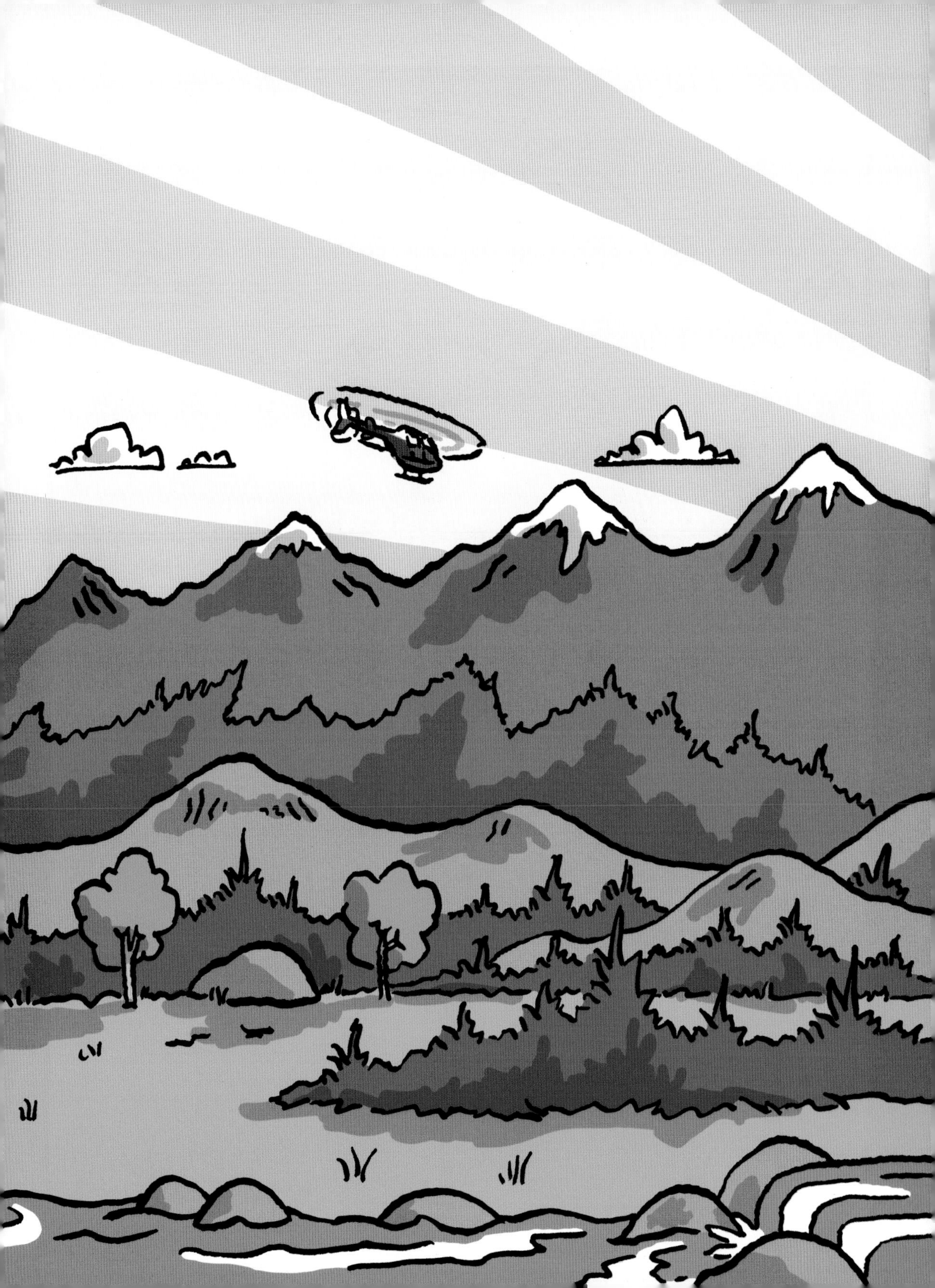

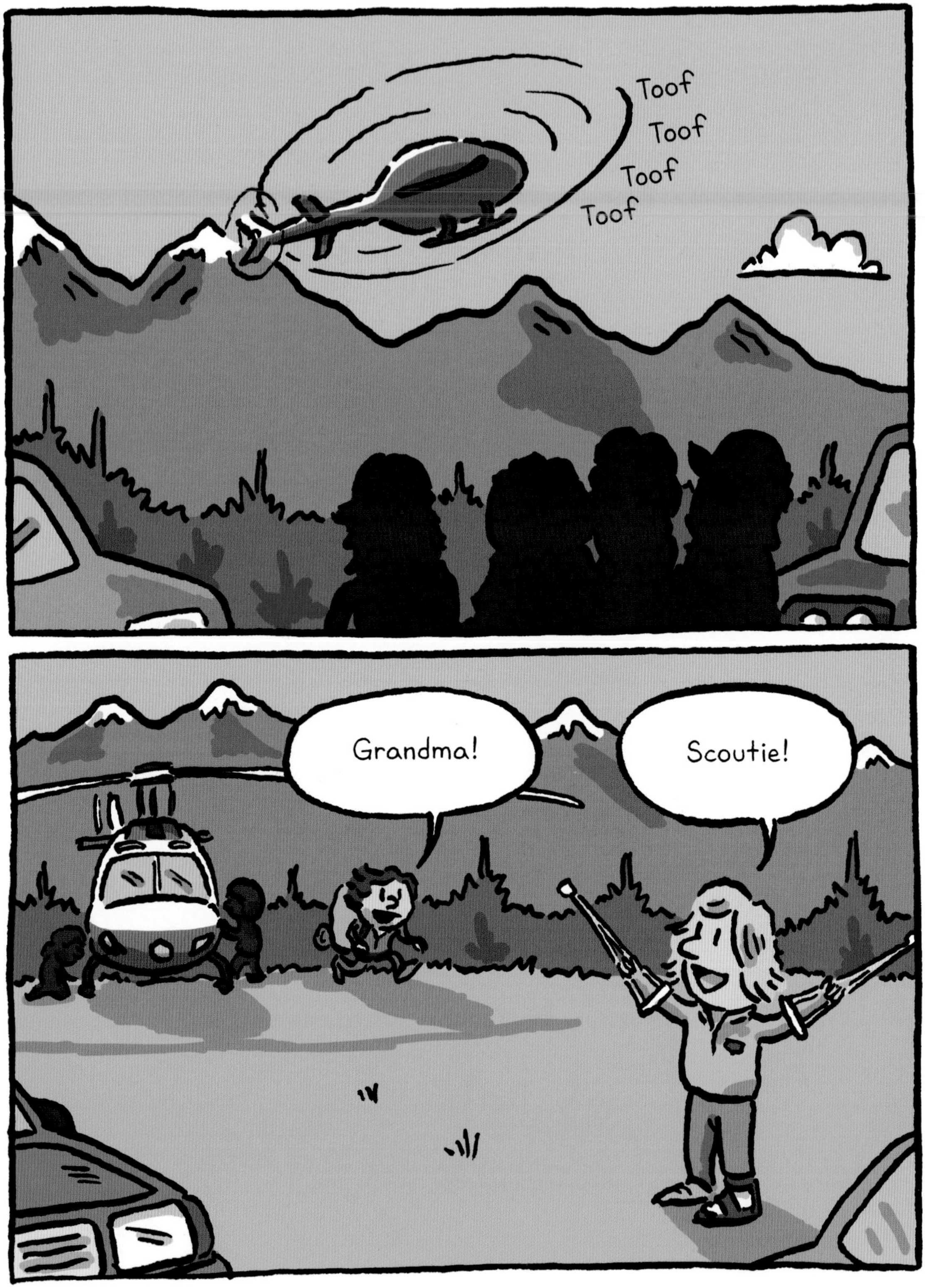
Toof
Toof
Toof
Toof
Grandma!
Scoutie!

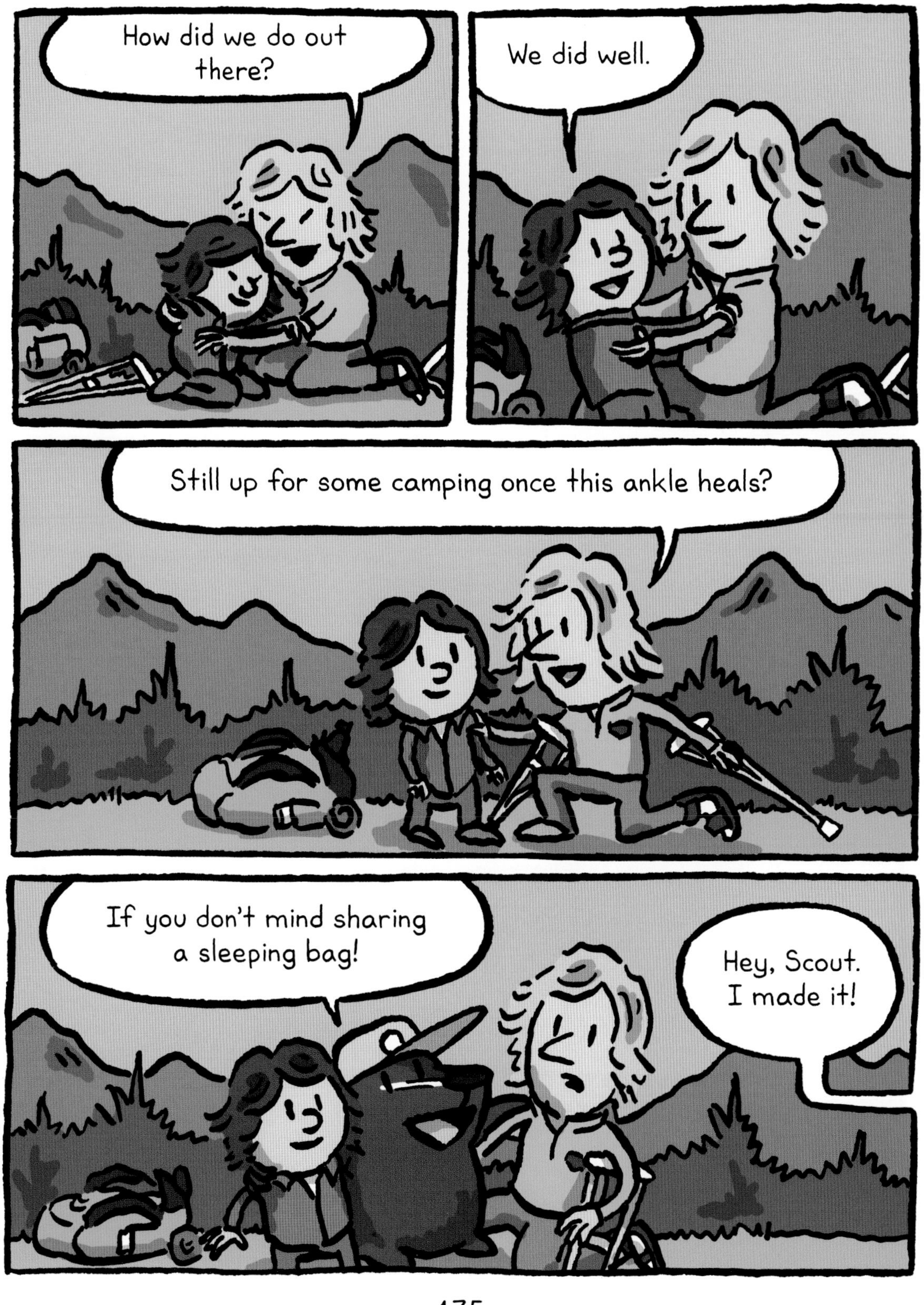
How did we do out there?
We did well.
Still up for some camping once this ankle heals?
If you don't mind sharing a sleeping bag!
Hey, Scout. I made it!

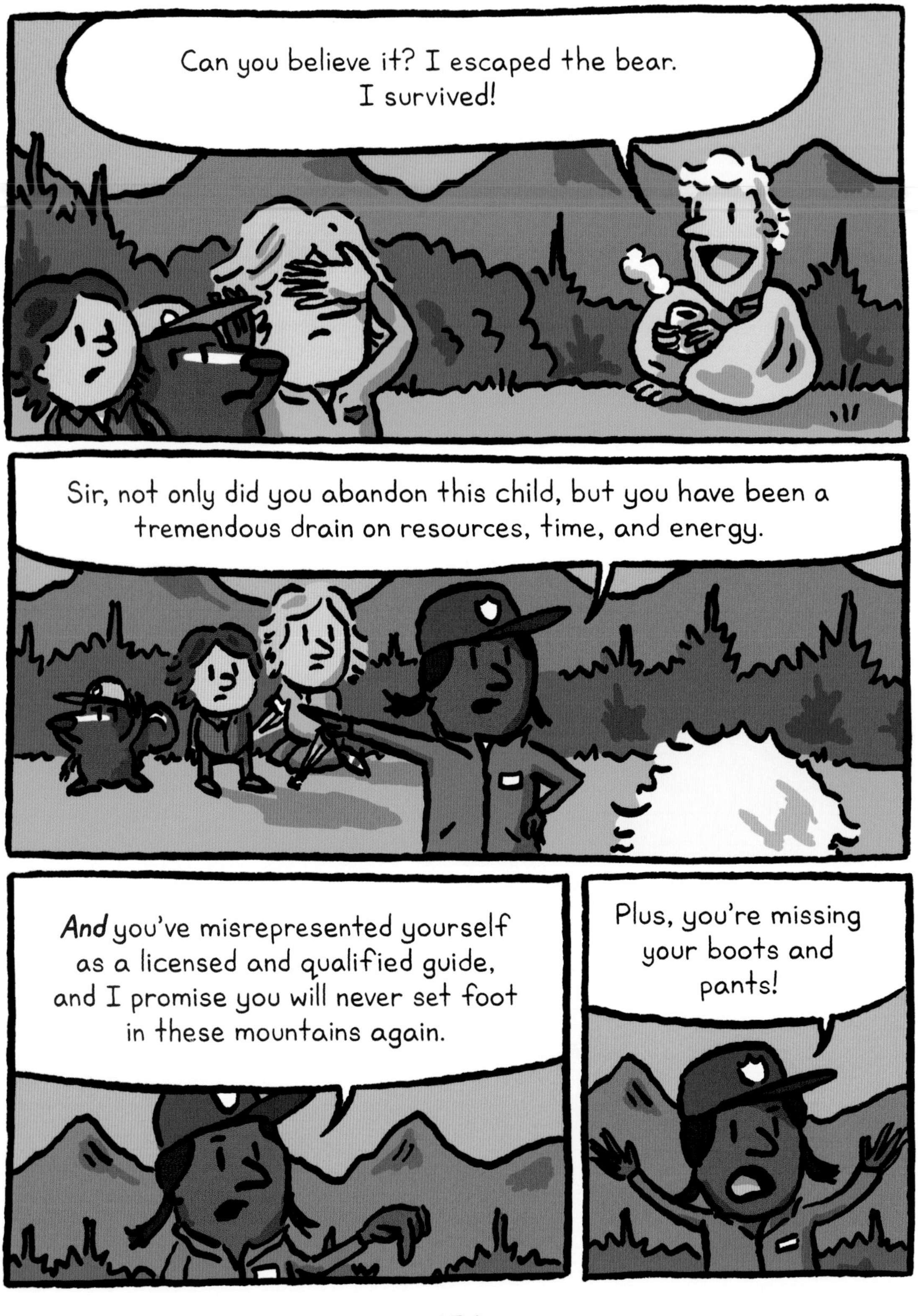
Can you believe it? I escaped the bear. I survived!
Sir, not only did you abandon this child, but you have been a tremendous drain on resources, time, and energy.
And you've misrepresented yourself as a licensed and qualified guide, and I promise you will never set foot in these mountains again.
Plus, you're missing your boots and pants!

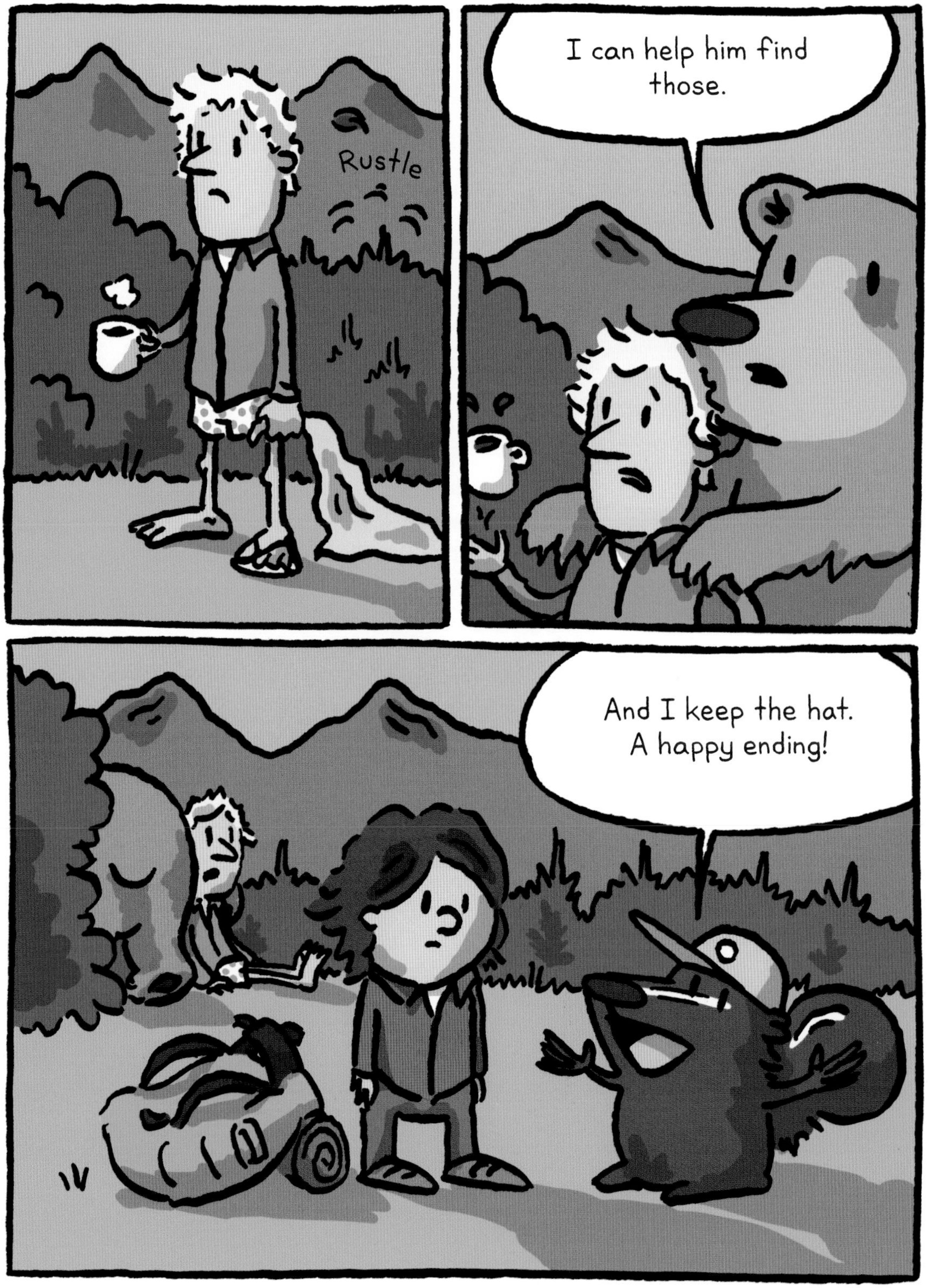
Rustle
I can help him find those.
And I keep the hat. A happy ending!

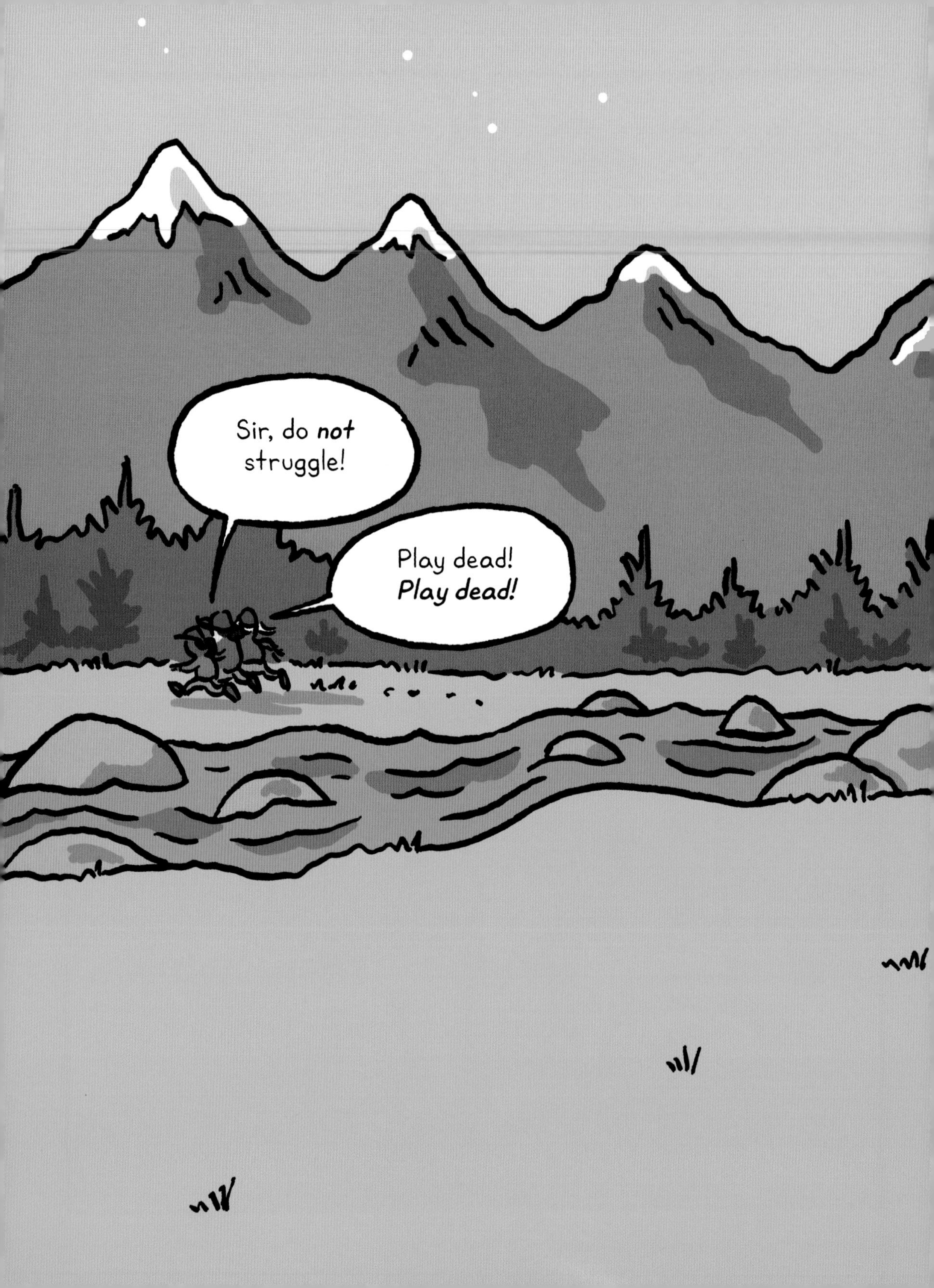
Sir, do **not** struggle!
Play dead! ***Play dead!***

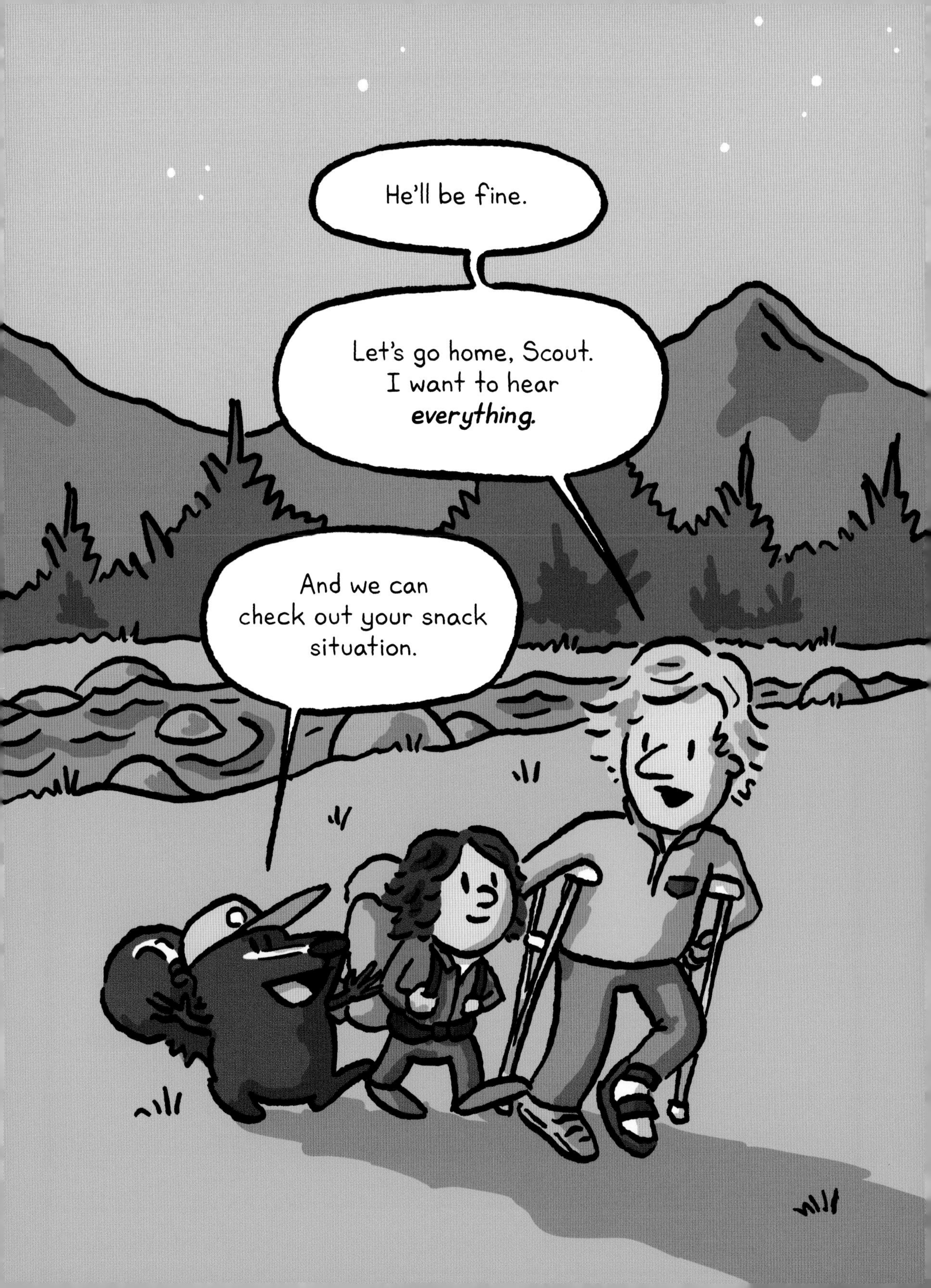
He'll be fine.
Let's go home, Scout. I want to hear *everything.*
And we can check out your snack situation.

Some handy knots

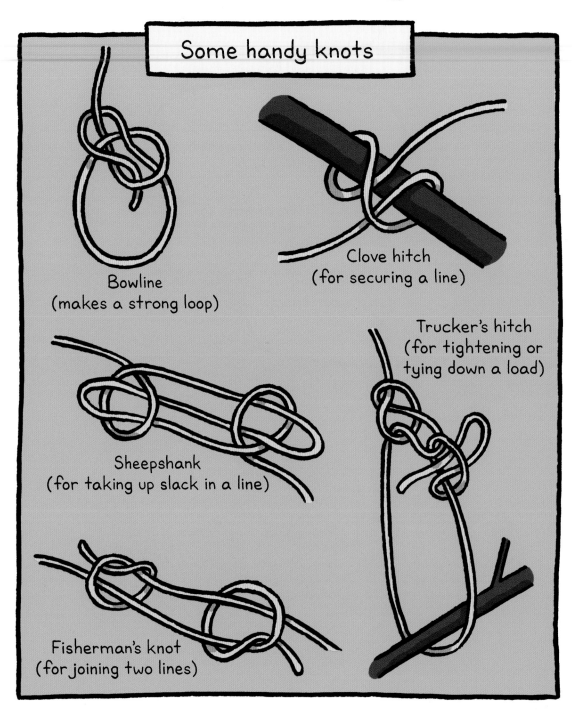

Bowline
(makes a strong loop)

Clove hitch
(for securing a line)

Sheepshank
(for taking up slack in a line)

Trucker's hitch
(for tightening or
tying down a load)

Fisherman's knot
(for joining two lines)

Wrapping a sprained ankle

Around the foot a few times

Around the ankle

Down around the foot and repeat

Tuck in the end and take it easy!

Morse code

A ·—	G ——·	N —·	U ··—
B —···	H ····	O ———	V ···—
C —·—·	I ··	P ·——·	W ·——
D —··	J ·———	Q ——·—	X —··—
E ·	K —·—	R ·—·	Y —·——
F ··—·	L ·—··	S ···	Z ——··
	M ——	T —	

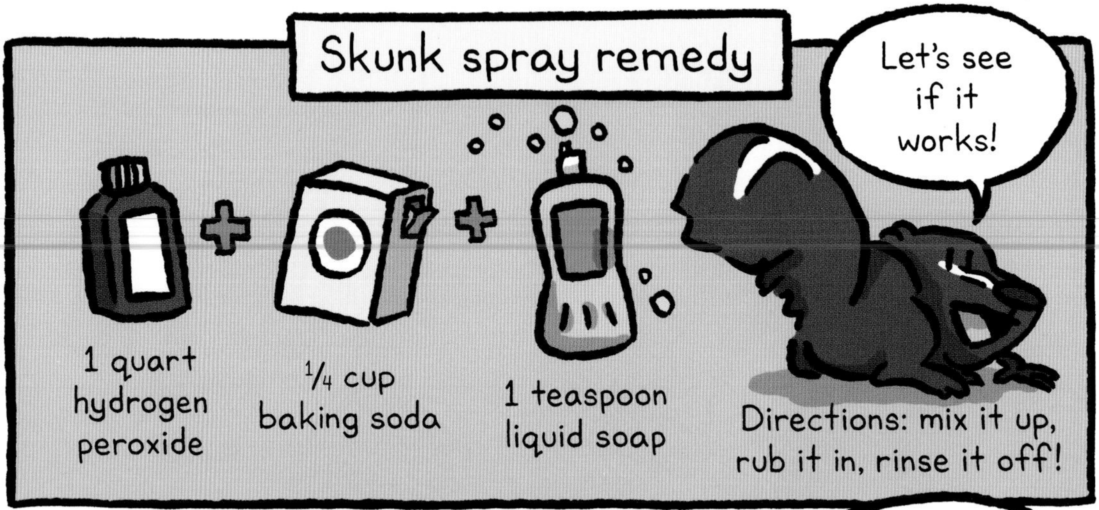
Skunk spray remedy
Let's see if it works!
1 quart hydrogen peroxide
1/4 cup baking soda
1 teaspoon liquid soap
Directions: mix it up, rub it in, rinse it off!

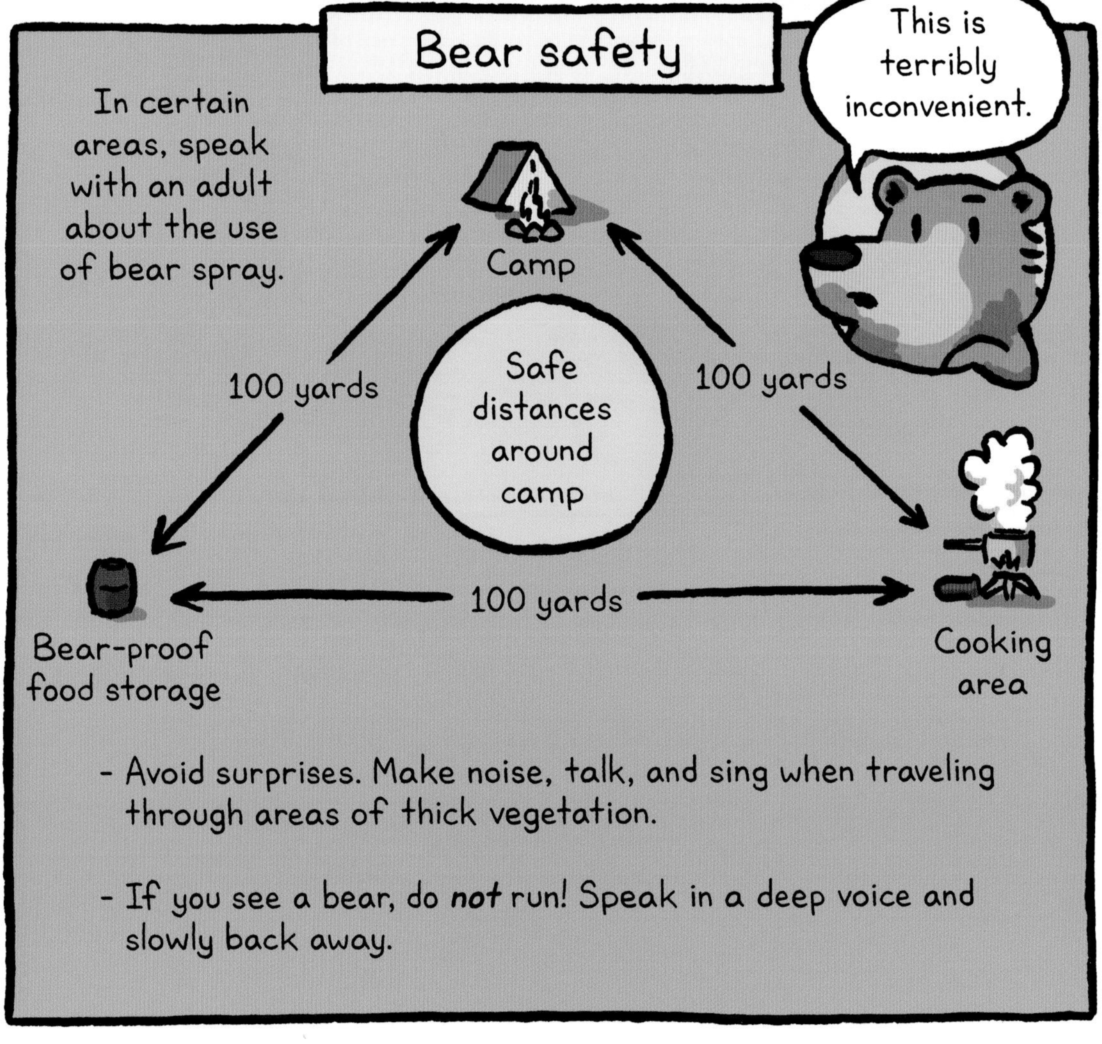
Bear safety
This is terribly inconvenient.
In certain areas, speak with an adult about the use of bear spray.
Camp
Safe distances around camp
100 yards
100 yards
100 yards
Bear-proof food storage
Cooking area
- Avoid surprises. Make noise, talk, and sing when traveling through areas of thick vegetation.
- If you see a bear, do *not* run! Speak in a deep voice and slowly back away.

Going to the bathroom

If you can't pack out your feces, use a "cat hole."

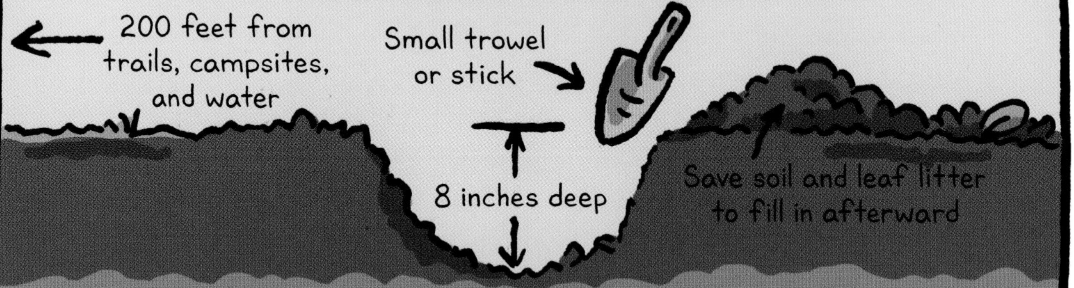
200 feet from trails, campsites, and water
Small trowel or stick
8 inches deep
Save soil and leaf litter to fill in afterward

- Toilet paper should be burned in the hole, if no fire danger. Preferably packed out in doubled-up ziplock bags.
- Urine can go on rocks or away from plants that may be damaged.
- Use some hand sanitizer to clean up.

For more on survival and camping in the mountains:

The American Red Cross First Aid and Safety Handbook, Kathleen A. Handal, Little, Brown, 1992.

Be Expert with Map and Compass, Björn Kjellström, Scribners, 1967.

Bear Essentials, John Gookin and Tom Reed, Stackpole Books, 2009.

Leave No Trace, http://lnt.org/why/7-principles/.

Mountaineering: The Freedom of the Hills, edited by Eric Linxweiler and Mike Maude, Mountaineers Books, 2017.

Peterson Field Guide to Edible Wild Plants, Lee Allen Peterson, Mariner Books, 1999.

SAS Survival Handbook, John Wiseman, Collins, 2009.

Wilderness Search and Rescue, Tim J. Setnicka, Appalachian Mountain Club, 1981.

United States Geological Survey, https://ngmdb.usgs.gov/topoview.

A Note from the Author

This is a fictional account of being stranded in the mountains and could have included injury, illness, extreme weather, or worse. Never enter a situation assuming you'll be rescued. Especially by a helicopter! Doing so puts yourself and others in unnecessary danger. The intention of this book is to lay a foundation for survival skills by emphasizing the manner in which Scout approaches this particular scenario and the logic behind each decision. All of the survival skills in the world mean nothing without a clear head and a positive frame of mind.

Stay safe out there.

Published by Roaring Brook Press
Roaring Brook Press is a division of Holtzbrinck Publishing Holdings Limited Partnership • 120 Broadway, New York, NY 10271
mackids.com • Copyright © 2023 by Maxwell Eaton III. All rights reserved. • Our books may be purchased in bulk for promotional, educational, or business use. Please contact your local bookseller or the Macmillan Corporate and Premium Sales Department at (800) 221-7945 ext. 5442 or by email at MacmillanSpecialMarkets@macmillan.com.

Library of Congress Cataloging-in-Publication Data is available.

First edition, 2023
Book design by Maxwell Eaton III & Molly Johanson
Edited by Emily Feinberg and Emilia Sowersby
Production editing by Kat Kopit
The artwork for this book was created with pen and ink on paper and colored digitally.
Printed in China by Toppan Leefung Printing Ltd., Dongguan City, Guangdong Province

ISBN 978-1-250-79046-0 (hardcover)
10 9 8 7 6 5 4 3 2 1

ISBN 978-1-250-79047-7 (paperback)
10 9 8 7 6 5 4 3 2 1